HORTICULTURAL ENGINEERING TECHNOLOGY
FIXED EQUIPMENT AND BUILDINGS

Science in Horticulture Series

General Editor: L. Broadbent, Emeritus Professor of Biology and Horticulture, University of Bath

Published in collaboration with the Royal Horticultural Society and the Horticultural Education Association.

This series of texts has been designed for students on courses in horticulture at the Higher Diploma or National Diploma level, but care has been taken to ensure that they are not too specialised for lower-level courses, nor too superficial for university work.

All the contributors to the series have had experience in the horticultural industry and/or education. Consequently, the books have a strong practical flavour which should reinforce their value as textbooks and also make them of interest to a wide audience, including growers and farmers, extension officers, research workers, workers in the agrochemical, marketing and allied industries, and the many gardeners who are interested in the science behind their hobby.

The authors are all British, but they have illustrated their books with examples drawn from many countries. As a result the texts should be of value to English-speaking students of horticulture throughout the world.

Other titles in the series are:

J. K. A. Bleasdale, *Plant Physiology in Relation to Horticulture (Second Edition)*
G. R. Dixon, *Plant Pathogens and their Control in Horticulture*
A. W. Flegmann and R. A. T. George, *Soils and Other Growth Media*
S. D. Holdsworth, *The Preservation of Fruit and Vegetable Food Products*
C. North, *Plant Breeding and Genetics in Horticulture*
M. J. Sargent, *Economics in Horticulture*
R. J. Stephens, *Theory and Practice of Weed Control*
E. J. Winter, *Water, Soil and the Plant*

and the companion volume to the present book

R. C. Balls, *Horticultural Engineering Technology — Field Machinery*

HORTICULTURAL ENGINEERING TECHNOLOGY
FIXED EQUIPMENT AND BUILDINGS

R.C. BALLS
ANCAE

*National Specialist Mechanisation Adviser with the Agricultural
Development and Advisory Service (ADAS) of the Ministry of
Agriculture, Fisheries and Food, U.K.*

M
MACMILLAN

First published 1986

Published by
MACMILLAN EDUCATION LTD
Houndmills, Basingstoke, Hampshire RG21 2XS
and London
Companies and representatives
throughout the world

Printed in Hong Kong

Typeset by
TecSet Ltd, Sutton, Surrey

British Library Cataloguing in Publication Data
Balls, R. C.
    Horticultural engineering technology: fixed
    equipment and buildings.
    1. Horticultural machinery
    I. Title
    635'.028   5678.7

ISBN 0-333-36435-X

CONTENTS

PREFACE

I have often felt that 'horticultural engineering' lies uneasily between the horticultural sciences and pure engineering. The horticulturist or plant scientist often finds engineering principles difficult to grasp, while the pure engineer usually lacks the practical knowledge of plant behaviour or requirements.

The modern horticulturist is heavily reliant on engineering by way of mechanisation at all stages from establishment to marketing. A working knowledge of engineering will help in three ways: awareness of what is available, ability to specify requirements in broad terms and improved efficiency of operating equipment.

In writing this book I have tried to establish the basic engineering principles of which the modern horticulturist must be aware, and to describe the equipment that is likely to be encountered. It is also hoped that students or practitioners of engineering will be able to grasp the basic applications requirements of the horticultural industry.

Obviously, as the book has to cover such a wide range of engineering sciences, some cannot be explored in great depth, and consequently the reader will have to continue by way of the books cited in the bibliography. Attention is also drawn to the companion volume: *Horticultural Engineering Technology — Field Machinery*. In line with the majority of the engineering industry, the two books are written entirely in SI (Système International) metric units; conversions to Imperial and other common units will be found in appendix A.

Houghton Conquest R. C. BALLS
Bedford

ACKNOWLEDGEMENTS

I would like to acknowledge the help given by colleagues in the Advisory Services and Research Stations, and also the information supplied by equipment manufacturers. The following companies and organisations have kindly allowed their drawings to be copied: CIBSE, London (figure 7.19); The Electricity Council, London (figures 6.5 and 6.6); Hamworthy Engineering Ltd, Poole (figure 4.3(b)); Spirax–Sarco Ltd, Cheltenham (figure 5.3(a)–(d)); and Woods of Colchester Ltd (figures 7.14, 7.15 and 7.17).

Full use has been made of my experience gained during advisory work on horticultural holdings throughout Britain, and I am grateful for the permission to draw on this work given by my senior officers in ADAS. Finally I am indebted to my wife for typing the manuscript.

1 PACKHOUSE DESIGN AND OPERATION

The design of packhouse equipment, and its layout, is often specific not only to the product, but also for the intended market. However, many operations in the various processes are widespread, and can be discussed under the following general groups of activity: reception; intake; cleaning; quality grading; size grading; preparation for market; weighing and packing.

1.1 RECEPTION

The produce will often arrive in containers which can be as diverse as 600 mm x 450 mm x 300 mm crates for celery, water-filled buckets for flowers, and 22 tonne bulk lorries for potatoes or onions.

These products will often need space for storage, as the packhouse usually cannot deal with a delivery immediately it arrives. There will be a minimum requirement for space to stand trailers, pallets and bins. This must be away from the areas of other activity, and often must allow for temporary storage of varying discrete lots, with access to each as might be required.

1.1.1 Weighing
In large packhouse operations the incoming produce will need to be weighed. This is normally done on a weighbridge of sufficient size to take the entire vehicle; modern lorries require a bridge deck at least 12 m x 2.7 m, with a weight capacity of 40 tonnes. The modern weighbridge uses an electronic rather than a mechanical system. This has several advantages, such as reduction in site work requirements, automatic taring and computer interfacing.

(a) Automatic taring enables a vehicle to be weighed when full, then empty, and the load weight automatically calculated, with all details being printed on a ticket. Some units have a 'memory' function, which holds details of several vehicles, and can recall the appropriate full weight when a vehicle returns after discharging its load.

(b) Computer interfacing enables all the weight data to be incorporated into the stock control system.

(c) Modern electronic weighbridges do not require to be sited over a deep pit to house all the levers; many electronic loadcells project less than 50 mm below the deck, so the whole weighbridge can be sited above ground level, with low access ramps each end.

Weighbridge siting must allow for access to vehicles entering and leaving the site, without generating blockages caused by vehicles waiting in the reception or dispatch area. Often when they are carrying produce from more than one grower, it is necessary to allow for incoming produce vehicles to return for reweighing, so that each lot can be weighed off separately.

1.1.2 Weather protection

Many products need to be protected from rain or the extremes of sun and cold. Where produce is left on trailers, tarpaulin sheeting can provide rain protection but will not be proof against frost unless both trailer body and sheet are thermally insulated. Tightly drawn sheeting can lead to high humidity and condensation spoilage in the crops beneath.

1.1.3 Conditioning during holding

Some produce, like onions, benefits from ventilation while in the holding area, to dry wounds caused during loading. Bulk trailers can be fitted with a fan and ducting; bulk bins can be stacked on to a force ventilation duct system.

1.1.4 Cold chain reception

Some produce quality requirements dictate that the produce is cooled as soon as possible after harvesting. In many instances the best opportunity for cooling is in a specialist cold store (see section 7.3) sited at reception. The cooling in most units will take a matter of hours, and it is normal to load the cooler one afternoon for packing the next morning. The cooler siting must allow access for both filling and emptying without conflict with other movements in the intake area.

1.1.5 Emptied container storage

Many bins occupy the same space when empty as they do when full. There must be provision for movement and storage of these while awaiting collection, and access to discrete lots for reloading on to transport.

1.2 INTAKE

The bulk of produce that arrives has to be broken down into a steady, even feed for the succeeding operations. The produce will often travel through the packhouse by conveyor, so the main intake operation will involve feeding this by one of the following methods.

1.2.1 Hand feed

Produce is transferred manually from the crate, bucket or bin to the intake conveyor. In operations where the first task involves mechanical processing, for example leek and celery trimming, the produce has to be laid out in correct alignment. The ease with which material can be handled depends on the state in which it arrives. A jumbled mass of celery sticks in a bin requires much sorting. If these have been placed systematically in a crate during lifting, they can be tipped on to the intake already aligned, and so need little further correction. The intake operators will often carry out primary grading, rejecting obvious rubbish or pre-sizing where a twin size intake is involved.

The material flow path must ensure that full and empty containers move freely within the intake. Roller conveyors can be used for small containers, with a separate one for full and empty ones. Large operations often employ one operator to take full crates from the pallet or trailer and restack the empty ones. Bins can be moved in by forklift or pallet truck, and manually pushed aside when empty.

1.2.2 Bulk bin emptying

Two methods are used to empty bins on to the line.

(a) The bin contents are tipped into a feeder hopper, which is a smaller version of that described in section 1.2.3, by either a forklift-mounted tippler, or a static tipping cage. Some static cages do not need separate power for tipping, the forklift tines being used to lift the rear edge.

To minimise damage when tipping any crop, the cage should tip the bin around its front edge (figure 1.1(a)).

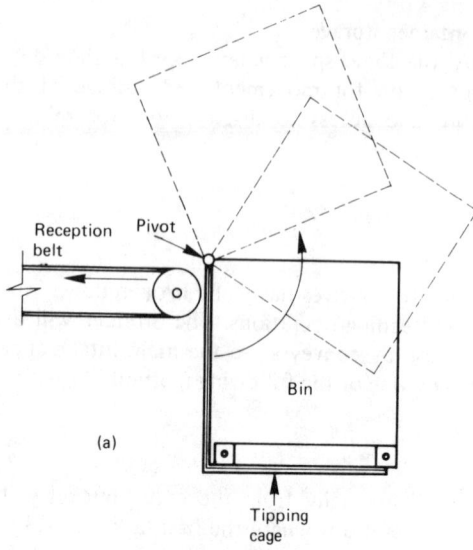

(a)

Reception belt

Pivot

Bin

Tipping cage

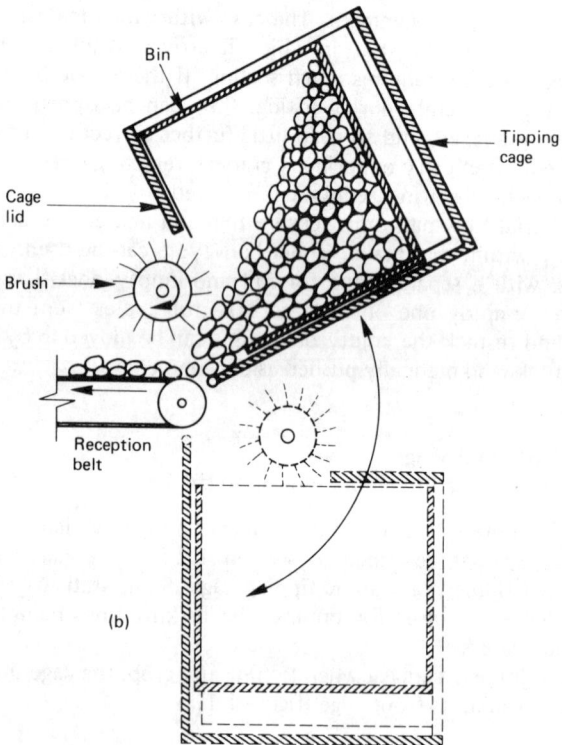

Bin

Tipping cage

Cage lid

Brush

Reception belt

(b)

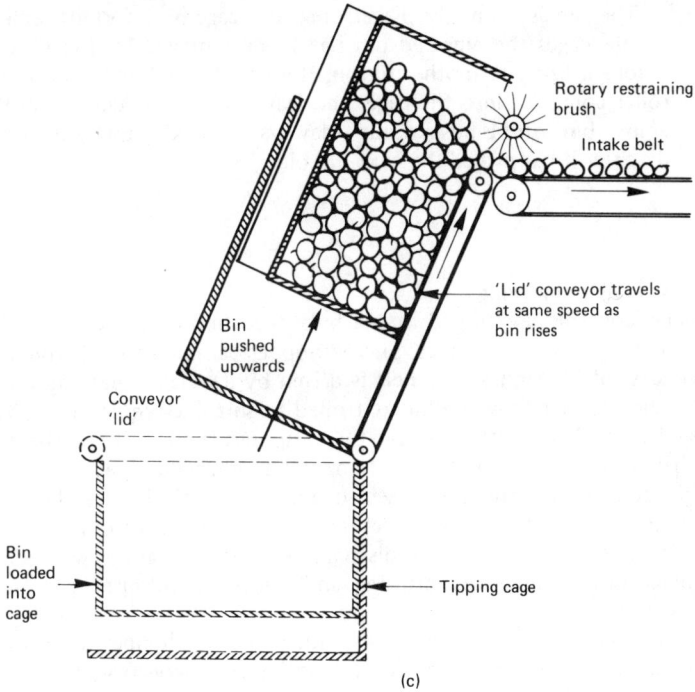

(c)

Figure 1.1 (a) Box tipping cage point. (b) Brush feeder/restrainer. (c) Apple box discharger.

(b) The bin is gradually tipped directly on to the intake conveyor, without an intermediate feed hopper. This uses a powered tip cage, controlled by either a crop flow sensor on the intake conveyor or manually by an operative. As fragile produce, like apples, can be damaged during rolling from a tipping box, a fruit bin tippler will often incorporate restrainers in the form of a large cylindrical brush which slowly rotates to feed out the fruit (figure 1.1(b)).

In one fruit bin system the box is placed in a cage with a conveyor 'lid' (figure 1.1(c)). The cage rotates until the box is on end, and the product is retained by the lid. The line intake is arranged to coincide with the top end of the lid conveyor in this position. The box is pushed upwards with the conveyor running at a matching speed, so the fruit rolls over the conveyor end on to the intake. By this method the fruit is neither dropped nor scrubbed as it leaves the box.

The bin is normally placed into the cage by a forklift, and in simple cages the emptied bin has to be removed by the forklift before it can put another bin in. It is possible to build a transverse roller conveyor into the cage, and leave one side open, so that the empty bin can be pushed out sideways for picking up by the forklift after it has placed the next full bin.

1.2.3 Trailer emptying

Trailer contents are tipped into a bulk feed hopper, which is a wide belt conveyor with tall sides. Such a hopper can hold from ½ tonne to in excess of 10 tonnes. The belt is driven by a variable-speed motor so that the product flow can be controlled to suit line requirements. The speed controller is often adjusted by a responsible operative on the line.

The most efficient bulk feed hopper design should have a 1.5–2.5 m wide belt to suit the trailer width and near-vertical sides. The belt should slope up at a gentle angle, rather than have a horizontal holding section and a steeply inclined discharge end. These features will reduce damage due to abrasion, bruising and crushing, and also promote a more even flow.

The trailer is normally tipped into the end of the hopper, so that the belt can be speeded to take away the material as it flows from the trailer end to avoid drop damage, and even adjustable lift can be provided to suit varying trailer height. Where both trailers and bins feed the same hopper, it is normal to position the cage tipper on one side.

1.2.4 Flotation

Crops that need to be washed, and top fruit (apples and pears), can be decanted gently by immersing the container in water so that they float out. For crops that are denser than water, like pears, special salts can be added to the water to increase its relative density. Fruit flotation is carried out in a relatively small tank, sufficient to hold one bin, with a special cage to push it down against its natural buoyancy. Root crops that are handled by trailer can use large tanks, into which the whole trailer is reversed. These flotation tanks double as pre-soakers, to soften soil for the wash process.

In both systems a pumped water circulation provides the currents to propel the produce towards the discharge elevator.

In some packhouses water is used to transport crops between the various stages of preparation (see section 1.8.1.2).

1.2.5 Conveyor discharge trailers

These are special vehicle bodies, fitted with a moving belt floor, which discharges the crop through a hatch at the rear end. The belt is normally 450–600 mm wide, and the remainder of the floor slopes towards this. The belt is often driven by an electric motor attached at the packhouse, which is controlled by the grading line, so that the feed rate is suitable for the rest of the line.

The belt is not designed to carry the full load in the trailer, and is protected from it in one of two ways:

(a) Loose boards laid across it, which have to be removed manually to suit the flow of the line.
(b) A 'bridge' or inverted Vee deflector, which is raised above the belt sufficiently to allow the crop to trickle under at a controlled rate.

As there is normally no line feed hopper in addition to the bulker, the line flow is disrupted each time an empty one is changed for a full one. In many installations there is provision for two or more trailers to discharge on to the line, thus ensuring continuity of feed.

1.2.6 Tipper trailer control

This is a version of the bin tippler in which a tipping bulk trailer is used to feed the line at its required rate. This is achieved by supplying oil to the tipping ram from a pump unit in the packhouse. The oil flow is controlled by sensors on the intake conveyor, which adjusts tip angle so as to maintain the line capacity.

1.3 CLEANING

1.3.1 Dry loose soil

This is accomplished by passing the crop over a series of small apertures, which allows loose soil and small clods to fall away. The crop is often agitated to help soil sift down through the spaces between the larger objects.

Several systems are used, the main ones being as follows.

1.3.1.1 Spaced bar conveyor (web)

This normally has bar spacings to suit the size of crop, being as wide as possible, without the crop falling through. In many instances a basic bar gap of, for example, 30 mm is used, and by adding 5 mm thick sleeving, the gap can be altered to 25 mm (alternate bars) or 20 mm (every bar). The web is normally agitated by running it over shaped idler rollers, which impart vertical bouncing. Research by the Scottish Institute for Agricultural Engineering (SIAE) has shown that agitating the web horizontally produces better soil removal with less impact damage to the produce. In the SIAE system the whole cleaner conveyor is mounted in a chassis, which is vibrated horizontally. The SIAE work shows that inducing vibration at right angles to the bars (in the direction of crop flow) is the most effective, but even vibration in the direction of the bars is better than vertical motion. An alternative method for inducing vibration in the direction of crop flow is to impose some uneven motion into the drive by, for example, a severely angled universal joint.

Material falling through the top run of web often has to fall through the return strand also. As some clods might not readily fall through the second time, a 'trap link' is fitted. This is a pair of bars mounted together so that they hang down when on the return strand, to provide a large opening.

1.3.1.2 Rollers
(a) Plain spools are either spaced discs or moulded diablo sections threaded on to a series of rotating shafts. Crop flows across the spool shafts, encouraged by their rotation; this also rolls each object, so creating agitation. These spools are relatively gentle to the crop, but the spaces between can collect mud and long material in wet conditions. Spools can also transfer mud or juice from rots to sound produce.

The disc or diablo spacing is fixed, but on some machines the shafts can be moved to provide aperture adjustment; however, this complicates the drive system.

(b) Star spools are a variation of the disc spool, where the 'disc' is in the form of a 4 or 5 armed star in stiff rubber. These are placed on the shafts, so that the stars from one bank are between those on the adjacent ones. The motion of each star arm pulls crop out of the gap between those behind. The star speed is such that normal crop momentum allows the crop to be carried from one bank to the next, without much falling into the gaps; but if the speed is too high, crop can be flicked upwards and be damaged by the impact on landing. The rubber stiffness is also important: too hard a rubber causes damage, too soft allows blockage to occur. As there is some deflection of the star arm, the effective gap will be larger than the static clearance. Star spacing along the shaft is fixed, but most star cleaners have adjustable shaft centres so that the cleaning aperture can be adjusted.

1.3.1.3 Rotary barrel
This uses a cylinder 600–1200 mm in diameter, with walls of spaced bars or large aperture mesh. The barrel rotates slowly (typically at

15-25 rpm), slightly tilted downwards to encourage the crop to tumble along to the discharge end. If the speed is too great, the crop sticks to the cylinder walls by centrifugal force. The crop is well agitated by the tumbling action, which can be too severe for delicate produce. The barrel can be made 'spoked' or 'spokeless'; in the former case it is mounted on to a central shaft by spokes. A spokeless barrel sits in a cradle of rollers around the outside or, if small, might hang from a rotating shaft by strong drive belts. The spoked barrel damages the crop passing through it.

1.3.1.4 Rotary brushing
The crop is passed over a series of cylindrical brushes. Most machines have brush bars at right angles to crop flow, in the same manner as spools; a few machines use a cradle formed from cylindrical brushes along which crop flows. The cradle is tilted, so that the crop is worked along by a rolling action.

The cleaning action of a brusher is determined by its bristle density and stiffness, but these have also to be related to any skin damage caused. In many machines the crop flow can be retarded by strips of canvas hanging down so that it can receive more brushing. Where the crop is likely to be covered in hard lumps of soil, the first few bars might have stubby rubber pintle fingers instead of bristles, as they are better able to remove lumps.

In all cases of dry soil removal, some will adhere to the crop so strongly that the force needed to remove them will cause damage. It must, therefore, be recognised that there is a limit to the soil-removal capacity of any method.

1.3.2 Light trash removal
This is material like the dry outer scales of bulbs, and is best removed by suction. The equipment normally consists of a small fan unit, with a fishtailed suction head over the conveyor. The air inlet speed can be 15-50 m/s, depending on the density of material to be removed. To aid separation the fishtail is often positioned over the drop point between conveyors so that the scales are not being trapped by heavier objects.

1.3.3 Washing
Many crops are washed to ensure good soil removal. These might be roots, like carrots and parsnips, celery and leeks, or fruit and ornamental stock where plant health requirements dictate a soil free root.

1.3.3.1 Washing theory

Most soil is removed as a result of the erosion caused by a fast-running stream of water. The bond between soil and the plant surface is reduced considerably when there is water between them. This is the main reason for pre-soaking and, where this is not done, the crop must be in the washer long enough for water to penetrate the soil. Sprays from high-pressure nozzles are less effective as the water droplets contain little energy, and any impact force is lost within a short distance of the nozzle. High-pressure systems use small orifices, which require fine filtration and higher pump power to provide the pressure.

1.3.3.2 Pre-soaking

This softens adhering soil and reduces its hold on the produce surface. Pre-soaking is usually carried out in a large, water-filled tank or pond. The crop is slowly propelled through by conveyor or pumped water currents. If the pre-soak pond is very large, it can be used as the main mud-settling pond for the washing system. Tank pre-soakers are normally fitted with a rotary cage or conveyor to hold the crop below the water level, to ensure complete immersion. It is also possible to pre-soak in the first section of a long washer barrel or in an additional barrel washer sited ahead of the main washer. Soil and stones settling out in pre-soaker tanks can be removed by an inclined perforated conveyor sited in the tank base.

1.3.3.3 Stone separation

Where a crop is harvested with stones, but does not require pre-soaking, a flotation separator can be used. This is a small tank of water, arranged so that the crop floats across but stones and heavy clods sink. A conveyor in the base removes settled material. Crops that are too dense to float naturally are driven across the tank by a high-velocity water flow. The water is introduced with the crop and leaves over a weir at the discharge end. The difference in level between the inlet and the weir lip is adjusted according to the depth that the crop will sink during its travel across the tank. An elevator is fitted to remove settled stone and clod.

1.3.3.4 Barrel washer

This is similar in construction to the barrel soil cleaner. The washing can be either by deluging or by immersion.

(a) The deluge washer employs a cascade of water, which flows from a supply pipe above or inside the barrel (if spokeless). The water and soil run out of the barrel base.

(b) In the immersion type, the barrel sits partially submerged in a tank of water. Sometimes paddles are fitted inside the barrel to create agitation and propel the crop through. The discharge end normally has an adjustable aperture to regulate the time the crop spends inside.

1.3.3.5 Conveyor washer
This is used for more delicate material like salad crops. These are carried on a perforated conveyor through overhead water sprays, sometimes with additional sprays from either side and upwards through the conveyor. The washing action is gentler, but less able than the barrel to remove hard or tightly held soil.

1.3.3.6 Leeks and celery
These crops can have dirt lodged further into their leaves by the random water flow in a barrel or conveyor washer. Specialist washers overcome this by presenting the stick to water sprays, stem downwards, so that dirty water runs away from the leaf axils. Some systems use small carrier baskets hanging from a chain conveyor, others a pair of high-level gripper belts. In both cases the sticks are placed manually, and most carrier basket models are manually unloaded also. The carrier basket chain is in a continuous loop, so allowing any produce that has not been properly washed in the manually unloaded system to go through the system again.

1.3.3.7 Pintle roller
This is used mainly on potatoes, and resembles the dry brusher roller with added water sprays. The combined action of water with gentle scrubbing by the rollers removes most soil, and can help remove scab lesions from the skin.

1.3.3.8 Scrubbing washer
This machine was developed for washing carrots, where the positive scrubbing action could produce an extremely clean root. In most machines the crop is brought into contact with a scrubber unit as it travels along a conveyor. The scrubber can be either a matting of heavy woven fibres or banks of bristles. It is positioned above the conveyor trough at a height to ensure that the crop is in intimate contact with it. Crop flow is encouraged by either reciprocating the trough beneath a static scrubber or oscillating the scrubber over a static trough. A flow of water along the trough also aids crop flow and cleaning. The distance between the trough and the scrubber is adjustable, to allow for size variations and to vary the scrubbing intensity.

This type of cleaner is highly effective but can also cause high levels of breakage damage.

1.3.3.9 Water consumption

(a) The majority of the water used for washing is recirculated from the washer discharge, following a period of settling and screening to remove the worst of the debris it carried. This saves on the cost of water used for washing, and reduces the amount to be disposed of. In most cases the recirculated water is not sufficiently clean to ensure that the product is fit for market, especially salad produce offered for direct consumption. There is, thus, provision for a final wash with cleaned, treated water, usually drawn from the mains. This water is used on the final stage of the washer, and after use is allowed to run into the main circulation, where it makes up for water lost from the system, and displaces some of the dirty water to prevent the system becoming completely fouled.

On the deluge barrel and spray washers, the clean water is added through a separate section of pipe at the end of the run. On the immersion barrel, the clean water sprays are positioned over the conveyor that carries the crop out of the tank.

(b) The water flow rate for washers is shown in table 1.1.

Table 1.1

Washer water consumption

Washer type	Water requirements (m^3/t)
Rotary barrel (deluge)	2.7–5.5
Conveyor	3.5–5.5
Conveyor and pre-soak	1.0–2.0
Rotary barrel (immersion)	0.2–0.4

The above examples using the higher flows will normally include a high proportion of recirculated water. The immersed barrel requires a relatively small amount of flowing water, and all of this can be provided as fresh water for the final rinse. The conveyor system following a pre-soak requires a higher flow than the immersed barrel to make up for the lack of agitation in the tank. The amount of fresh water needed by the partial recirculation types will depend on the soil being removed, and the intended market for the produce.

1.3.3.10 Drying
This is desirable on some products, like potatoes and apples for pre-packing, to avoid creating rot conditions in the pack. The common system is to run the crop across a bank of sponge rollers. Water collecting in the sponges is squeezed out by a metal roller pressing against the underside of each one. Hot air also can be used to dispel the water, but the time and energy needed to evaporate droplets is considerable. This results in long drying conveyors to give the required time, and high inputs of air and heat to provide the energy.

1.3.4 Automatic separating methods
Several systems are used to identify differences between plant material and minerals (soil and stones). The common ones are as follows.

1.3.4.1 Translucence
(a) Short-wave radiation — X-rays and Gamma-rays penetrate plant matter more readily than mineral matter.

(b) High-intensity light beams which can shine through certain plant material. A sensor, on the opposite side of the crop to the source, 'sees' mineral objects as dark shadows, but does not see plant matter. The intensity of the radiation or light is adjustable to take account of both crop density and soil cover.

1.3.4.2 Light reflectance
The flesh of most crop matter is more reflective than soil, either to visible light or non-visible light like infra-red.

In all cases the material is first viewed on a conveyor, or as it falls from the end, and the relative positions of the rejects in the stream are memorised. The stream then flows or falls past a series of rejector fingers, activated by the memory, which deflect the rejects into a separate conveyor.

1.3.4.3 Crop density
The crop falls on to a bank of carefully sprung or balanced fingers. Vegetable matter, being lighter than clod or stone, is deflected by the finger; a heavy object forces the finger down, so that it drops into a reject conveyor below.

Systems involving a fall past sensors need adequate time for the signal to activate the deflector fingers. This is achieved by placing the rejectors some distance below the sensors, 200–300 mm being required to give sufficient time. This drop can lead to damage in some crops; the greater fall distance to the reject conveyor can cause so much damage to 'good' items that it is not worth trying to recover them. The stream must pass through the sorter in a single layer to avoid confusing the system. This limits the flow capacity. One system for increasing capacity pre-sizes the sample, so that any crop objects larger than the majority of clods and stones can bypass the sensor.

1.4 QUALITY GRADING

This involves both the rejection of unsuitable produce, and subdivision of acceptable material into a range of grades.

1.4.1 Mechanical sorting

Many of the decisions are too complex to be analysed mechanically, although in some cases one aspect is capable of identification, enabling partial mechanical separation. The best example of this is colour analysis. Tomatoes can be graded into 'ripe' and 'unripe' by measuring the amount of red or green present. On peeled potatoes a black bruise is discernible against the white flesh. The colour difference as it appears to the human eye in daylight might not be sufficiently strong to activate the selector. It is often necessary to use light of one colour (monochromatic) or two colours (bichromatic) to make the definition of the difference more dramatic.

Work is being carried out at the SIAE to determine the spectral analysis of the various defects of a potato. Such defects as greening, blight, scab, bare flesh and black rot have been defined in terms of a spectral wavelength 'fingerprint', which could eventually form the basis for a multi-defect sorter.

1.4.2 Manual sorting

The crop is presented to an operator on some form of conveyor. The workrate and accuracy of the operator is influenced by certain aspects of the conveyor design.

1.4.2.1 Object flow rate

Research in the U.S.A. has shown that the optimum flow of material past the operator is between 250 and 450 objects per minute. The mass flow rate of a crop on a sorting table should be a function of the size of its constituents. Examples of this are shown in table 1.2.

Mass flow is determined by varying the intake feed rate. On some lines this is under the control of the sorting operatives; on others it is fixed by the supervisor, to suit each sample.

Table 1.2

Mass flow rate of produce at 300 items/minute

Crop	Count per tonne	Mass flow rate (t/h)
Onions, 40/60 mm	15 000	1.2
Onions, 60/80 mm	7 500	2.4
Potatoes, seed	16 000	1.1
Potatoes, ware	8 000	2.3
Potatoes, baking	3 500	5.1
Brussels sprouts	125 000	0.14

1.4.2.2 Object presentation
Each object should be rotated slowly while passing the operator, so that all its facets can be seen. The normal method is a roller table, where the conveyor is made of free-running rollers placed between side chains. Each roller rotates either by running along a strip of frictional material beneath the table, or by means of gear teeth on one end which engage with a rack. Some simple potato sorters use a flat conveyor belt with strips of rubber hanging over at intervals, which roll the tubers backwards as they pass beneath.

U.S. research has shown the most effective method of rotation for near-spherical objects to be a flat belt conveyor, with a wide pitch rod link conveyor running about 50 mm above. Both conveyors run in the same direction, the rod link one travelling faster than the belt, thus causing the objects to rotate forwards as they progress. The speed of either conveyor is adjustable, to vary both the rate of flow past the sorter and the number of object rotations.

1.4.2.3 Crop presentation to the operator
There are two ways of doing this, the most common being 'sideways presentation', with the operators standing to one side of the belt, and the crop passing across the line of vision. The alternative is to place the operators at the end of the belt, so that all the material flows towards them. In the sideways presentation the operators frequently turn to view the oncoming produce, but this is uncomfortable for arm movements needed to pick off the conveyor. Forwards presentation is more effective, as the head and body are operating in the same direction, and has shown higher grading efficiency at fast flow rates compared with sideways presentation.

The other major consideration on a sideways table is whether all the crop flows past all the sorters, or whether each has a discrete flow. The first system is simpler, but results in the same crop being viewed by each operator in turn. Single-operator sorting does not allow a second person to take out anything missed by the first, but enables individual quality control assessments, training and bonus schemes to be conducted. Sideways presentation tables need special laning to permit single-operator flows, whereas this is automatic if forward presentation is used.

1.4.2.4 Sorting table division
Figure 1.2 shows the lane divisions for sorting crops into two grades plus an outgrade.

1.4.2.5 Manual select/mechanical rejection
Systems exist where the sorting operative simply identifies the object to be removed, and the equipment notes its position in the crop flow and removes it. The removal might be by powered deflector fingers as the crop falls from the conveyor or a small pneumatic piston beneath the conveyor, which punches the reject off the table. Most systems require the operator to stand at the sorting table and point to or touch the reject. At least one system allows remote selection by means of a television picture of table flow, from which the operator identifies the reject by touching its image on the screen with an electronic pointer.

1.4.2.6 Illumination
The operator's ability to recognise crop defects is influenced considerably by the illumination level over the sorting table. In many instances this involves artificial lighting, and both the quantity and the quality of this light are important.

The recommended illuminance level (quantity) over the table is 500–750 lux; this compares with a recommended 100–150 lux for general packhouse illuminance. This latter level is also important to sorting table operators, because following a spell under the high illuminance a poorly lit packhouse will appear dark, and the operators will be unable to see dangers. Artificial light usually involves fluorescent tubes mounted parallel to the table. A 2.4 m, 125 W tube at a height of 0.5 m should provide the recommended illuminance over a 0.6 m wide table, so two tubes should be regarded as the minimum for a double-sided table.

The spectral quality of the light is important for the ease with which the faults may be seen. Tubes of the wrong colour rendering can mask faults, while certain colours might exaggerate a fault beyond its appearance in natural daylight. Each crop will have its own spectral rendering requirements, but published data exist for very few. The recommendations for apples are a natural colour matching tube (such as Kolor-rite – Thorn-EMI Lamps Ltd) at 750 lux, and for potatoes a level of 500

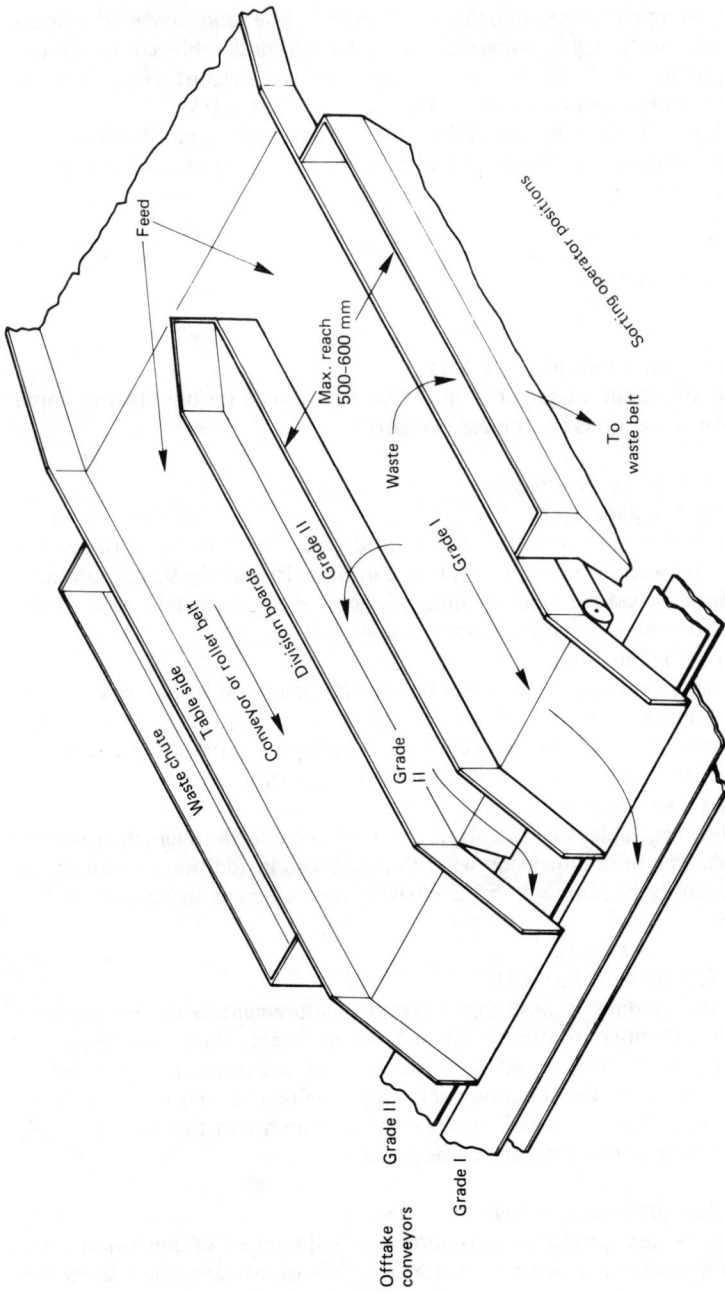

Feed

Max. reach
500–600 mm

Sorting operator positions

Waste

To
waste belt

Grade I

Grade II

Division boards

Conveyor or roller belt

Table side

Waste chute

Grade
II

Offtake
conveyors

Grade II

Grade I

Figure 1.2 Sorting table lanes.

lux, using either a combination of 'warm white' and 'daylight' colours or all 'north light' coloured tubes. Background table colour is also important, for example, apples are seen best against grey, potatoes against white or natural wood and carrots against black.

While a good level of illumination is necessary, excessive levels can cause eyestrain and will tend to mask wet or shiny products by bright reflection.

1.5 SIZE GRADING

1.5.1 Definitions of size grades

The size grade of an item might be determined by one, two or three linear dimensions or its mass (weight).

1.5.1.1 Sizing by dimension

(i) Single dimension

This is determined by the minimum distance apart of a pair of parallel bars between which the produce can pass. Irregularly shaped produce cannot be graded well by single dimension, as large, thin objects will take the same grade size as smaller spherical ones.

(ii) Two dimensions

These are determined by the distance between the sides of a square hole or diameter of a circular hole, through which the produce can pass. This removes much of the problem caused by flattened objects, but will still not distinguish between long and short cylindrical produce.

(iii) Three dimensions

A few vegetables like carrots might have to conform to length as well as girth. The third dimension will often be taken in addition to a square or circular hole standard, by a separate measurement using parallel bar gaps.

1.5.1.2 By mass (weight)

Weight grading is a straightforward measurement with the produce being presented in gramme (ounce) weight ranges. Thus a baking potato might be in the 170–200 g range. Weights and measures legislation in the U.K. does not condone pack weight being declared by multiplying the weight grade of the produce by the number in the pack. Instead, the final pack weight must be declared.

1.5.1.3 Grade terminology

In many cases produce size is quoted in 'millimetres' of dimension, only one measurement being given for two-dimensional sizing by a square or circular hole. Grades quoted in the form '40/60' indicate that all produce will pass through a 60 mm bar gap or hole, but none through one of 40 mm. Certain crops have the convention of being measured by length of their equatorial perimeter (circumference) rather than diameter. Thus a narcissus bulb of '16 cm' (160 mm) size is 51 mm diameter.

1.5.2 Size grading methods

1.5.2.1 Bar screens
This is the simplest form of grader, consisting of parallel rods, which grades the produce in one dimension only. The bars can either be fixed into a 'frame' or the crossbars of a conveyor. Crop flow on the fixed bar screen is promoted by either steeply angling it or shaking it when near horizontal. The latter system provides the best grade out of undersized produce, as the crop stays on the screen and is orientated during the shaking. On the fixed screen the crop normally flows along rather than across the bars. The main problem comes from objects near to the grade size, which can wedge between the bars and so interrupt flow. The conveyor bar screen carries the crop, and thus is less likely to block, but there is less chance for full orientation of the produce unless it is violently agitated, which makes its grading accuracy less efficient.

1.5.2.2 Perforated and mesh screens
This is the commonest method for two-dimensional grading and, like the bar screen, is made either as a rigid screen or in the form of a conveyor.

(a) The normal rigid screen is a grid of heavy wires accurately fixed together to produce the required hole dimension. The crop is shaken across the screen, thus serving both to transport the produce, and to re-orientate each object, so that it can have many 'tries' to fit through a hole. The riddle is either mounted on a slight slope, in the direction of crop travel and rocked horizontally, or held horizontal and caused to jump violently to throw the crop forwards in small increments.

The grader screen will normally have square holes, but for some crops other shapes are preferable, for example, slotted for narcissus bulbs and round for tulips.

Where circular or oval holes are required the screen will be made of flat rubber or plastic, with the holes cut in. As there is a significant amount of material between the holes on which the produce might sit, the holes are often made in rows along the screen, and low wooden strips fixed between each row to ensure that the product travels only over the perforated parts.

(b) Conveyor screens are formed of stepped wire sections, clipped together with flexible fasteners to form a conveyor belt. The screen conveys the crop and, with the help of agitation, undersized produce falls through. This action is more gentle to the produce than causing it to flow by jumping across a fixed screen, and with correct agitation the grading efficiency is similar. The screen holes are usually square, but rectangular and hexagonal ones are possible. The screen runs around a large, soft-faced roller at the discharge end. This helps to push out any objects that are partially wedged in the screen holes. Being a continuous band, the undersized produce falls into the centre of the band, and has to be removed by a transverse conveyor, rather than having to pass again through the underside return strand.

Screens of plastic mouldings held together with thin transverse pins are under development. These should lessen crop damage by presenting a surface of larger radius than wire, on to which the produce drops.

Either screen type can be obtained in a wide range of screen hole sizes, commonly in 2 mm increments between 20 and 95 mm.

The rigid screen is mounted in the grader in such a way that it can be easily exchanged for one of a different size. The conveyor screen contains a joining link to permit its easy removal from the grader.

1.5.2.3 Diverging belt

These grade in one dimension only, but quickly and gently transport the crop. The 'belt' is commonly a roller chain with plastic mouldings on the top for the produce to rest on. The chain runs in a guide channel to provide the lateral restraint needed to maintain the grading gap accuracy. The belts are in pairs, which diverge from the minimum grade gap at the on-feed end. The degree of divergence is normally fixed to take account of all the possible size categories. The desired grades are selected by the position of the discharge chutes beneath the belt.

Where more than one belt pair is used it is possible to mount them in a divergent (fan-like) pattern, so the crop is graded between any pair of adjacent belts. It is more common to mount the belt pairs in parallel, with the space between them blanked off to cause the crop to run only between the divergent belts.

Irregularly shaped objects have to be re-orientated as they sit on the belts, to provide the maximum chance for sizing. This can be done by flexible fingers hanging over the belts, which cause the object to roll as it runs beneath. Better orientation is achieved by running one belt faster than the other, to turn the object slowly during its travel.

1.5.2.4 Diverging aperture fruit graders

To avoid damage by the drop from between the belts, fruit graders are designed so that it rolls away from the aperture. This is aided by the spherical shape of the fruit. These types are often known as 'spinning sizers', because of the way that the fruit rotates as it is graded.

(a) Apple graders use a single flat belt lying over at an angle, with a smooth bar above (figure 1.3). The fruit is prevented from rolling off the belt by the bar until it reaches a point where the bar is high enough to let it roll under. The grader normally is divided into sections, with a bar height being adjustable over each, so that several grades can be taken. In the pear grader the bar is replaced by a moving belt to give a diverging belt action.

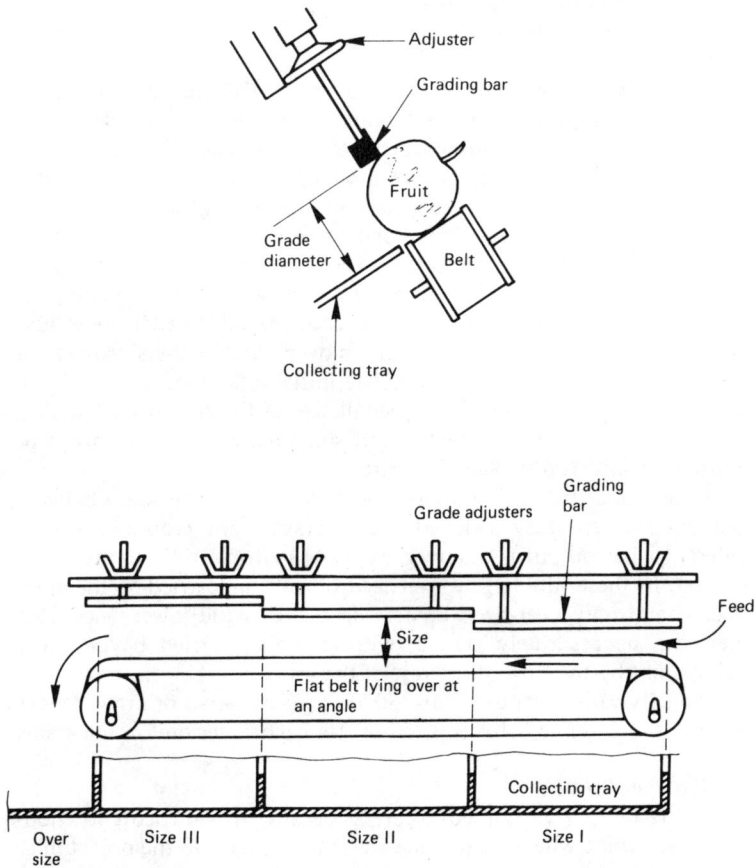

Figure 1.3   Spinning sizer fruit grader.

(b) Simple tomato graders do not use a moving belt, instead the fruit is placed on a large turntable with a stationary aperture bar around its perimeter. This bar is made of a number of sections, each placed at a progressively increasing height above the table and each height step corresponding to a desired fruit diameter size. The table is slightly convex so that the fruit rolls towards the perimeter, where it is retained by the aperture bar until its height above the edge is suitable for it to escape on to a sectioned tray around the edge. The sections of the tray correspond with the aperture bar steps. The fruit is picked from the trays for hand packing.

There is normally one section without any aperture bar to allow any oversize fruit to roll off the table.

1.5.2.5 Diverging roller

These are single-dimension units, grading on diameter, and are used predominantly for root crops (carrots and parsnips) in the U.K. although some versions have been produced for tomatoes. The rollers are placed along a sloped grading bed, so that the crop flows from one end to the other. In the simplest form, each 'channel' consists of a pair of rollers set closely together at the in-feed end, with the gap diverging towards the out-feed end (see figure 1.4(a)). The roller rotation and inclination causes the crop items to flow along, until the gap is sufficient for each to fall through. A series of chutes beneath the table catch the efflux, and the division between each can be moved to alter the size range of the objects falling into that chute. The initial roller spacing and divergence can be adjusted to suit the overall size of the crop being handled. Inclination is normally set to $10°$, but some machines allow this to be adjusted to suit crop flow characteristics.

Higher capacity machines have 3–10 roller sets. The space between each set is covered by a ridged cap to prevent any crop escaping the rollers. Higher output is obtained by using multiple roller units (figure 1.4(b)). In these, the largely oversized objects are carried on the upper rollers, and only near-sized objects drop on to the lower ones. Here they can be accurately graded, without being carried beyond their sizing point by the flow of the rest of the product.

Capacity varies between 250–350 kg/h for tomatoes or other delicate objects and 1 tonne/h for root crops, for each roller unit in the grader.

1.5.2.6 Parallel belt

Diverging belts have limited accuracy because it is difficult to choose the exact point where each grade starts and ends, and the object might not be rotated to its minimum dimension by the grade change. The parallel belt is more accurate since the gap is constant, and an object is correctly sized anywhere along the belt where it is orientated to its

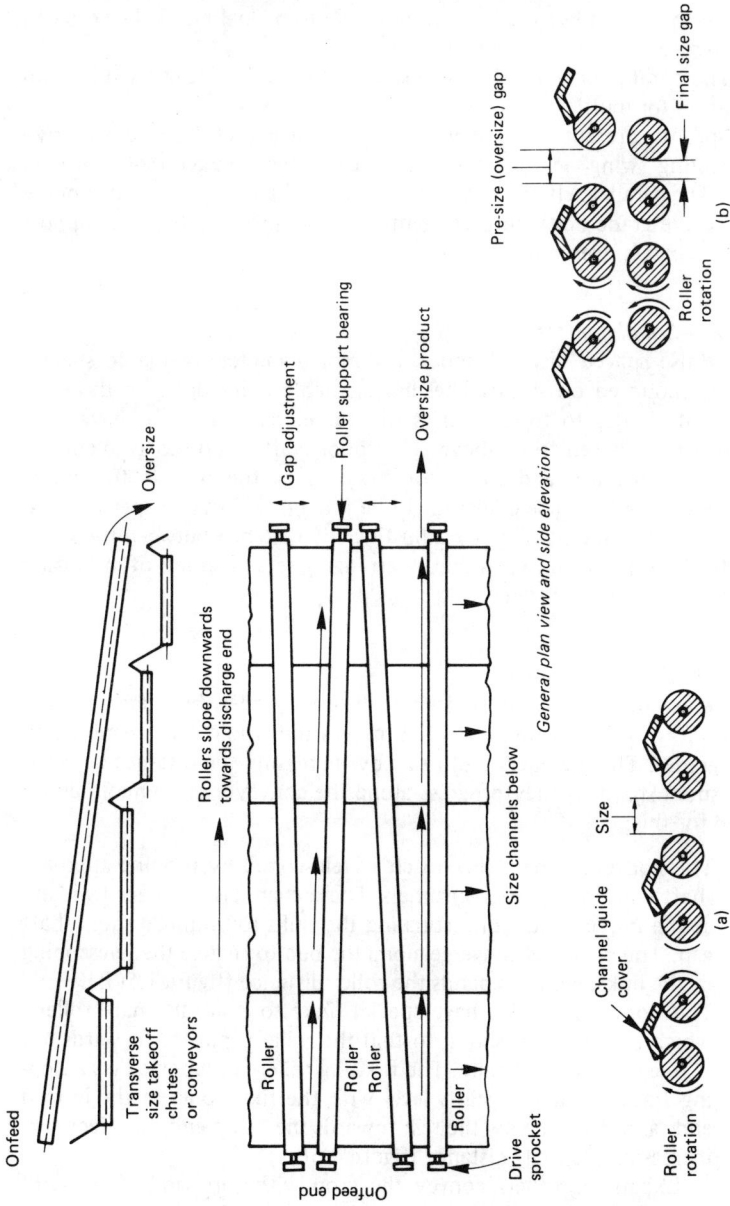

Figure 1.4 Diverging roller sizer: (a) single roller, (b) double or deep trough rollers.

minimum dimension. These units retain the differential belt speed to rotate the object but the belts do not have to be 'paired' — the crop can run between any two in the bed.

The parallel belt unit is single size, and several must be used in combination for multi-sizing.

Sprouts present a particular problem since they have one or two projecting 'wing' leaves which make them seem larger than the base size. The parallel belt unit can be fitted with a light roller or belt running above the grade belts, to press gently on the sprout so that the support of its wings is overcome.

1.5.2.7 Spool graders

These use spaced discs of about 150 mm diameter, or diablo shaped rollers mounted on shafts. The disc or diablo coincides with those on adjacent shafts, to form a series of square, rectangular or hexagonal holes when viewed from above. The spool shafts rotate so as to convey the crop forward, and this also re-orientates the objects for better grading efficiency. The grader might be fixed or adjustable aperture, the latter being made possible by adjusting the distance between the spool shafts. Multiple sizing is possible by arranging sets of spools of increasing aperture in the same frame.

1.5.2.8 Expanding roller

These use the same spool shafts as the spool grader, but here they are fitted into a chain conveyor which moves the whole roller bank along the grader. These graders multi-size by increasing the distance between the spool shafts as they progress along the conveyor. Two methods are used for this:

(a) The conveyor chain link pitch is telescoped by running alternate shaft ends in two track channels. These channels are spaced widely, at the in-feed end, concertina-ing the links for minimal spool shaft gap. The channels converge along the bed to reduce the telescoping of the links, which expands the roller distance (figure 1.5(a)).

(b) The conveyor chains have special links to hold alternate rollers, which have vertical slides, so that the roller is pushed forwards but is free to float vertically. The floating roller is supported on a sloping track, so that it starts level with the fixed ones at the in-feed end, and drops below the rest towards the other end, so effectively increasing the shaft distance (figure 1.5(b)).

Expanding rollers convey the crop with care, and offer multi-sizing with the ability to change sizes by altering the cam track or support track angle.

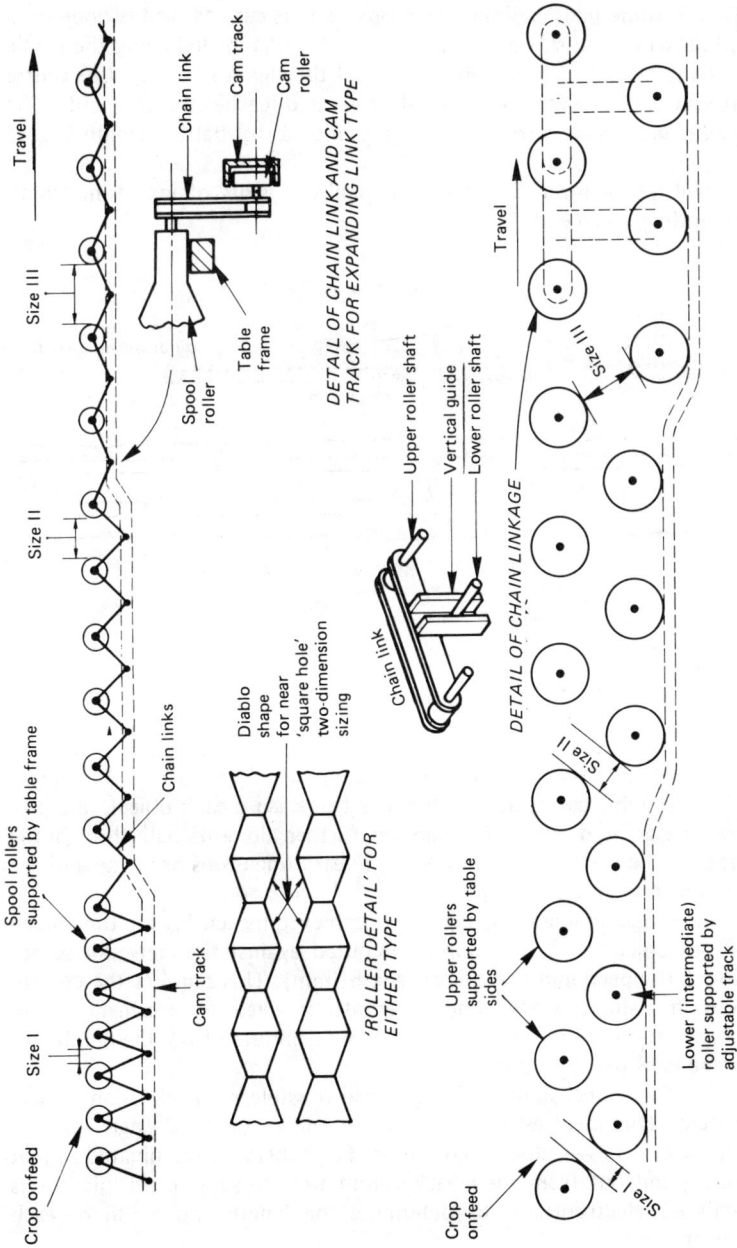

DETAIL OF CHAIN LINK AND CAM TRACK FOR EXPANDING LINK TYPE

'ROLLER DETAIL' FOR EITHER TYPE

Diablo shape for near 'square hole' two-dimension sizing

DETAIL OF CHAIN LINKAGE

Upper roller shaft

Vertical guide

Lower roller shaft

Chain link

Upper rollers supported by table sides

Lower (intermediate) roller supported by adjustable track

Crop onfeed

Travel

Size I

Size II

Size III

Spool rollers supported by table frame

Chain links

Cam track

Spool roller

Table frame

Chain link

Cam track

Cam roller

Figure 1.5 Variable aperture (expanding roller) sizer mechanisms.

1.5.2.9 Length grading

This is sometimes desirable in crops such as carrots, and is done on a riddle with long slot holes. The product is channelled along the riddle in its longitudinal direction. It will fall through a slot only if its centre of gravity goes over the edge before its end reaches the other side. The length grade will correspond roughly with a slot half its length (figure 1.6).

Multiple sizing is possible with banks of slots of increasing length from the in-feed end.

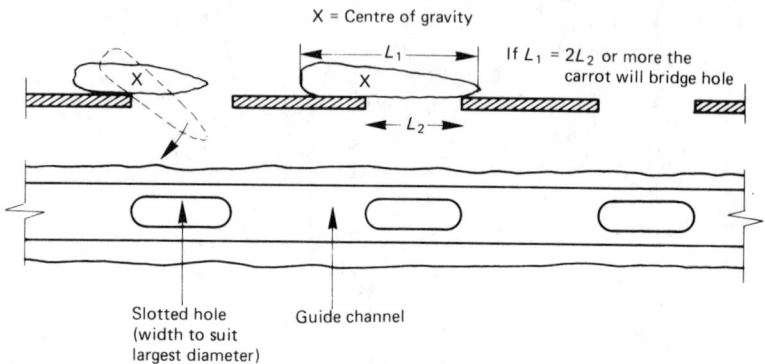

Figure 1.6 Length grader.

1.5.2.10 Electronic size measurement

These systems use optical techniques to measure each object, and programme grade diversion mechanisms further along its path through the grader. The systems measure either linear dimensions or the area of the shadow that an object casts.

(a) Single-dimension sizing can be achieved by sensing the time taken for an object to pass a point, computed against the conveyor speed: time (s) × speed mm/s = object length (mm). This requires the crop to flow in a single, spaced line. Alternatively a television camera system can be used, with the object size being computed from the number of frame lines that it occupies.

(b) Two-dimensional grading is also possible on a television camera system. This involves a camera looking down on to a single layer of tubers as it passes along a conveyor. The tubers are illuminated so that they stand out from their background and the subsequent 'picture' is analysed electronically to determine the length and width of each object.

(c) Volume is measured in one system by projecting the object, at a known velocity, through a biplanar light beam measurement device. The light beams measure the object's height and width, from which a cross-sectional area can be determined. These cross-sections are measured at intervals during the object's passage through the beam unit and, because the velocity is known, each interval corresponds to an increment of object length. This has the same effect as slicing the object into thin discs, the area of each being measured and then multiplied by the disc thickness to find its volume. The equipment determines the whole volume by summing the 'disc' volumes.

(d) Recent work at SIAE has shown that a potato can be graded optically by measuring the area of the shadow it casts. This has been found to correlate more closely with its mass (weight) than one or two linear dimensions.

(e) Objects with a wide variation in shape, such as Conference pears, cannot be graded well on a mechanical sizer and close grade conformity to a certain shape is not possible by weight grading. It is however possible, using a three-axis optical sizer linked to a specially programmed analyser which determines the stalk axis, to select fruits within a certain ratio of major to minor equatorial diameter.

Grade division techniques depend on the way in which the crop is conveyed. The television system, with a flow spread across the width of a conveyor, uses the same fall diversion fingers as in the waste rejection system. In the single file length measurement system, the crop is maintained in single file on a narrow belt, and deflectors mechanically push it sideways at the appropriate grade point. In both systems the object's position on the conveyor is noted, when it is measured, for diversion further along the system.

Most optical systems rely on the sensors clearly 'seeing' each object as a separate entity. This means that it must have sufficient contrast against its background, and not touch its neighbours. Contrast is especially difficult in root crops which might be grown in a variety of soils, from near-white limestone to black fen.

1.5.2.11 Arrangements for multiple grades

This is easily done on systems with divergence or expansion abilities. Other systems are of single aperture size only, and these must be used in multiple arrangements to produce a number of size grades.

(a) Sequential layout involves each grader feeding on to the next. As the oversize flows on to the next section each time, the system must start with the smallest aperture. The crop flow is linear with each undersize being taken out at right angles.

(b) Stacked layout involves the undersize from one screen falling on to the next. In this, the system starts with the largest aperture. A stacked system is more compact than a sequential, but the crop flow is more contorted, to keep each screen grade separate.

1.5.2.12 Grader accuracy and operation
The results of tests* on various types of potato grader are summarised in table 1.3.

Table 1.3

Potato grader accuracy (N.I.A.E. data)

Mechanism	Percentage grading accuracy				Damage
	Long-oval tuber shape		Flat-round tuber shape		
	low feed rate	high feed rate	low feed rate	high feed rate	
Spool	92.9	91.9	94.6	94.7	Negligible scuffing
Conveyor screen	98.5	98.5	99.1	99.3	6 per cent scuffed
Reciprocating screen	98.6	99.3	99.0	99.2	Less than 10 per cent scuffed

These results show that the long-oval tubers were slightly more difficult to grade than the flat-round. The spool type was marginally less accurate but gave the least damage. It was noted that the damage level increased as the feed rate fell or became intermittent; this was because tubers remained between the spools or were severaly agitated on the screens. It was also found that there was little difference in accuracy between a low feed rate and one that was 3 or 4 times greater (higher).

The basic findings on accuracy and damage in relation to throughput hold true for most types of grader, thus any installation should not be vastly oversized and the feed should be even.

1.5.3 Weight grading
This offers a more reliable system for close discrimination of product sizes, where even slight shape variation would confuse linear dimen-

*User testing scheme: National Institute of Agricultural Engineering, Silsoe, Bedfordshire.

sion graders. In the weight grader each object must pass the weigher head separately, with sufficient space from its neighbours to allow the system to react fully. The main mechanisms are as follows.

1.5.3.1 Mechanical balance systems
In most machines of this type the product is carried in specially supported cups, which tip when the prescribed weight is exceeded.

In the most common type the front edge of the cups is supported by transverse rods spanning between carrier chains. The remainder is supported by a projection which runs along a track; this has gaps at intervals corresponding to the cross discharge conveyors for each grade. The gap is spanned by a weight-sensing arm. If the cup is lighter than 'set', it is supported on to the next section of track. If the cup is heavier than 'set', the arm allows it to drop and tip its contents. The weight setting of each arm decreases progressively along the bed, so the heaviest is discharged first. At the end of the bed any remaining cups tip into the 'undersize' discharge; the cup belt returns beneath the grading bed and the cups are reset as they reach the filling point. On some graders the cups discharge directly to the cross conveyor, on others a trailing flap beneath each cup reduces the fall.

A simple system uses cups supported by their rear edge from a horizontal chain, and the weight of the produce is counterbalanced by a sliding weight on an arm projecting from the cup. At the in-feed end, the weight is pushed to the far end of the arm, thus giving the maximum counterbalance force. A small rail set at a convergent angle to the conveyor moves the weight inwards as the conveyor proceeds along its track. This reduces the counterbalancing effect on the cup, and when the product weight overcomes the counterbalance the cup tips its contents. An alternative is for the cups to slide across weight-sensitive supports, which reduce in force from the in-feed end. These allow the cup to tip when the weight of its contents overcomes the support restraint.

The nominal capacity of these types of grader is 0.75–1.0 t/h per lane of cups, but this range can be seriously reduced if singulator feed is poor.

1.5.3.2 Electronic weighing
The majority of electronic graders use the same cup track principle as the mechanical types, except that the cup contents are weighed by load cells at the in-feed end. The weight in each cup is used to program the opening of the appropriate track gap. In this system the product can be discharged in any order of grade, and it is also possible to subdivide the most common grade bands to avoid overcrowding on the discharge conveyors.

It is possible to combine a semi-automatic quality selector (see section 1.4.2.5) into the weight programme, so that two or three quality grades can be split into their desired weight bands on the one machine.

Low rates of flow can be dealt with by a single-head 'checkweigher' system. This carries the items in spaced single file over a scale platform, the weight being used to programme the appropriate deflector to knock the item off into the weight sector. These machines can deal with 30–100 items per minute.

In any electronic system the weigher head is constantly monitoring the weight on its tray, so the weight will be seen to rise as the item runs on, remain constant when all its weight is on the tray, and then diminish as it leaves. The electronics are programmed to search for this consistently high weight before the diversion mechanism is set. Some units also automatically reset their empty tare weight, by looking for the constant minimum weight period between each item, and calling this 'zero' for the next item. This allows for a build-up of dirt or moisture on the conveyor belt without affecting accuracy.

1.5.3.3 Singulation of product feed

The produce must be fed singly over any weigher system. The mechanical method for this is to channel it into a single stream in a chute of Vee section, and deposit it on to a cupped singulator conveyor feeding the weigher. Spacing on the singulator is achieved by running it faster than the channel feed, so that each item is taken away before the next one drops. The cups on the singulator are shaped in an attempt to allow them to hold only one item, so that doubles and trebles are eliminated. This is often aided by sloping or vibrating the cups. Hand correction can be applied at this stage. The singulator and weight grader tend not to run at 100 per cent cup filled capacity. This better ensures that each cup contains only one item.

1.6 PREPARATION FOR MARKET

Several types of fruit or vegetable need to be trimmed or undergo some other process to make them fit for marketing. The main activities are as follows.

1.6.1 Onion topping

This removes the old, dried foliage to leave a neatly finished neck. Two systems are used.

(a) The roller topper uses a pair of contra-rotating rollers, one of which is fitted with a sharp-edged spiral. The spiral both moves the onions along the roller and re-orientates them, to give the maximum chance for top to be drawn into the rollers. The size of the rollers is such that the spherical bulb sits on top of them, but any long material is drawn between them and broken off. In the commercial topper between two and ten pairs are fitted into a framework, the shape of which can be altered so that a crop that tops easily can run across quickly while a difficult one is restrained. The typical output is 1–2 tonnes/h per pair of rollers.

(b) The fan topper is built around a large propeller fan which is sited beneath the onions as they sit on a screen. Long material is drawn into the fan blades, which are sharp edged, and impact cut it. The onions are vibrated across a bar screen above the fans. This re-orientates as well as propels them, so that there is maximum opportunity for the top to be drawn through.

The roller topper is simpler in operation, and is capable of ingesting a high percentage of the top. However, the scrolls can damage the bulb skin, and the wrenching action of the roller can pull the necks from onions whose tops are not completely brittle. The fan topper is gentler on the onion but its success at ingesting top is less, especially on a crop with short foliage following field topping. The blast of air created by the fans can cause dust problems in the packhouse.

1.6.2 Radish topping
Roller toppers with appropriately sized rollers have been used successfully to top radish.

1.6.3 Bulb cleaning
The roller principle is used to remove skin and husk from gladiolus corms and the old flowering parts from tulip bulbs. The rollers are usually smooth and rubber covered, and grip the bulb waste by friction. This is sometimes aided by keeping the rollers dampened by a light water mist. The cleaning action is a combination of rubbing the husk and pulling the longer material. The rollers revolve slowly and in multi-roller machines they are driven so as to rotate for 3 or 4 revolutions in one direction, and 3 or 4 in the other. This allows each roller to react against that on either side alternately, and avoids the need to restrict flow to between specific pairs.

It is sometimes advantageous to pre-condition the bulbs by, for example, leaving them in a warm, wet atmosphere for the mechanical cleaner to work effectively.

1.6.4 Leek and celery trimming

This involves the removal of the part of the base plate that contains the roots, and cutting back the upper growth to the marketable part of the stem. The crop is passed through a pair of saw cutters for this, the spacing of the saws being equivalent to the average marketable stem length.

(i) Horizontal presentation

The stems are fed through the saws, laid across a flat belt. The crop is placed on to the belt by hand, with the root ends aligned to a guide. The cutters are vertical circular saws and, to prevent the stem moving while being cut, a second conveyor or soft roller is mounted above to press it on to the belt. The root is trimmed to the datum set by the guide, but as the topping saw is at a fixed distance from the root saw, all the stems are cut to the same length irrespective of the amount of marketable length each contains.

(ii) Vertical presentation

This uses a vertical in-feed, with the material placed by hand between gripper belts. There is no need to place the stem accurately, as an automatic root plate sensor is used to align them. This consists of a spiked belt pressing on to the root; the spikes are sharp enough to penetrate the root hairs but not the root plate, so they push it downwards to a fixed level. In this machine the cutting is by handsaws running across several gripper belt units.

(iii) Cutter wear

The saws need specially hardened teeth to resist abrasion from the soil carried among the roots. A blunt saw will make a ragged cut and can push the stem out of line, so that it trims at an angle instead of straight across. The normal tooth material will be a metallic carbide, which is very wear resistant, but care must be taken to choose the correct type, as some are very brittle and would be broken by hitting small stones.

The crop is normally washed after trimming to remove debris.

1.6.5 Sprout trimming

Some sprout harvesters leave small heels of stem attached to the butt of the sprout. It is possible to machine trim the butt square and remove this heel. The trimmer consists of a Vee-shaped guide with an open bottom along which the sprout is rolled by a conveyor belt pressing from above. The rotation causes the sprout stem to poke through the guide base at intervals, and cutters running beneath the guide trim any projecting material. The system works best on spherical sprouts, where the only part to project below the guide is the stem; pear-shaped sprouts can be over-trimmed if the machine is not carefully set. The sprouts have to be within a close size range, 2–5 mm is suggested, having been graded on a machine working at a pressure equivalent to that of the conveyor belt used to propel the sprout. The pressure grader will ensure that soft or winged buttons are not pushed further into the trimmer guide than their grade requires.

1.6.6 Apple polishing

These machines are designed to buff the naturally occurring waxes on the fruit's surface. Two methods are used, brushing and wiping.

The brusher is similar to the dry brusher described in section 1.3.1.4, the fruit flowing across a series of softly bristled rollers. This action can achieve an acceptable finish, and is relatively kind to spherical fruit, but there is a risk of the bristles marking the surface of more irregularly shaped fruits.

Wiping is carried out by soft cloths which are attached to rotating shafts mounted above the crop at right angles to flow. The crop is carried on either a conveyor or a roller brusher, similar to that mentioned above. This type is less popular than the roller, owing to the risk of the cloth tips becoming loaded with surplus wax and other dirt and so marking the fruit.

1.7 WEIGHING AND PACKING

Most horticultural produce is sold in packs of declared weight, with the remainder by declared quantity (count). Produce is sold in either bulk packs for redistribution by the retail trade, or ready for direct customer sale (pre-pack). There is no firm definition of what constitutes a bulk pack or a pre-pack, but normally quantities for direct sale of under 5–7 kg are termed pre-packs. The weighing and packing equipment for pre-packing differs from bulk packing, because of both the material used for the pack and its size.

1.7.1 Bulk packs

1.7.1.1 Bulk bin and sack weighers/fillers

These will normally be between 10 kg for sprouts and carrots, and 25 kg for potatoes. The pack is a pre-formed sack of paper or netting, which is closed after filling by tying or stitching. Most bulk weighers operate on the inclined belt principle, where the produce is lifted from a hopper to the weighing head by a belt inclined at 40–50°. The belt has flights which are designed to carry only a single layer of produce, any excess rolling back as a result of the inclination. The weigher often incorporates two belts, a wide one for rapidly filling the sack to near the desired weight and a narrow one taking only a single line of product for 'making up' the final weight. The sack is fixed on to a weighing scale, which incorporates two micro-switches. One controls the main belt and is set to cut off when within 1–2 kg of the final weight, the other acts to stop the make-up belt at the final weight. The point of action of the make-up belt switch has to be adjusted to take account of product 'in flight' between the belt and the sack, which will depend on the product mass. The twin belt machine is capable of weighing to comply with U.K. weights and measures legislation. Single-belt machines will place approximately the correct weight more rapidly, but need subsequent manual recorrection. These are often termed 'auto sack fillers' to avoid confusion with the 'weights and measures approved' twin-belt machine.

Some of the single-belt types incorporate a dial scale, so that the operator can adjust the weight while the sack is *in situ*, on others the sack has to be placed on a platform scale for final correction. Weighers that fill directly into the sack impose a limit on capacity, as the machine has to wait for the sack to be changed. Capacity can be improved by using an intermediate weighing pan which the machine fills while the sack is being changed, and dumps its load rapidly into the empty sack.

The sack is held on the filler by friction clamps and has to be placed manually in most machines, although one type will automatically open and place certain types of sack. The clamps are often operated by compressed air so that both the operator's hands are free to place the sack; the sack is released by a foot pedal while picking up and opening the next.

Output is 200–300 packs per hour where the bags are placed and removed manually, 350–500 packs per hour where the bag is placed manually but fed under the weigher and released automatically, and 500–600 packs per hour where the bag is handled automatically at all stages.

In some cases produce will be reloaded into bulk boxes for transit to another site for packing or processing. These boxes will need to be loaded without damaging the produce. Several methods exist for this, the most common being as follows.

A descent elevator, which can be raised as the box fills.
A zig-zag 'fall breaking' discharge chute from a horizontal conveyor, raised as the box fills.
Tilting the box so the conveyor can commence filling into the bottom corner.
A descent conveyor with height adjustment and having a rotating distributor at the bottom end (primarily used for apple bins).

1.7.1.2 Apple box fillers

It is possible to fill both cell packs and trays by mechanical means.

On the tray filler the fruit is encouraged to roll down a chute on to the trays as they pass beneath on a conveyor. The chute angle and fruit flow are arranged to allow a single layer to amass at the lower end of the chute, so that the lowest row is continually carried away by becoming lodged in the tray depressions. The chute is oscillated gently to help fruit flow and to aid its distribution into the depressions. The filled trays move to a position from which an operator can place them in the outer box. On current machines the trays are also placed manually, but automatic destackers and loaders are under development. Tray placing normally requires an operator, in addition to the one for box filling, but in some types the tray feed is arranged so that trays are loaded at the same end as the box filling, to allow one operator to do both jobs. There is also a need for some manual correction of the filled trays. Although this is sometimes done by the tray loader or box filler, high capacity lines use a separate operator.

In the cell pack filler a thick foam conveyor replaces the trays; holes in the foam correspond with the final positions of the fruit in the cells. The cell dividers are fed from a roll, in a continuous 'honeycomb', and drop over the fruits in the foam conveyor holes, so that one fruit is positioned within each cell. At the end of the foam conveyor the fruits are drawn from their holes by the cell matrix which continues forwards. Immediately following the foam conveyor is a flat belt, which carries the layer of paper used to separate the cell layers in the box. The loaded cell matrix runs on to this and the assembly is carried forwards to an operator, who cuts the cell matrix and its paper undersheet into lengths to fit the box. This system requires one person fewer than is needed for the tray filler, but the output is slower; typical rates are 40×14 kg (30 lb) boxes per hour for the cell type and 60×18 kg (40 lb) for the tray type.

1.7.2 Pre-packing

The equipment for this falls into two sections, weighing and packaging.

1.7.2.1 Weighing systems

(a) Most mechanical scale weighers work in a similar manner to an inclined belt bulk weigher, and can have single or double belt feed. Produce is run into an open pan sitting on a dial scale. In the single-belt unit only the approximate pack weight is run into the pan automatically, and has to be corrected by an operator before it is discharged into the pack. The double-belt system works as in the bulk weigher, with the second belt being a low-capacity make-up to final weight, after the main belt has stopped; these units can weigh to legal standards automatically.

A method for increasing output per operator is to place several pan and scale units on a turntable. Each unit passes beneath a product feeder, to be filled automatically to the approximate desired weight. It then rotates to pass before an operator for correction, before the pan tips automatically into the bag, and the finished pack is then discharged on to the offtake conveyor.

In most systems another operator is needed to place the empty bags on to each scale unit, but at least one system can take its bags automatically from a feeder unit, provided that they are special wicketed types. The single-head unit will produce up to 10 packs/operator/ minute, whereas the multi-head will pack up to 40 packs/operator/ minute.

A few weighers use horizontal vibrating chutes instead of a belt to feed the product to the weighing pan. The vibration of the chute settles the produce into a single layer, and some might be channelled to regulate the flow even more. The vibrating chute is a very gentle method for conveying and singulating the product, but is less positive if it tends to flow badly. The flow is rapidly stopped by dropping a flap across the chute end without damage to either product or conveyor.

(b) Computerised electronic systems have been developed to overcome the mechanical weighers' inherent minimum accuracy of one unit of produce. For example, if potatoes weighing 120 g each are used to fill a 2 kg pack, the weigher will only be able to fill the pack to within 120 g of the desired weight. Thus its best accuracy will be 120 g/2000 g or 6 per cent. As each pack must contain at least 2 kg to comply with weights and measures legislation, the producer will 'give away' up to 6 per cent of the produce being packed.

Some weighers now use micro-computer technology to achieve tolerances of less than one unit. The machines operate by weighing either each piece of produce or small batches of it, and computing the best combination of these to make up the final weight.

The single-piece system uses a cupped conveyor, carrying one product in each cup. Like the fruit weight grader, each cup is weighed, but this is done several cup spaces ahead of the discharge point. The empty pack is first filled to around 75 per cent of its final weight by taking all the pieces of produce from the cup belt while summing their weight to know how much is in the pack. The difference between the part weight and the final is then used to calculate the closest combination of product weights remaining between the weigher and the discharge, these being taken and the remainder recirculated to the intake. If there is not a suitably close combination, it will continue to run until one is found.

In practice the system will only work on a product with a diverse weight range, as very closely graded material will cause the machine to run for a long period 'looking for the correct combination'.

In the batch system the feed mechanism dispenses about one-quarter of the desired pack weight into 10 or 12 weigh pans. The computer then decides on the four pans that will best make up the final weight. The product feed into the weight pans need only be crudely controlled by switching off the main conveyor flow as the desired pan weight is approached, without using any fine feed to finish making a set weight. This has the twin advantages of speed and less damage, as no singulation is needed in the feed.

The batch machine is complex and expensive, as each pan needs an accurate weighing unit. However, when annual throughput is high, expenditure on these types of computerised weigher can be justified on the saving in 'give away' over conventional units.

1.7.2.2 Packing equipment
Produce can be packed into nets, plastic film bags or rigid punnet trays.

(a) Bag-filling equipment is simple in construction and operation. It normally consists of a chute or funnel around which the bag mouth is secured. The bag is normally hand opened and placed, but can be released automatically by a foot pedal while the operator is picking up the next one. 'Wicketed' bags are made specially for automatic opening and even placement. In this system the bag has one side longer than the other; bags are threaded on to a pair of horizontal rods by holes in their longer side, so that the front bag in the batch tends to hang open like a pouch. The opening is sometimes aided by an air jet. Wicketed bags can also be used horizontally for packing produce like leeks where a fan jet opens the topmost bag, and a chute at bag height guides the produce in. The bag is normally torn from its support rods after filling, automatically exposing the next empty one.

(b) The net sleeve machine forms its bag by gathering the end of the sleeve and clipping it to form a base; when the produce is in place the sleeve is gathered above and two clips are placed, one sealing the existing bag, the other forming the base of the next. The net is then cut between the two clips. The net is stored in a large ruck around a long tube down which the produce is tipped into the clipped bag end. The sleeve is loosely held, so that the produce weight draws the net off the tube; its descent is halted at a point where the top of the net can be gathered. The clipping head is activated by each filled bag end dropping away from the tube end.

The tube holding the net sleeve is detachable from the pre-packer, so that it can be replaced by another when its net is exhausted, and the empty one refilled without loss of running time.

The polyethylene sleeve unit works in a similar manner, except that it is heat sealed into a flat end, rather than being bunched.

(c) Punnet tray fillers consist of a carousel or pocketed conveyor which during manufacture is held under tension while it cools. This or conveyor is indexed by one tray space at each weigher cycle; there is usually a sensor to prevent product from being discharged if a tray is absent. In simple systems the trays are placed and removed manually; more complex machines can automatically de-nest a stack of trays and pass filled ones to the lidding station. Some fillers for discrete objects, like apples and tomatoes, can place the required number of fruits into a celled tray, with one in each cell.

Lidding machines vary in complexity, and often their design will be closely related to the lid-fastening system. Some lids snap on to projections on the tray, while others are glued with heat-activated adhesive. The latter system is a more versatile lid but the glue can be affected by wetness or dirt on the product. Simple, manually fed carousels can be used for glued lids, the lid and tray being placed at the first station, rotated into the heat press station and unloaded at a third station. Punnet trays can also be covered with film, using the equipment described in section 1.7.4.

1.7.3 Counters

Some products like flower bulbs and seeds are sold as a declared number rather than a declared weight. These require a packaging machine which counts out the desired batch. The most common system is for the object to interrupt a light beam which operates a pulse counter. Many systems use infra-red, to avoid normal daylight or artificial light interfering with the optical detector head. The product has to pass through the light beam in a single row, and there must be a gap between each object to allow the light to hit the detector to reset the pulse switch. The counter subtracts one from its set total each time an object is sensed. When it reaches zero it activates a flow switch, and when the pack is replaced the counter automatically resets to its original total for the next batch.

1.7.3.1 Bulbs

The bulb counter has a bed of Vee-shaped channels which are vibrated to cause single lines of bulbs to move along them. The feed on to the chutes is slow enough to allow the bulbs to space themselves in transit. The sensor heads are just below the discharge, so that the bulb falls through the light beam. The pulses go to one counter, which activates small flaps on each channel end to halt the flow when the prescribed number has passed.

1.7.3.2 Seeds
Seed-counting systems normally use a vibratory bowl feeder to provide a single line of spaced seeds. The bowl has a small track spiralling gently up the inside of its wall. When the bowl is vibrated the track acts as a small vibratory conveyor to cause a line of seeds to climb out of the bowl. Various profiles in the track ensure exclusion of any seeds not climbing in a single line, and a change in track slope towards the top speeds up the line to space it. The seed line falls past the counter head which, when satisfied, operates a flap to divert the seed stream back to the bowl.

A clear gap to allow the beam to shine on the detector is essential to the counter operation. If any debris bridges this gap, or dust occludes the detector, the counter will not sense the gap and will continue to count only 'one' until the detector receives another burst of light. Dust and free debris can be removed pneumatically, and sometimes adhering debris can be discounted by increasing the beam strength to shine through it.

1.7.4 Wrapping

1.7.4.1 Overwrapping
This normally refers to wrapping fruit and vegetables in transparent film. It is increasingly being used for semi-prepared produce, such as peeled white cabbage, broccoli spears and sweet corn cobs, or soft fruit in punnets offered for direct sale. Most produce is overwrapped manually because of its shape and frailty.

(a) In the manual system a film dispenser unit is used to simplify the provision of film lengths to the correct size. In this the film is pulled from a roll, and when the correct length is reached the pull is relaxed, and the film sags on to a hot wire which cuts it. The dispenser is normally fitted to the rear of a table on which the overwrapping is carried out. The table can also be fitted with a hot plate to heat seal the film ends around the product.

(b) A more mechanised dispenser uses a pair of conveyor chains fitted with grippers to pull the film from the roll, and a powered cutter. The cut length of film is carried across a flat table with a hole in the centre and released across the hole. The product is pushed through the hole by hand, taking the square with it. It is caught beneath with the other hand to finish the folding of the free ends manually. The conveyor speed is adjusted to keep time with the rest of the operation.

(c) In at least one machine the heads are pushed mechanically into the film squares. The wrapped portion is then gripped in a cup, which allows a system of small rollers finally to fold the free flaps over the base and seal them.

1.7.4.2 Shrinkwrapping

This is used on some salad crops like cucumbers. It uses special film which during manufacture is held under tension while it cools. This produces an in-built elasticity, which is released only by rewarming the film. The shrink film is normally produced in the form of a sleeve of suitable width for the product to be inserted easily.

The product in its length of sleeve is passed through a heated tunnel. This warms the film and allows its elasticity to pull it tightly on to the product. A high level of heat is used, so that the film is rapidly warmed, but the heat has no time to penetrate into the produce.

1.7.5 Bundle tying

1.7.5.1 Twine systems

Products like nursery stock bushes are often tied into bundles for ease of handling and the assembly of sale packs.

(a) The tyer normally uses string which is fed around the bundle by a long curved 'needle', into the jaws of the knotter. The string is fed to the needle through spring-loaded plates, which impart a tension to it. The string tension is used to pull the bundle together, before knotting. It is possible to use elasticated twine, so that material like flower stems which cannot be compressed without damage can still be bound into a tight bundle.

(b) Some products are assembled into bunches manually, and placed into the tying machine where the needle and knotter are worked by a stroke from a foot pedal. Other tying machines use a conveyor to feed material into an assembly yoke within the needle arc. The bundle formed in the yoke is then tied and discharged automatically, before the tyer resets for the next. The bundle size is either regulated by its increasing diameter triggering the needle, or regulated by the number of objects passing under a sensor wheel, which trips the knotter once each revolution.

1.7.5.2 Taping

Bundles of fresh vegetables look better if tied with tape rather than twine. The taping machine consists of a curved guide arm, around which the tape runs, and a sealing/cutting unit at the point where its outer end meets the base. When the arm is raised a strand of tape runs from its outer end to the sealer. The bundle is pushed against this tape, and the arm is brought down to wrap the tape strand around it, finally sealing the ends and cutting them when it meets the base. The tape feed tension can be adjusted to give the required bundle seal.

1.7.6 Carton and bag sealing

1.7.6.1 Sacks and bags
The tops of these can be sealed by stitching or tying.

(a) The stitcher is in the form of a small electric sewing machine either fully portable and run across the bag top by hand, or mounted on a stand over a conveyor which carries the bag through its jaws. The latter machine can be sited immediately after the bagger unit, so that the filled bag is dropped on to the stitcher conveyor and the top flaps pulled up and guided into the stitcher.

Stitching can be done on paper or netting bags, although the latter might need a strip of plastic across the sewing point to hold the stitches against the net.

(b) Tying normally involves bunching the top of the bag, and winding a length of wire around it. In manual operations the wire is placed around the neck and the two ends twisted together. Usually a simple tool is used to twist the tie; this consists of a spirally grooved shaft mounted in a barrel handle, while a hook at the end of the shaft engages in loops at each end of the tie. As the handle is pulled away from the neck the shaft rotates, thus twisting the tie; a ratchet in the handle allows it to return without the need to turn the shaft to repeat the twisting operation. The automatic wiring machine forms a ring of heavy wire (4–5 mm diameter) around the bunched neck, the ring resembling a simple keyring. The machine forms the rings from a continuous length of wire, the mechanism carrying out bunching, cutting the wire to length, and forming it round the neck in one operation.

1.7.6.2 Cases and boxes
Cases can be sealed by self-adhesive tape or stapling.

(a) Self-adhesive tape systems work best on dry packed materials, and are likely to fail totally on cases of freshly washed produce.

Taping machines unroll self-adhesive tape across the joint of the top flaps. The tape is fed under slight tension, to achieve a tight seal. The taper might be hand held and drawn over the case, or frame mounted with the case passing beneath on a conveyor.

(b) Staples positively fasten the case flaps, but can damage produce directly beneath, and require to be rust resistant for wet produce.

Some stapling machines resemble those used in offices, with an anvil plate which is held beneath the cardboard, to clinch the staple legs. The anvil must be mounted on an arm which passes under the case flaps.

As there is a practical limit to the length of the anvil arm which is sufficiently rigid to clinch the staple, non-anvil 'carton staplers' are also available. Instead of the anvil, these incorporate a pair of clinching fingers which follow the staple in from the top, and twist inwards to turn the staple legs over. These can work on any size of carton, but the produce must be kept below the legs of the staple as it passes through the lid and is clinched.

Simple anvil staplers can be fully portable and hand operated, or mounted in a simple frame and foot pedal operated. In the latter type, it is possible to mount several staplers in one frame, and operate them all with a common bar from the foot pedal.

Carton staplers are often power operated from either compressed air or mains electricity.

1.7.6.3 Pre-pack sealing
These are often sealed by taping, using a hand dispenser which applies a ring of self-adhesive tape around the bunched neck. Other methods include clipping, in the same way as the net sleeve filler, heat sealing film bags and putting small plastic clips around the bunched neck.

1.7.7 Weight/price ticketing
Pre-packed produce can be prepared fully for retail sale by adding a ticket stating its description, weight and price. These can be produced automatically by a printer directly connected to the weigher unit assembling the pack. If the pack is hand assembled its ticket is prepared by the pack passing over a flow weigher scale connected to the printer. The pre-packer ticketing unit normally produces a small label, which is clipped into the pack seal. The flow weigher uses a self-adhesive sticker, which is either automatically applied to the pack, if the shape is suitable, or if not, presents it to an operator in synchronisation with the product passing him on the flow weigher discharge conveyor.

1.8 PACKHOUSE LAYOUT AND DESIGN

1.8.1 Materials handling
This is one of the biggest influences in packhouse efficiency. A normal operation will have the following material flows.

IN	OUT
Raw product A	Packed produce in trays
Raw product B	Packed produce on pallets
Raw product etc.	Second-grade material
Boxes for bulk produce	Waste plant matter
Paper/plastic packaging	Waste soil, stones etc.
Empty supermarket trays	Dirty washing water
Pallets	
Clean water	

There will also be numerous sub-flows within the packhouse.

1.8.1.1 Conveyors and pallets

Some of the product will move on conveyors, and some on pallets or in bins which will involve movement of forklifts or pallet trucks.

(a) Most conveyors require straight runs with definite angled turns, and are unable to snake around other pieces of equipment. In many cases transfer from one conveyor to the next involves a small drop, and consequently there is a loss of height towards the outflow end. Raising the incoming product to a height which will accommodate this series of downward steps is preferable to keeping to one level, with numerous small elevators between each item of equipment.

(b) The flow should preferably be in one direction, with intake to outlet at opposite ends of the building. If only one access is used, the handling flows will often be found to conflict, especially where the packhouse is being used for fresh produce, where later harvestings will be received at the same time as earlier batches are dispatched.

The dispatch area often requires more planning than the intake as there will be many separate orders to be assembled and removed as and when transport arrives.

(c) Where there is significant movement on pallets, a level flat floor is required to permit hand pallet trucks to operate. This will make the packhouse and dispatch more compact and safer for the workforce than if forklifts have to be used.

(d) Waste is often removed by conveyor or water flume channel. The flume will have to be at, or below, ground level, and needs careful design to prevent the waste settling out or clogging it. The conveyor might be at this level also, or pass high across the tops of the equipment. In many instances the waste handling will need to pick up from several points on the line, and discharge to a point separate from intake or dispatch. This can often involve the conveyor crossing the shed at right angles to the main product flow, and a floor level installation will cause an impediment to through traffic by wheeled vehicles.

(e) Congestion around the packaging equipment can be reduced by feeding the packaging in as it is used, rather than storing it within reach of the operators. This can be done by installing a second (mezzanine) floor above the packing area, where packaging materials are stored and, after any making up is done, fed directly down chutes to the packers. An alternative is to use a neighbouring building to store and make up materials, with a recirculatory overhead conveyor running to the packer, carrying the materials on hooks. The materials are removed as required, and the remainder recirculated after empty books have been refilled. One conveyor can travel over all the packing lines, carrying the full range of packaging.

(f) The area needed for placing the packs on pallets can be minimised by having only one palletising point, fed from all the packing lines, rather than one for each line. This involves combining the packs on to one conveyor, and resorting them for the appropriate pallet. This is practical only where the different packs are easily discernible.

1.8.1.2 Water channel (flume) handling

This technique is an extension of the flotation emptier (section 1.2.4), where water is used to convey the product into and around the packhouse. Fluming can be used both for crops which are to be washed and for gently handling top fruit.

Flume water velocity must be matched to the crop; for example, laminar flow is essential if fruits are to be prevented from bumping together, while stronger flow will be needed to prevent soil from a root crop settling in the bottom.

American recommendations* for potato flumes can be summarised as follows.

Water/crop volume ratio 8–10:1 for optimum performance; maximum ratio 6:1.

The best practical shape is either square (water depth = width) or trapezoidal (side slope about 1:12).

Water velocity should be 1 m/s in straight main flumes and 0.5 m/s in branch flumes and at intersections.

Intersections and bends should be at a sharp 90° angle, lesser angles and radiused bends cause more damage.

The bottom should slope at 1:220 for flumes less than 15 m long; 1:180 for 15–50 m, and 1:140 for longer flumes.

Where the base slope is insufficient to prevent sedimentation, mud sumps should be installed at convenient points.

Gentle, laminar flow can be achieved by discharging the water over a weir at the crop discharge end, and introducing the water sufficiently ahead of the crop feed for turbulence to subside. The crop should be removed by a perforated elevator across the flume width, ahead of the weir. Sparge jets might be needed to assist root crop flow, but must be avoided for fruit.

Because, in most flumes, the water is recirculated there is a real danger of the water becoming heavily contaminated with crop debris and micro-organisms; this can lead to shortened shelf-life. Water treatment is essential to prevent this becoming serious.

---

*'Designing Flume Systems' in Orr and Hunter, *The Potato Storage*, Michigan State University, 1976.

1.8.1.3 Flow regulation

There are often times when the product flow rate does not suit certain sections of the line. There will be times when the line is empty because of intermittent box tipping or bulker changeover. The quality of each batch might demand more or less attention to trimming or sorting, and overfeeding or starving the packers, or the packers might halt the line periodically to change pallets or packaging.

One simple, short-term accumulator used for fruit and tomatoes consists of a transverse rod conveyor, in which the rods are free to rotate. Under normal flow conditions the rod/side chain friction and lodging in the inter-rod spaces are sufficient to move the crop, but when flow is obstructed the rods freewheel and the conveyor runs freely beneath the crop.

Where holding times exceed the capacity of this type of conveyor accumulator it will be necessary to install proper storage arrangements at strategic intervals along the line. These might be surge accumulators, holding only 10–20 minutes' worth of line capacity; or buffer hoppers, holding maybe two or three consignments' worth of a certain grade.

As the final product is increasingly being demanded to tight specifications, which often do not amount to economic flow rates for sophisticated packaging equipment, this latter system allows one such machine to sequentially pack several grades on resupply from the stock bulks.

Modern 'cold chain' distribution systems require that produce be delivered to the retailer at specific temperatures. In many cases it is cooled prior to packing, and during its time in a warm packhouse can rewarm to above acceptance temperature.

1.8.1.4 Avoiding damage

Much of the damage in the packhouse can be attributed to the movement between machines or processes by conveyors and elevators. The main points to consider are the following.

(a) Keep the number of elevators to a minimum, as it is often preferable to lift the produce to full height at the in-feed and allow all other stages to be by descent. Flights and large drive drums increase the fall distance.

(b) Chutes and other joining devices can accelerate the crop and increase impact damage.

(c) Very fragile products, such as apples, can be damaged by congestion where flows are turned or decreased in width. This factor increases with the less spherical shapes of certain varieties of fruit.

1.8.2 Produce flow for manual operations
An essential part of trimming and packing operations is the feeding of
raw product to an operative, and conveying away the finished product,
waste and down-graded material. Normally this involves several people
working side by side, so the conveying systems must service each one,
without hindering their actions.

1.8.2.1 One-way feed
In this system the product is fed along a wide belt with operators to
one or both sides. The feed belt brings produce from the intake, and
each operator takes it off at its own rate. Normally the belt discharges
to waste, so that any produce not taken by the operator is regarded as
unsuitable for market.
   The main problem is ensuring an even feed to all operators. The flow
might be too heavy, so that much of the product accumulates by the
last two or three operatives. They might be able to stop the belt to
allow time to deal with the backlog, but are still given an unfairly high
workload, or else good crop is wasted if they do not bother to stop the
belt. If the feed is too slow, the later operatives get little material, or
the earlier ones take the easiest items, leaving the more difficult for
those down the line.

1.8.2.2 Recirculatory feed
This overcomes the above problem by returning any items to the in-feed
end, which pass all the operators again.
   (a) The simplest system is a rotary table, where the produce is carried
in a band around the edge. The operators sit around the table and take
off the items for trimming, and any which are left go round again. The
produce is fed on to the edge at one point, or on to a shallow cone in
the centre to roll to the edge.
   (b) To cater for a large number of operators, twin contra-running
conveyors can offer a better building utilisation than a large rotary
table. Transfer from one conveyor to the other is by either a deflector
plough, or a 'U' bend conveyor at each end.
   All recirculatory systems allow random choice for each operative,
and each can work at its own rate. In the cone-fed rotary all the produce
can flow to any point, so that there is no 'first pick' or 'last pick' position. Because the system is recirculatory all the material eventually
must be removed by hand, as there is no 'end' point for rubbish discharge; there is also a risk of the crop becoming increasingly damaged
by repeated cycling.

1.8.2.3 Accumulation of packed material
The rotary table is often used as an accumulator at the dispatch end of the line to allow the operator assembling the packs time to change the pallet or bin, without hindrance of line flow.

1.8.3 Environmental factors

1.8.3.1 Atmospheric conditions
In many operations involving a cleaning process, quantities of dust or dirty water droplets are liberated into the atmosphere. This can seriously affect the working conditions of personnel in adjacent areas. There are two ways of reducing this problem.

(a) Segregation of the building into 'clean' and 'dirty' areas. The dirty area should contain such operations as box/bulker unloading, soil extraction, washing/dry brushing, onion topping, and any application of chemicals. The clean area can contain the sorting, packing and dispatch areas. If the dirty area is smaller than the clean area, the dirty atmosphere can be contained within it by enclosing it, and installing a suction fan to create an inflow of air at 10–15 m/s at all openings where conveyors or other machines pass through the walls.

The dirty area suction fan needs only to have sufficient capacity to prevent dirt egress through the openings, rather than trying to remove all the dust from inside it. If the clean area is relatively small and compact, it is easier to enclose it and install a system which provides a positive pressure of clean, warm air. The walls separating the two areas can be canvas sheeting with Velcro sealed joints, so that it can be opened easily for maintenance of the equipment inside.

(b) Where dust or spray is created at only one or two points in the line, the problem is best solved by fitting a dust suction system to each point, so that the problem is solved at source.

There is no satisfactory way to remove dust from the general packhouse atmosphere by installing extraction fans in the outside walls. The air velocities needed to capture the dust particles will result in uncomfortably high currents of air, and very large fan systems.

A clean environment is also essential for many modern packaging machines, as dust can seriously affect the delicate mechanisms and precision components. Where there is no 'clean area' in which the machine can be installed, a dust-proof enclosure with filtered air supply can be used.

1.8.3.2 Temperature

(a) Temperature requirements for the various operations of the packhouse will differ. For example, operatives handling boxes and bags will find a lower temperature more comfortable than those standing at a sorting or trimming table. The building effectively can be divided into 'sedentary' and 'active' areas, running at temperatures of, for example, 20°C and 15°C respectively. This can also help the 'cold chain' system, as produce is more likely to be stood in the cooler intake and dispatch areas and move quickly through the warm sorting/trimming area.

(b) The heating system should provide the best environment, without excessive use of fuel. It is normally considered in air conditioning design that the feet need to be warmer than the head. A contrary effect is created by natural convective heat distribution, where warm air rises, resulting in a warm roof area and a cold floor. This effect is often exacerbated where warm air is blown in at a high level.

Where possible the heat should be put in at a low level by, for example, underfloor heating. In an existing packhouse the operatives should stand on a false floor, raised above the concrete high enough for warm air to circulate beneath. Convective heat rise can be contained by fitting vertically blowing fans in the roof.

In a badly designed system the roof area of a packhouse can rise to over 30°C where heat is applied to maintain a temperature of 15°C at the floor. This can lead to a high fuel consumption, without producing the desired operator comfort. Loss of heat and comfort through draughts from open doors can be reduced by strip curtains which create a reasonable air seal, but allow free movement of vehicles. It is preferable to design the produce flow so as not to involve vehicular access into the main working area.

Insulation of the walls and roof will reduce not only the heating requirement but also solar heating during summer months.

1.8.4 Workplace layout

The manual operation might involve trimming and overwrapping a cabbage, bunching flowers, bagging lettuce or assembling a weight of bean pods.

(a) Normally it is done on a small table adjacent to the feed conveyor. The finished product is returned to a second conveyor, often running parallel to the feeder. This also must be within reach of the operator, to avoid the product being thrown on the conveyor hence suffering damage. On rotary tables a separate lane ring can be fitted to take finished product, this being unloaded either manually or by deflection to the discharge conveyor if it is the outermost ring.

The waste conveyor commonly runs beneath the feed conveyor, so that waste and trimmings can be pushed down a chute on to it from the table. The rotary table can have a lower tier for waste, with a scraper into the waste conveyor at one point.

(b) Second-grade produce is not normally catered for by a further separate conveyor; instead it might be distinctly identified (class I cabbage wrapped, class II left bare), and put on to the finished product conveyor or, if apparent at the in-feed end, the first operator might pick it off into a bin.

(c) Some crop treatment that involves two operations, like cabbage trimming and wrapping, can be made easier by concentrating on one part of the job for a time, then the other. For this, the table must have a holding rack, so that a number of items can be stored after the first task, to await the operator's change to the second.

2 GLASSHOUSES AND TRANSLUCENT PLASTIC STRUCTURES

These are used to provide the necessary artificial environment for the production of crops for which the climate is unsuited. Certain crops are grown in opaque structures; these are discussed in section 3.5.2, chapter 3.

2.1 CONSTRUCTION
These buildings were formerly known under the generic name of 'glasshouses', but an increasing number use plastics or other translucent materials. The construction is still largely peculiar to the type of cladding, the two basic types being glasshouses and plastic-covered tunnel structures.

2.1.1 Glasshouses
There were formerly many different shapes and sizes of glasshouses, including aeroplane, cucumber, vinery and dutch light. Most of these have been superseded by two main categories, widespan or multispan.

2.1.1.1 Widespan
This has a single pitch of roof covering an area as wide as 20 m. In order to give the roof sufficient pitch to shed rain and snow, the ridge is high above the ground, and a large part of the house volume is contained within the roof triangle. This can be advantageous in providing a large volume of air above the crop which is better able to absorb changes in humidity and temperature. The drier, more buoyant atmosphere suits tall flower crops, such as roses and carnations. There is, however, a slight tendency for any added heat to rise and accumulate in this space, although this effect and any steps taken to remedy it are very dependent

50

on the heating system design. The widespan house has all the weight of its roof carried by trussed frames which rest on stanchions along each side, and thus there are no internal supports to obstruct machinery and crop layout. The widespan can offer better overall light transmission than the multispan, as there are no intermediate gutters to stop light. In the U.K., few true widespan houses have been built in recent years.

2.1.1.2 Multispan

This is built up from a number of smaller span units normally either 3.2 m or 6.4 m wide. These houses have a lower roofline than the widespan, and thus there is a smaller volume of air above the crop which can be advantageous for those requiring higher humidities; crops requiring drier conditions can be accommodated by using extra ventilation. In most houses roofs are supported by a row of stanchions beneath each gutter, the exception being the 'floating gutter' type in which the gutters are supported by a series of transverse beams, which are in turn supported by stanchions placed at spacings wider than one span. (figure 2.1).

The stanchions can prove an impediment to machine working, although there is still a clear path at least 3 m wide along each span, and the floating gutter house offers even wider clear paths. This type of construction does not require the heavy foundations of the widespan, as the weight is spread over more stanchions. However, the stanchion

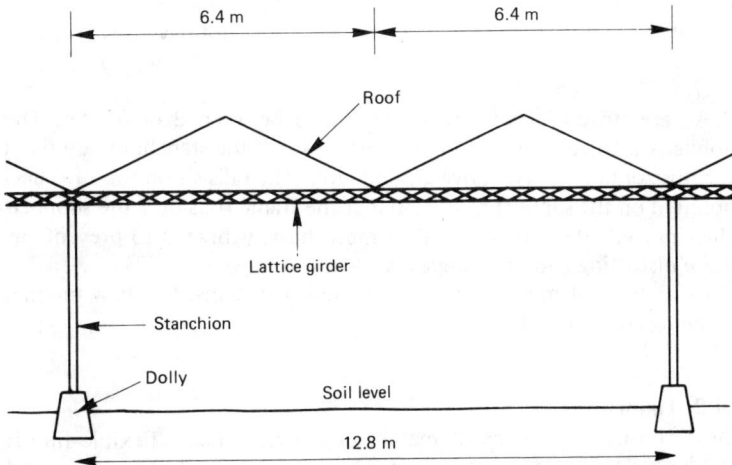

Figure 2.1 Floating gutter glasshouse roof.

bases must offer sufficient anchorage to prevent the house being lifted in strong winds. The rows of stanchions allow for easy subdivision of the house, and can provide supports for heating pipes and crop wires. The lower roofline reduces heat loss into the unproductive upper areas of the house, but the gutters between each span block some of the light falling on the house.

These houses are often known as Venlo types, after the region of Holland where they were first popular, and were a development of the 'Dutch light' house. This latter type consisted of independently framed glass panels (lights) mounted on a support structure. The 'light' is usually made to a common size of 1.70 m x 0.76 m, and this gives rise to the basic Dutch light house dimension of 1.8 m eaves height (one light on a row of concrete blocks) and widths of either 3 m (two lights angled together to form the roof) or 6 m (four lights). This type of house is easily constructed and moved, but suffers from lower light transmission than a Venlo because of the thick timber frames. Few Dutch light houses are built in the U.K. now.

Most of the structural metal is steel, protected from corrosion by galvanising. The zinc in the galvanising corrodes very slowly in relation to the steel it covers. However, even very dilute acidic contaminants in the house atmosphere produce soluble zinc salts on the galvanised surface. These can be washed on to the crop beneath by condensation drips, and cause zinc toxicity problems (zinc drop symptoms). This can be prevented by coating the galvanised surfaces with a water-repellent paint, such as calcium plumbate; normal paints, especially bituminous, should be avoided, as their petroleum-based solvents are also toxic. The aluminium used for other components does not have this problem.

2.1.1.3 Mobile houses
These are structures which can be moved between 2 or 3 sites. The mobile is a Dutch light or Venlo type in which the stanchions are fixed to a horizontal rail just above ground level. The rails sit on top of rollers mounted on the support blocks, so that the frame rolls over the supports when moved, the structure being more heavily braced to prevent the house distorting and breaking glass when it is moved.

As a result of modern intensive cropping systems, few new mobiles are being erected in the U.K.

2.1.2 Tunnels
These consist of a series of metal hoops over which a flexible film is stretched. The hoop spans between 4 m and 7 m, and can be arranged as a single span or multispan units. These latter consist of hooped roof members supported on vertical stanchions. The hoop is normally made

of 25, 32 or 40 mm nominal bore (nb) water pipe, and should be of the U.K. 'blue band' classification which has a wall thickness of 3.25 mm, although narrow tunnels might use 20 or 25 mm outside diameter, drawn metal tubing. Spans up to 5 m use a plain hoop, while wider ones incorporate bracing members into the upper area, to increase the snow and wind carrying capacity.

In small tunnels the hoops are made of one continuous length of pipe, as joining two shorter pieces by welding or screwing can seriously weaken the hoop at that point. In the braced wider tunnels the tube between each bracing point and the lower brace and the floor is also in a complete length. Attachments of bracing or longitudinal members are made with special tube clamps (Kee Klamp) rather than welding or using screwed pipe joints, a wide range of these being available to cater for most combinations of tube number and angle of divergence.

Commercially made tunnels use machine rolled hoops. A do it yourself construction is possible by bending the pipe around a semicircle of heavy posts, or using a hydraulic pipe bender, but in both cases considerable trial and error is needed to arrive at the correct profile.

Tunnels can be constructed on bare soil sites by bedding a flat plate with a vertical steel spigot on to firm subsoil, or by fixing the hoop ends directly to railway sleepers. To aid construction, the spigot is made to slip inside the hoop pipe and be retained by a pin. Whatever system is used, it must also be designed to prevent the tunnel being uplifted by wind.

The cladding sheet can be fixed by special clamping strips, but the simplest method is to dig the sheet into the soil either side of a single tunnel or to roll it twice around a timber batten and bolt this to the framework. This latter method can be used to join sheet to any part of the frame, and is used as the gutter fixing on multispan units. Sheets are usually used in a single width, as jointing by adhesive or heat welding is seldom satisfactory. The maximum sheet width of 11 m normally is the limiting factor to the width of single tunnels or each span of the multispan.

Attempts have been made to construct a mobile tunnel, using a similar horizontal ground rail to support the hoop ends. These have been moderately successful, but as the tunnel lacks the weight and rigidity of a glass construction, it has to be longitudinally braced, and also have holding-down points at each location.

2.2 LIGHT TRANSMISSION CHARACTERISTICS

The light required for photosynthesis, more correctly termed 'photosynthetic active radiation' (PAR), must pass through the cladding. Not all the PAR existing in outside daylight passes through the cladding. The most suitable materials transmit between 82 and 92 per cent, some plastics with lower transmission values being unsuitable for most crops. These figures relate to the translucent material itself, in single thickness and in clean or clear condition. Mounting the material on a frame reduces the overall transmission value because of the shading effect of the framing; for example, the crop in a Venlo glasshouse clad with glass of 87 per cent transmission might receive only 65 per cent PAR. The loss effect of multiple layer cladding is accumulative; for example, in double glazing using two sheets of glass, with a light transmission efficiency of 87 per cent, the outer one will transmit only 87 per cent of the PAR and the inner one only 87 per cent of that, meaning a composite transmission of only 76.6 per cent.

Light transmission into a structure is also influenced by the angle of the sun's rays to the glass. As most houses have a large roof to wall area ratio, the slope and orientation of the roof is more important than that of the walls. It is accepted that a roof should run east/west rather than north/south to collect as much sunlight as possible in winter when solar angles are low. A single house with a north/south orientation will receive the maximum summer sunlight and this can be advantageous for crops which grow into the upper parts of the house, such as cucumbers and tall flowers, because both slopes of the roof are equally exposed to light.

As most of the light not transmitted by a multispan roof is lost by reflection, the NIAE* have devised a glasshouse roof shape which reflects the lost light downwards, through the next north-facing slope (see figure 2.2). For example, the 17 per cent of light which might be lost by reflection shines on the next roof, which transmits 83 per cent of it, so that only 17 per cent of 17 per cent, that is 2.9 per cent of available light radiation, is lost — all by reflection from the second roof slope.

All materials are liable to get dirty, and often this dirt becomes ingrained through the action of chemical pollutants which etch the surface; plastics also occlude as a result of degradation caused by ultraviolet radiation. Glass and rigid plastics can be cleaned by pressure washing with detergents, and ingrained material removed by a solution of hydrofluoric acid, which etches off a layer of glass surface to a depth below the grime. Commercial plastics often contain ultra-violet inhibitors (UVI); these are mostly absorptive compounds, and when they are replete, degradation will set in.

*National Institute of Agricultural Engineering, Silsoe, Bedford, U.K.

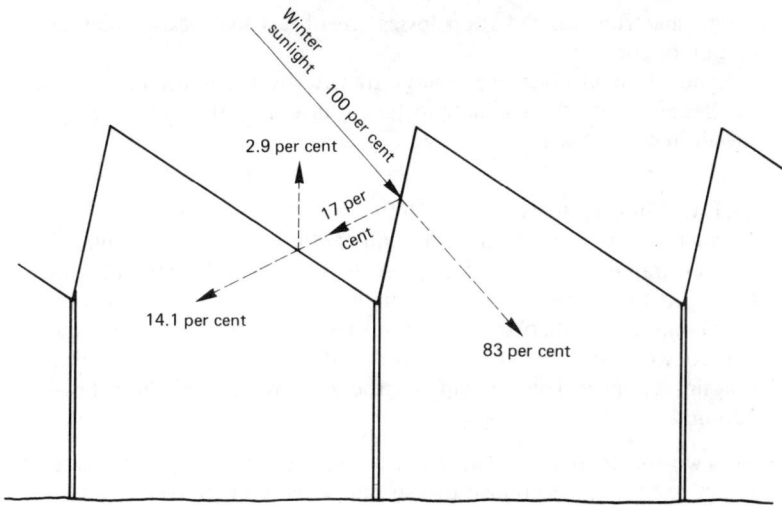

Figure 2.2 Asymmetrical glasshouse roof for maximum light gain.

2.3 SOLAR HEATING EFFECT

Most translucent materials allow radiation energy in the visible and ultra-violet parts of the spectrum to pass, but reflect energy in the longer wavelength, infra-red part of the spectrum. Sunlight contains mostly visible and ultra-violet radiation, which passes into the structure and heats the crop; this converts the energy to infra-red radiation, which is trapped within the structure.

2.4 HEAT LOSS REDUCTION

Heat can be lost from the structure by three means, convection, radiation and conduction.

Convective loss is largely governed by the airtightness of the structure, because warm air will rise towards the roof and escape through any gaps there, and be replaced by cold air leaking in through the lower parts of the walls. This can be minimised by sealing all possible gaps, although if the house is heated by an appliance which draws its combustion air from within the house, due allowance must be made for fresh air induction.

Radiation losses are due to long-wave (infra-red) energy emissions from warm objects in the house. However most translucent materials are opaque to all, or a large part, of the emissions in this part of the energy spectrum, so radiation losses are of less significance than conduction or convection.

Conduction involves heat energy transfer by the house air warming the cladding, and the cladding in turn transferring its heat to the outside air in contact with it.

2.4.1 Cladding systems

Conductive loss can be reduced significantly by 'double glazing'. This involves trapping a layer of air, which is a relatively poor heat conductor, between two sheets of material. The optimum air gap is 15-25 mm; if less than this it will not be fully effective, and if much wider it will allow air to circulate within the gap and so its effectiveness is again reduced. The air gap is produced by one of the following methods.

(a) Two sheets of glass. These can be flat sheets held apart by spacers or one flat sheet bonded to a second sheet with cranked edges. This latter unit is only the thickness of two sheets at the edges, enabling it to be fitted into most 'single pane' glazing bars.

The added weight of the second sheet of glass might produce loadings beyond the design strength of the framework. Light transmission will be reduced by the second sheet of glass, and this effect is worsened if thicker structural members are needed to support the extra weight. These systems can save 40-50 per cent of the heat loss suffered by single glazed structures, the exact value being dependent on the effectiveness of the air gap seal.

(b) Double skin rigid plastic, normally available as a composite moulded or extruded unit, consisting of the two sheets and thin spacing ribs between. The two main materials are polycarbonate or acrylic (PMMA); others such as polypropylene, polyethylene and PVC have been tried, but appear to suffer from greater ultra-violet degradation or light loss than the two accepted materials.

The air gap for most sheets is only 4-8 mm (polycarbonate) or 15-20 mm (acrylic), but any loss of effectiveness is partially compensated by its being in larger sheets, which have fewer joints to let in draughts. The sheets are lighter than double glass, and thus do not over-load the framework. Some materials are also sufficiently flexible, when new, to bend to fit tunnel hoops. The sheet length allows many sizes of tunnel to be clad with a single sheet from apex to ground level. These materials are stronger than glass when new, but ultra-violet degradation can cause embrittlement; in some types this has occurred within two or three seasons. Despite a potential heat loss saving equivalent to 50 per cent of the transmission of a single glazed house, these materials have yet to become widely used in the U.K.

(c) Underdrawing with transparent polyethylene sheeting. This both creates the necessary static air gap, and reduces draughts coming through joints between the panes or the glass and the frame. The sheeting is normally fixed inside the framing, giving a nominal air gap thickness of the back of the glazing bar, but this will vary as the sheet sags. Some films have matrices of air bubbles trapped within. These add slightly to the insulation value of the sheet, but their big advantage is in acting as spacers to maintain the minimum air gap from the glass. Other translucent film insulants use two layers of sheet separated by encapsulated bubbles, to create a composite air gap insulation material. These materials will save 35–45 per cent of the heat loss suffered by single glazed structures.

Light transmission is reduced by the layers of polyethylene sheeting, especially if they are left *in situ* for two or three years to accumulate dust and become increasingly opaque from ultra-violet degradation. Where this degree of light loss proves detrimental to a crop, the grower might line only the house walls. The potential heat loss savings from this will be reduced to between 5 and 10 per cent, depending on the ratio between the roof and wall surface areas.

(d) Heat loss from structures with flexible plastic cladding is reduced by using two layers of sheeting, and spacing them by means of air pressure from a small fan.

In tunnels, the inner sheet is supported by the frame, and the outer sheet is pushed away from it by the air pressure.

In glasshouse-type framed structures, the films are made up of twin skinned panels that fit between the glazing bars as direct glass replacements. In both types the gap can be reduced to bring the two film surfaces together; this aids cooling on hot days by increasing conductive heat loss potential, and improves light transmission by combining the two refracting surfaces.

Condensation can occur between the films if the inflation air is drawn from inside the house. If drawn from outside, it is warmed by heat coming through the inner sheet, and is raised further from its dewpoint so that condensation does not occur.

The foregoing 'double glazing' systems can also cause a rise in relative humidity within the house. This is mainly due to the inner surface being warmer, hence raising the dewpoint temperature of the surface and reducing the amount of moisture removed from the air as condensation. In addition, methods (b), (c) and (d) will reduce air exchange.

2.4.2 Thermal screens

Where a permanent 'double glazing' system would cause an unacceptable light loss, or its installation proves impractical, it is possible for the secondary layer to be in the form of a temporary screen, commonly termed a 'thermal screen', drawn across the crop at night and opened in the morning.

Thermal screens might be made of polyethylene film or light-weight woven materials. The main requirement is to segregate layers of air, although the material's heat conductivity (k) value can have a marked effect on fuel savings.

The screens normally rest on single filament nylon cables stretched tightly across the house. These must be positioned so as not to impede access by man or machine, but to be below anything in the roof which might obstruct movement, such as vent gear. In multispan houses the screen is divided into sections, each drawing across or along a portion of the house. Even in single-span houses the screen might need to be divided to pass supports or braces. Despite screens being in several sections, they are drawn simultaneously by a common winch system to which the leading (moving) edge of each is fixed. To ensure that each section opens and shuts fully, its leading edge is only loosely clamped to the winch wire. The winch winds about half a metre further than should normally be required to move the sheet. As each leading edge comes to a stop at its open or closed position, the clamp allows any excess wire travel to slip through. This ensures that all the sheets are fully drawn either way, without the need to finely adjust each leading edge to the winch. Each wire in the system is drawn by a common motorised winding tube running across or along the house; one wire is fitted with catches to operate the motor control stops.

Condensation and rain leaking in can collect on top of an impervious drawn screen, to form ponds which can seriously over-load the supporting cables.

Because light level is important to most crops, the drawn back screen should create the minimum of shading. 'The drawn screen can cause an overall light loss of 2–3 per cent on an overcast day, but with heavy localised losses under the material stowage positions. For this reason also, the screen is normally drawn back soon after dawn, to allow the maximum period of daylight exposure, but on frosty mornings this can lead to a mass of cold air falling from the roofspace. This can be prevented by pre-warming the roofspace using heating pipes placed above the screen.

Other designs of thermal screen system have been tried, the most common being a series of 'lay flat' tubes, positioned in the roof so that they touch when inflated. These are, however, difficult to deflate fully and when hanging limp, create a louvred effect which reduces light transmission.

While the major heat savings can be effected by screening the roof, there is also interest in fitting curtains of similar materials to the sides and end of the house. Many materials have been tried, either as permanent curtains with a relatively good translucence or more opaque materials which can be drawn back. To be effective the roof screen must make a good seal with the wall curtains; this is usually achieved by arranging that the screen edges trail over the top of the curtain.

The main value of a thermal screen is in heat savings; these can range from 35 per cent for clear polyethylene to 66 per cent for a double aluminised polyethylene, *when the screen is in position.* The overall seasonal savings of the higher value materials (drawn, saving 50–60 per cent) has been measured as 25–30 per cent, but with the penalty of a small reduction in crop yield. One further advantage observed during early trials was a reduction of radiation heat loss from the crop canopy, resulting in an increase in canopy temperature of 0.5–1.0°C. This has implications for reducing the house air temperature when the screen is in position.

2.4.3 Partially opaque structures

A few crops, such as narcissus and tulip flower forcing, or sprouting potatoes, require only low levels of light, but still need heat for development. These crops will tolerate a structure where up to 85 per cent of the cladding is opaque insulated material, to combine the maximum fuel saving potential with natural daylight input. Several versions of these exist.

(a) An insulated structure where a small area of the roof is fitted with translucent sheets.
(b) A mushroom tunnel with a strip of clear plastic cladding along its apex.
(c) A structure with translucent clad walls and insulated roof.
(d) A glasshouse with rigid opaque insulation placed inside either under the roof or against the walls.

In many cases the translucent portions are double skinned, or can be underdrawn with insulated shutters, so that they also contribute to heat saving.

These types of building can reduce the potential heat loss of a single glazed structure by 60–85 per cent.

3 BUILDINGS

3.1 STRUCTURES FOR STORAGE OF CROPS IN BULK

The first consideration when designing or specifying the building for bulk crop storage is its ability to resist the lateral pressures generated by the heaped crop.

3.1.1 Calculation of thrust wall forces

When a crop is heaped without using retaining walls, the sides slope rather than stand vertically. The angle of this slope (measured from the horizontal) is termed the 'angle of repose'. Angles of repose are well documented for seed crops, but root crops have varying angles, according to cleanliness and shape of the product, and it is normal to assume an angle of 40–50° where this is not given.

The lateral thrust is governed by crop depth, angle of repose and bulk density; some values for bulk density are shown in table 3.1.

Table 3.1

Bulk density of some common crops

Crop	Bulk density (m³/t)
Carrots	1.7–1.9
Onions, as lifted	2.5–2.8
Onions, dried and clean	2.1–2.2
Potatoes	1.6–1.7
Red beet	1.7–1.8
Peas	1.2–1.3
Cabbage seed	1.4–1.6

The relationship between these three factors is calculated as follows. From figure 3.1(a), the force (F) generated by level storage is due to the mass of material (M) in the triangle XYZ formed by the repose angle (R), sliding down the repose face.

The volume (V) in the triangle per m of wall $= \dfrac{h^2}{2 \tan R}$ (3.1)

where h = depth of crop.

$$\text{Mass } M \text{ tonnes} = \frac{V}{\text{bulk density}}$$ (3.2)

The mass is converted to force in Mega Newtons (MN) by multiplying by gravitational acceleration, g (9.81 m/s^2). Therefore

Force (F) MN $= M \times 9.81$ (3.3)

This force acts down the slope face; to extract the horizontal component multiply by the cosine of the repose angle.

Horizontal thrust force $= F \cos R$ (3.4)

Combining these

$$\text{horizontal thrust in MN} = \frac{h^2 \times 9.81 \times \cos R}{2 \times \tan R \times \text{bulk density}}$$ (3.5)

For example, if the wall was to hold 3 m of dried peas at a repose angle of 40°, the thrust per metre length from eqn (3.5) would be 33.5 MN, but if the wall was to hold 4 m of potatoes at 50° angle, the thrust would only be 26.5 MN.

The thrust varies from a maximum at the base of the wall to zero at the top, if the heap surface is flat. 'Surcharging' (piling above wall level) increases the thrust (see figure 3.1(b)) so that there is still a finite pressure at the wall top. The centre of lateral thrust pressure acts at one-third the height of the wall, which is the reason why most of the strength is required at the base of the wall.

3.1.2 Construction of thrust walls
The main methods of thrust wall construction are as follows.

3.1.2.1 Free standing
This relies on the 'bookend' principle, where the weight on the foot prevents the section overturning (figure 3.2). Such walls are often used to form a temporary storage area or to hold up the loading end of a heap in a store with permanent side walls. Where this wall is required to withstand thrust from both directions, the section is in the form of an inverted T.

(a)

(b)

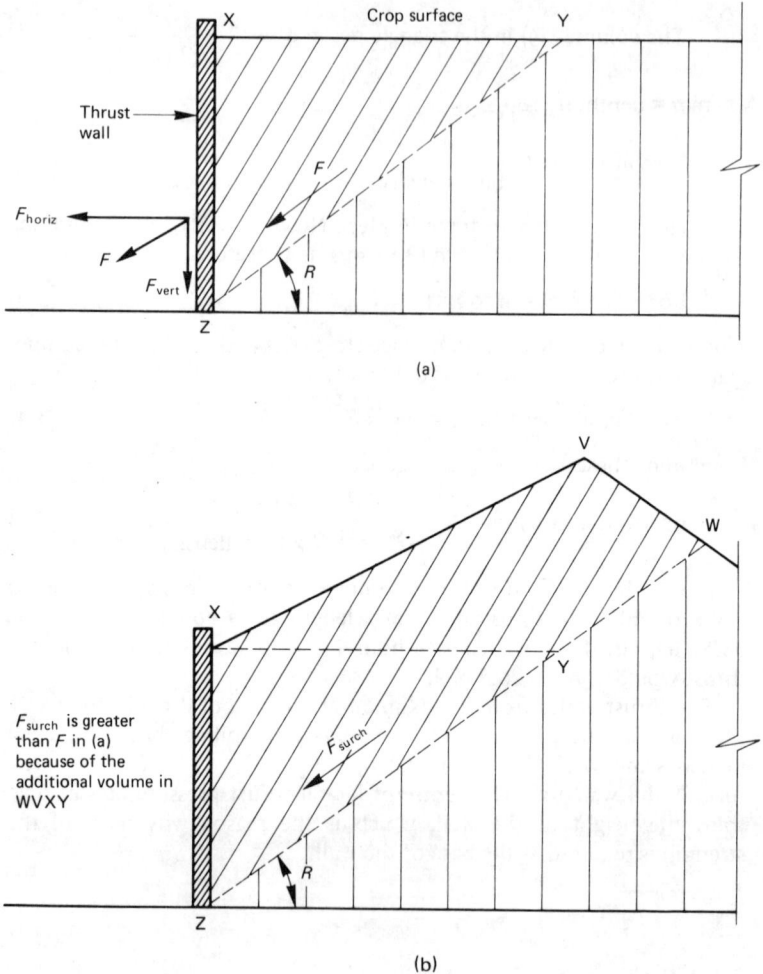

Figure 3.1 (a) Thrust forces in level loading. (b) Thrust forces in surcharged loading.

3.1.2.2 Bins

Bins are self-supporting because the horizontal thrust forces act equally in all directions. The walls are thus formed into a cylinder or rectangle. The walls of the latter, however, need sufficient horizontal strength to prevent their bowing outwards. This is normally achieved with deep

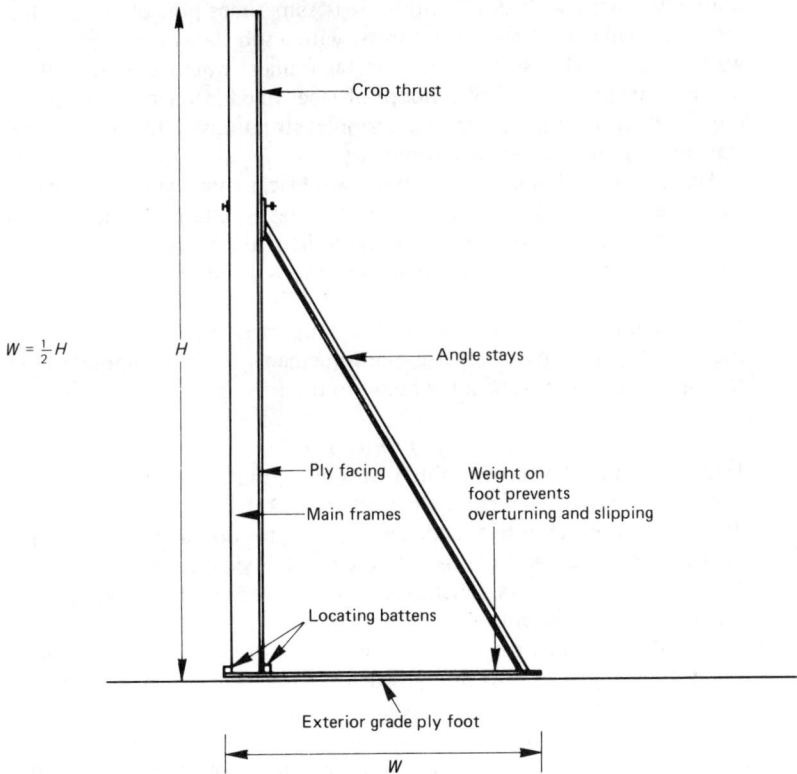

Figure 3.2 Free-standing thrust wall.

horizontal corrugations. The circular bin can be up to 12 m diameter, but wall rigidity limits rectangular bins to around 5 m, unless additional cross ties are fitted.

The walls of a tall bin can be tailored to the decreasing thrust, by making them strongest at the base and gradually reducing to light-weight panels at the top. Bins are normally restricted to materials which flow and can be moved in and out by conveyor, as the walls are perma-nently fixed.

3.1.2.3 Thrust walling integral with the building frame
Building thrust walls are normally made to be supported against vertical stanchions or piers. The wall is reinforced horizontally to prevent its bowing outwards between the vertical supports. These supports are

64 Horticultural Engineering Technology

normally placed at 2-3 m centres. It is sometimes possible to use the building frames as alternate supports, with a sub-stanchion or pier half-way between. This system uses 'portal frames' where the strength is obtained from a continuous 'hoop' of steel fixed into large foundation blocks at each end, rather than simple structures with two vertical stanchions tied together by a roof truss.

Brickwork walls are normally built two bricks thick without a cavity, with the bricks laid in 'English bond' — that is, alternate bricks being laid across the wall. Reinforcement material is also placed in the mortar joint every second or third course, and the wall bonded into the piers and stanchions.

In some buildings the only vertical support is the main frame; here the thrust panels have vertical reinforcement, and are supported by strong horizontal rails spanning between the frames.

3.1.2.4 Temporary divisions and thrust barriers

Temporary thrust walls forming divisions within buildings can be supported by vertical stanchions placed in socket holes in the concrete floor. The floor slab is not sufficiently strong to support the stanchions, so the floor concrete depth is increased in the vicinity of each socket. This arrangement allows stanchions to be removed and the holes plugged when the division is removed.

Thrust barriers across doorways are usually made from strong horizontal timber placed into slots down the door frames. The crop thrust presses the timbers too tightly against the door frames for them to be removed, thus the lower boards are placed in angled slots so that they can be removed for the crop to be drawn out through the base of the barrier (figure 3.3).

3.1.2.5 Mass walling

Mass walling is unreinforced and relies totally on its weight to withstand the crop thrust forces. It can be made of thick concrete, masonry or even earth backing to a simple wall. Walls of bagged fertiliser or crop in boxes should not be regarded as safe, because of potential slippage between the bags or boxes.

3.1.2.6 Structural air supply ducts

Main air supply ducts normally need to be thrust supporting. They have an open rectangular cross-section to allow access by personnel and for airflow, and the strength is gained from heavy bracing in the corners to prevent the tunnel being deformed into a lozenge shape. Very large air tunnels can be constructed from two self-supporting thrust walls with an airtight top between.

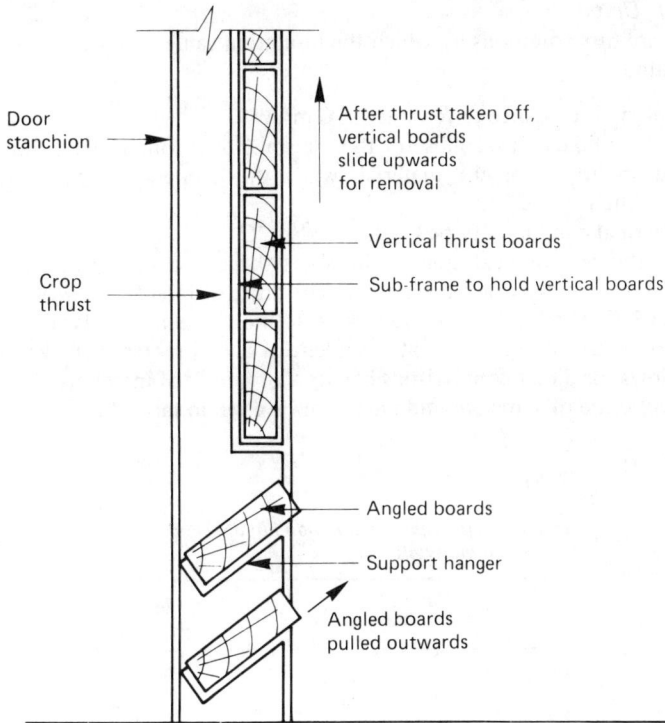

Figure 3.3 Doorway thrust boards.

3.2 INSULATION

Most horticultural crops are stored at a temperature different to the prevailing ambient, therefore an important building design consideration is the thermal barrier that it is able to generate to hold the desired conditions.

3.2.1 Theory of insulation

Building insulation relies on air entrapped within materials of poor thermal conductivity. In order to specify such materials, one must first appreciate the units in which insulation is measured and then consider the suitability of the material for the application.

3.2.1.1 Units

There are three methods by which the insulation value of a material can be quoted.

(a) Thermal resistance or R value — $^{\circ}C$ m^2/W

This is time taken, in seconds, for the transmission of one Joule through one square metre of the material, when the temperature difference between the faces is $1^{\circ}C$.

(b) Thermal conductivity or k value — W/m $^{\circ}C$

This is the rate of heat transfer in Watts through a square metre of material 1 m thick, when there is a temperature difference between the faces of $1^{\circ}C$. The k value is quoted only for individual materials and not composites. As its units are independent of actual material thickness, this allows for direct comparisons between a number of materials.

The k value of some common materials is given in table 3.2.

Table 3.2

Insulation (k) value of common building and
insulating materials

Material	k value (W/m $^{\circ}C$)
Brickwork	0.84
Asbestos cement sheeting	0.36
Dense cast concrete	1.40
Concrete block (medium weight)	0.51
Plywood	0.25
Timber	0.14
Roof tile	0.84
Roofing felt	0.19
Plastic-covered steel sheet	50
Aluminium sheet	210
Glass	1.05
Expanded polystyrene	0.033
Glass fibre quilt	0.040
Polyurethane board	0.025
Ureaformaldehyde foam	0.040
Polyisocyanurate foam	0.023
Woodwool	0.09
Light-weight concrete block	0.19

(c) Thermal conductance or U value — W/m^2 $^{\circ}C$

This is the rate of heat transfer in Watts through a square metre of a single or composite material of specified thickness, when there is a temperature difference between the faces of $1^{\circ}C$. U value is used in calculations to determine the likely heat gain or loss through a given material. It is the most common unit by which designers of heating or cooling plant specify the standard of insulation to be used, leaving the architect to decide how it is best achieved.

3.2.1.2 Calculation of insulation values

U value of a material is found by dividing its k value by its thickness t in metres;

$$U = \frac{k}{t} \tag{3.6}$$

For example, for 50 mm expanded polystyrene, k value 0.033

$$U = \frac{0.033}{0.05} = 0.66 \text{ W/m}^2 \text{ }^\circ\text{C}$$

The U value is also the reciprocal of the R value

$$U = \frac{1}{R} \tag{3.7}$$

The insulation value of a composite is calculated by adding the *thermal resistances* (R values) of each material, also including the thermal resistance formed by the layer of air lying against the two outer surfaces. The resistance of these layers can be taken as 0.12 m^2 $^\circ$C/W for the sheltered surface inside (R_{in}) the building, and 0.055 m^2°C/W for the surface outside the building which is exposed to wind (R_{out}). Where a structure is insulated by means of an unventilated air cavity, its thermal resistance will range from 0.15 m^2 $^\circ$C/W for a 5 mm cavity, to 0.25 m^2 $^\circ$C/W for a 20 mm cavity. These figures include the inner surface resistances of both faces of the cavity. Thus the composite thermal resistance (R_{comp}) made of materials a, b and c would be

$$R_{comp} = R_{in} + R_a + R_b + R_c + R_{out} \tag{3.8}$$

The thermal transmission value is then easily calculated, because

$$U = \frac{1}{R}, \text{ so } U_{comp} = \frac{1}{R_{comp}}$$

Where the U value of each material is given instead of its R value, the composite value is obtained by adding the reciprocals of each U value, plus the air layer resistances.

$$\frac{1}{U_{comp}} = R_{in} + \frac{1}{U_a} + \frac{1}{U_b} + \frac{1}{U_c} + R_{out} \tag{3.9}$$

Where k values are quoted, the composite U value is

$$\frac{1}{U_{comp}} = R_{in} + \frac{t_a}{k_a} + \frac{t_b}{k_b} + \frac{t_c}{k_c} + R_{out} \qquad (3.10)$$

Example: a wall consists of 110 mm brick, 50 mm expanded polystyrene and 10 mm thick plywood. Its composite U value is calculated as follows.

Brick $k = 0.84$, $t = 0.110$, $\frac{t}{k} = 0.13$.

Expanded polystyrene $k = 0.033$, $t = 0.05$, $\frac{t}{k} = 1.52$.

Plywood $k = 0.25$, $t = 0.01$, $\frac{t}{k} = 0.04$.

$$\frac{1}{U} = 0.12(R_{in}) + 0.13 + 1.52 + 0.04 + 0.055(R_{out}) = 1.865$$

Therefore

$$U = \frac{1}{1.865} = 0.54 \ W/m^2 \, ^\circ C$$

3.2.2 Insulation materials

3.2.2.1 Masonry blocks
These are either made from porous aggregate or are foamed during manufacture, to entrap air. Insulation blocks vary in thickness from 110 mm to 250 mm, with corresponding U values of 1.9–0.76 $W/m^2 \, ^\circ C$. They are easily built to form non-thrust-bearing walls, with a degree of insulation, but even the thickest block cannot give the level of insulation needed for long-term cool storage.

These blocks are porous to water and thus require additional protection; a skim of cement rendering or plaster will help to protect the block from liquid-phase water, such as rain, but will not exclude water vapour.

3.2.2.2 Composite concrete slabs
These are made of either a matrix of vegetable fibres (woodwool or straw) bonded with cement, or autoclaved porous concrete.

The cement/fibre slabs are not strong enough to form thrust-bearing walls, but have sufficient compressive strength to be used as an insulating face for other types of thrust wall.

Autoclaved concrete can be reinforced to form structural walling for bulk crop stores.

A 100 mm thickness (2 slabs) of woodwool has a U value of 0.9 W/m^2°C, and 200 mm of autoclaved concrete 0.95 W/m^2°C. While these materials are unsuitable for constructing long-term cool stores, they are suitable for protecting potatoes and other root crops from frost damage or low levels of ambient heat.

Woodwool and straw slabs are not closed cell, and so require a vapour barrier; this is usually either plasticised sheet or rendering. The autoclaved concrete is reasonably resistant to moisture.

3.2.2.3 Cavity wall injection

Cavity infill materials increase the U value of a cavity by dividing it into a large number of tiny air pockets. Suitable materials are expanded polystyrene beads, mineral wools or *in situ* foamed ureaformaldehyde. The k values of these materials enable insulation values to be attained, with a suitably wide cavity, that are suitable for cold stores.

Expanded polystyrene is sufficiently closed cell to require no further vapour proofing; the other materials should ideally be used in conjunction with vapour proofing of the walling.

3.2.2.4 Glass fibre

Glass fibre in blanket form is widely used. It can be laid between two skins of cladding material during building or used to line internal surfaces. The fibre must have vapour barriers installed to prevent ingestion of water. Steps must be taken to prevent the blanket from being compressed by the weight of the outer cladding, or working its way to the base of the cavity when installed in roof slopes or walls. The k value of uncompressed blanket is 0.035 W/m °C, which allows cladding suitable for crop stores if 100–150 mm thickness is used.

3.2.2.5 Cellular plastics

Foamed plastic slabbing is usually made from either polystyrene or polyurethane. The latter is not closed cell, consequently it is factory coated with vapour barrier materials, which can range from plasticised paper and aluminium foil to oil-tempered hardboard and plasterboard. These slabs are made in either the common building board size of 2.4 x 1.2 m or 0.6 x 3.0 m in the case of refined expanded polystyrene. The k values allow normal cool store U values to be achieved with 50–100 mm panel thickness.

Specialist 'cold store' panels are made from a 150 mm thick core of foamed plastic, between two sheets of aluminium. These can be locked together to form the walls and roof of a cold store without further cladding or structural framing.

Foamed plastics can be sprayed on to the surface of other building materials. The most common material is polyisocyanurate, which is supplied to the spray head as two chemicals, which combine in the nozzle and form a foam as they land on the surface. The foam is closed cell and thus requires no vapour barrier. Its k value allows insulation to cold store standards with 50–100 mm thickness. The material is highly suited to the insulation of existing structure, as it adheres to most surfaces, easily flows around frame protrusions, and seals the building against air in-leakage. The foam should not be sprayed over power cables attached to the building frames, as it insulates these against heat loss and effectively derates their current capacity.

3.2.3 The effects of water on insulation

Air is a poor heat conductor, while water conducts heat relatively well. If the air spaces in the insulation become filled with water, much of the insulation properties will be lost; therefore these air spaces must be protected against ingress of water. Water occurs in the form of vapour in the atmosphere, as well as 'free' water from, for example, rain. The former is the more difficult to exclude, as it is carried into the material with air infiltration. There are two basic methods for excluding water vapour and free water. Traditional building materials, such as brickwork or asbestos cement sheets, can be porous to vapour although appearing to be proof against rain.

3.2.3.1 Closed cell materials

'Closed cell' materials have an internal matrix of separate air cells, with no connection between each other or the outside surface, through which water can penetrate. These materials can be cut or pierced without increasing their tendency to absorb water.

3.2.3.2 Vapour barriers

The 'vapour barrier' is an impervious membrane applied to the surface of the insulant which can be in the form of metal or plastic sheet, or bituminous compounds. Some insulation boards made from non-'closed cell' materials have a vapour barrier fitted to both faces during manufacture. While by this means the barriers are fitted at the same time as the insulation, the material is prone to damage during handling and construction.

Any vapour barrier must completely seal the insulation; this is simple on large areas of flat surface, but more difficult when it has to be fitted around obstacles and building frame members. There is also risk of puncturing the barrier membranes by nails or sheeting bolts during fixing.

As most pre-sealed insulation boards have a barrier on the faces only, the edges and perimeter of any cut areas must be sealed. This is usually done with self-adhesive tape, although most tapes can peel off after a time. If the building is to be maintained at a temperature above or below ambient, only one vapour barrier need be used. This is fitted to to the 'warm' surface because it will always be slightly cooler than the adjacent air, and therefore can cool the air in contact with it to below its dewpoint.

The vapour barrier will be effective in trapping moisture inside the insulation also. While this might not be sufficient to lower insulation values, it can promote dry rot in any timberwork which might be included within the barrier; therefore any timber likely to be in this situation must be pressure treated against decay.

3.2.4 Fire resistance
Many light-weight plastic insulation materials can be a dangerous source of fire. The material might either burn and fuel the fire or break down under the effects of heat and give off harmful fumes.

There are two fire rating properties of building materials, each being given a 'class' number following testing to Fire Research Station standards. In most cases a Class 1 rating will be required by insurance companies and fire authorities. The two properties are

(a) Self-extinguishing capacity. This refers to the ability to suppress combustion after the material has been ignited and the source of ignition then removed.
(b) Prevention of flame spread. The material might decompose under the effects of heat, and so provide combustible products which allow any applied flame to spread across the face of the sheet. Even if the foam is 'self-extinguishing' it can still allow fire to run from one part of the building to another.

Materials that are not of sufficiently high rating in regard to self-extinguishing capacity or flame spread prevention can be 'proofed' by a film of inert material applied to all exposed surfaces.

3.2.5 Thermal bridging
This refers to the transfer of heat through insulated surfaces by conduction into structural steelwork. This can occur where the insulants are placed between frame members rather than completely enveloping them, or where the steelwork protrudes from the insulated covering of a stack.

The localised areas of heating or cooling can cause deterioration of crop, and condensation formed on members can run back into the crop and initiate rotten areas.

The problem can be solved by ensuring that all non-insulated steel-work or masonry is either totally inside or totally outside the insulated layer. Where this is not possible, any members which traverse the insulation must be insulated independently. Condensation on roof members might be cured by a layer of cork-based insulating paint.

3.3 AIR LEAKAGE

Air leaking through a building can cause a high rate of heat loss or gain from the ambient air.

3.3.1 Definitions and values

Leakage is normally measured in 'air changes per hour', one air change being equivalent to an airflow rate through the building equal to one empty volume per hour. All buildings, except for controlled atmosphere stores, undergo some degree of air leakage. This can be caused by wind pressure, vertical convection currents set up by the heating system or the expansion/contraction as the air within the building changes temperature. The notional air leakage rate of a building depends on its volume. In a small building the area of walls to internal volume is greater than in a large building, so any leakage holes in a small building cause a more rapid air change. The design air changes for a range of building sizes are given in table 3.3.

Table 3.3

Air infiltration rates into buildings

Room volume (m³)	Empty vols/h
28	1.44
140	0.60
280	0.40
560	0.30
1130	0.20
2830	0.12

The heat transfer due to air exchange is dependent on air volume flow rate, m³/h, air temperature difference, °C and the specific heat of air on a volume basis, kJ/m³ °C. This latter varies with air temperature and density but a mean value for the range of U.K. ambient conditions is 1.3 kJ/m³ °C.

The heat transferred by leakage is thus

$$kW = \frac{\text{no. of volumes/h} \times \text{specific heat } (1.3) \times \text{temperature difference}}{3600}$$

$$(3.11)$$

3.3.2 Methods of reducing air leakage

(a) Sprayed foam insulation will effectively seal against air leakage.

(b) Sprayed foam gap-filling materials can be obtained in aerosol form, with an injector tube to direct the filler into the crack.

(c) Points where corrugated sheets join flat surfaces can be sealed with pre-formed plastic extrusions, shaped to fit the corrugations.

(d) Sheet and slab insulation board joints can be sealed with adhesive tape, mastic or by the sheets having a tongue and groove edge. Another common method is to use two sheets each of half the required final thickness, and lay them so that the outer layer covers the joints in the inner layer.

(e) Vents and doors can seal on to rubber gasket strips.

(f) Sliding door edges can be fitted with brush bristle strips. These are well suited to form a seal against an irregular shape, and easily flex sideways when the door is moved.

(g) Sliding doors can be fitted with special hangers or track. The former allows the door to be clamped inwards against the frame, to be against a gasket. The latter system track is notched at the closed position, so that the door drops as it reaches this. The notch shape and angled bottom guides force the door inwards as it drops, so that it wedges on to the frame. It is opened by a lever system which forces the door back on to the track.

(h) Doors that have to remain open for access can be partially sealed with strip curtains or rubber flap doors. Both of these allow a vehicle to drive through, and the curtains or flaps fall back into place once it has passed.

The building fabric sealing methods (a)–(d) are prone to damage by birds and rodents. Old cracks can be re-opened and new ones formed, as the building structure moves by thermal expansion and contraction; similar problems occur in timber as it wets and dries.

3.4 CONTROLLED ATMOSPHERE (CA) STORAGE

Many top fruit crops and some vegetables are stored in a modified atmosphere of oxygen and/or carbon dioxide to reduce crop losses and delay maturity. This requires a building that is totally sealed against air exchange in addition to thermal insulation described previously.

3.4.1 Methods of sealing

(a) Walls and ceiling are normally sealed with sheet metal, bituminous compounds or rubberised plastic membranes. The metal sheets are over-lapped at their joints and smeared with a generous layer of petroleum jelly before fixing, to ensure an air seal. Further petroleum jelly is smeared over any other potential leakage points. Bituminous compounds are trowelled over the internal surfaces. These require to be carefully inspected each year, as some compounds can crack and the materials are easily damaged. The membrane is formed *in situ*, from coats of various resins applied to a glass fibre base. The compound requires to be bonded to a suitably prepared surface. The aluminium sheet/foam sandwich panels described in section 3.2.2.5, can be locked together with suitable gasketing, to form prefabricated CA stores.

(b) Doors and access hatches can be made with metal sheeting on suitably rigid framework, sealed in a similar way to the wall sheeting. They are sealed to their frames with double rubber gaskets. A removable threshold is fitted across the doorway, for the door base to butt against; this is removed for forklift access during filling and emptying.

(c) Pipework and cables pass through the wall at one point, in a special 'service' panel. This is a steel plate sealed into the wall, with each pipe or cable passing through in a gland sealed both to the plate and the cable or pipe wall.

(d) Floor surfaces are sealed with a special compound and also sealed to the base of the walls, as normal concrete finishes are not gas-tight. Extra attention must be paid to the foundations, to prevent the floor cracking as a result of settlement and to prevent large slabs cracking under thermal contraction.

(e) Condensate drainage pipes need a water trap seal.

(f) Vent pipes are installed to allow foul air to escape and fresh air to be introduced. These are fitted with valves so that the store can be resealed after venting. Some form of venting must be used whenever the store temperature is being altered, to take account of the expansion or contraction of the air. A change of $1^\circ C$ can produce a pressure change of 400 Pa, which is sufficient to damage the store structure.

3.4.2 Store testing

The normal method for testing that the store is air-tight is to pressurise or evacuate the store slightly and see how long this pressure difference takes to change. The accepted method is to start with a pressure difference of 187 Pa and measure the time taken for it to reduce to 125 Pa. These times range from 1 min, 10 s for stores to hold oxygen levels of 16 per cent or above, to at least 7 min for stores to hold oxygen levels of 2.5 per cent.

The store can be pressurised or evacuated using a domestic vacuum cleaner, and the test conducted with a suitably accurate manometer. The pressure difference to atmosphere in the tests should never exceed 250 Pa, as this can cause damage to the materials, thus increasing leakage problems.

3.4.3 Leak detection

Leaks can be detected in a number of ways; the most common methods are listed below in descending order of leak size.

(a) Detector gas. If refrigerant gas is introduced to a pressurised store, large leaks can be detected with a refrigerant gas detector lamp. This is done from outside the store and cannot pinpoint the position of small leaks as the gas can move laterally within the insulation before emerging.
(b) Directional microphone and amplifier. This is used inside the store to listen for the 'hiss' of the leak. A stethoscope can be used to listen for the more pronounced leaks.
(c) Candle flame. The air movement caused by air leaking into an evacuated store will deflect a candle flame held near the suspected area.
(d) Soap bubbles. A soap solution is painted over the suspected area.

Checks (b), (c) and (d) are carried out within the store. This entails one person entering it and a second person sealing it and controlling the vacuum cleaner.

Most simple leaks can be cured with liberal applications of petroleum jelly over the suspect area.

3.5 BUILDING APPLICATIONS

3.5.1 Crop storage

There are two basic crop storage methods, in bulk, or in boxes.

3.5.1.1 Bulk storage

This method is suitable for most root vegetables or dry seeds, but not for delicate and leafy crops like cauliflower, lettuce or apples.

Storage depth is limited by both the resistance of the crop to crushing and its requirements for air movement, to prevent spoilage. Some examples of recommended storage depths are shown in table 3.4.

Table 3.4

Storage depths for bulk stored crops

Crop	Circumstances	Recommended maximum height (m)
White cabbage	All	2
Beetroot	Unventilated	2
	Force ventilated	3
Narcissus bulbs	During drying	2.5
	After drying	3
Potatoes	Unventilated	2
	Naturally ventilated	2.5
	Force ventilated with ambient air	3.5
	Force ventilated with added humidity	6
Peas	During drying	2.5
	After drying	10

The table shows that a lower height of some crops is needed during drying or if a forced air supply is not used. Resistance of potatoes to crushing varies according to the amount of moisture existing in the cells (turgidity), fully turgid tubers showing the greatest resistance to crushing.

Storage depth can also be limited by the strength of the support walls (see section 3.1.1).

The size of a store to hold a given tonnage of crop depends on its bulk density. Bulk density is a measure of the volume (m^3) occupied by 1 tonne of the crop; the figures for some common crops are shown in table 3.1. It is suggested that, for store volume design, the higher figure is used as this will give the building size most likely to hold the crop in all situations. When determining design tonnage from a given volume, use the lower value.

For example, a store to hold 100 tonnes of potatoes will need a volume of 170 m^3. If the crop is to be stored at 2.5 m depth, it will require a floor area of 68 m^2.

The crop's angle of repose must be taken into account when designing stores with no retaining wall on one or more sides — for example, where a store has a retaining wall at the back and either side but the heap slopes to the floor at the front. This will have the effect of increasing the heap length by $H/2$ tan R, where H = crop depth and R = the angle of repose.

3.5.1.2 Box storage

'Box' or 'bin' normally relates to a pallet-based container holding up to 1 tonne of produce. The shallow depth of crop in a box compared with when it is in a bulk heap allows fragile products to be stored without risk of crushing. Because the box sides support all the thrust from the produce, the box storage building does not need its walls or air distribution ducting built to withstand crop thrust. However, the store structure should be of sufficient strength to protect the insulated cladding when the boxes are being handled in the store. This usually involves strong, closely spaced sheeting rails, together with a curb at the base of the walls. Despite this, the cost of a box store will be less than that of a bulk store of similar capacity, but the additional cost of the boxes will make the two prices similar.

The most popular sizes of box are

(a) 1 m x 1.2 m x 0.9 m overall height
(b) 1.2 m x 1.2 m x 1.2 m overall height
(c) 1.8 m x 1.2 m x 0.9 m overall height
(d) 0.9 m x 1.5 m x 0.8 m overall height

The overall height includes a 150 mm high pallet base.

The first three are based on pallet sizes recommended under British Standards, the latter is popular among potato growers in the eastern counties and is often called the 'Lincs. pattern box'. The mass of produce that a box holds will depend on the product's bulk density, but it is common for boxes to be classified according to their potato capacity. By this method boxes (a) and (d) would be called 'half tonne' and (b) and (c) '1 tonne'.

Most boxes are designed to be stacked in the store. In most cases the stack height is limited to 5 or 6 boxes, owing to building headroom and forklift capacity, but systems with stacks up to 12 boxes high are in existence, using special forklifts with triple extending high lift masts. Safety is a major factor in tall stacks. Boxes which stack squarely when new can form stacks that lean dangerously after a period of use, when they are beginning to suffer damage and lose rigidity.

The gross bulk density of a product stored in a box will be around 30 per cent less than the same product in a heap. This means that boxes will have to be stacked at least 4 high to give the same floorspace utilisation as a 3 m high bulk heap.

3.5.2 Mushroom and rhubarb sheds

Because mushrooms do not photosynthesise, a lighted building is un-
necessary. Rhubarb and other crops, such as chicory, are 'forced' in
the dark to achieve rapid elongation, without formation of green chloro-
phyll. Therefore growing sheds for these crops can be fully insulated
with opaque materials. There are two basic forms of growing shed.

3.5.2.1 Rigid structures

These are normal buildings made of materials like brickwork or asbestos-
clad steel frames, and which are insulated.

The insulation can be in the form of rigid foamed plastic, spray-
applied foam plastic, or fibreglass or thermal building blocks. These
have been described in section 3.2.

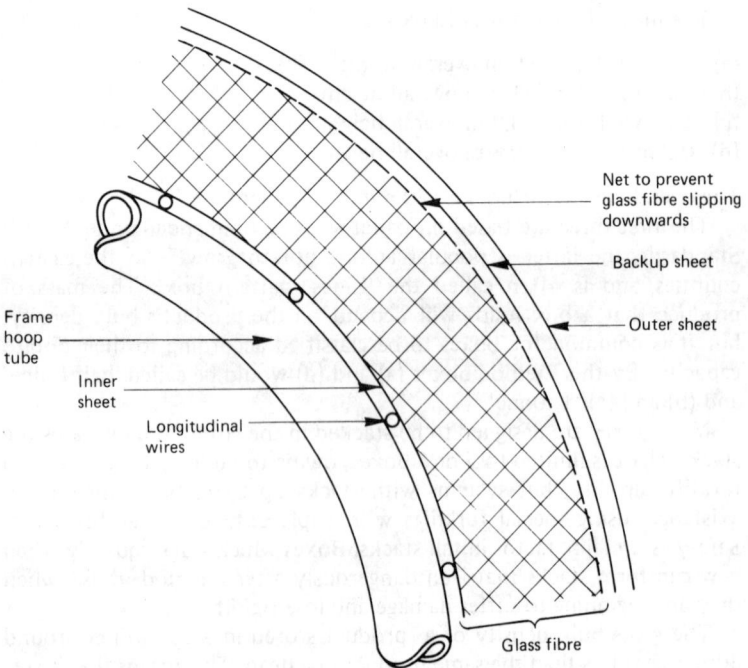

Figure 3.4 Mushroom tunnel insulation.

3.5.2.2 Flexibly clad tunnels

These have the same hooped framework as the translucent tunnel, clad with two layers of plastic film, having 75-100 mm of glass fibre sandwiched between (see figure 3.4). Black film is used as it is more resistant to ultra-violet degradation than clear film, and the potential time between recladding rises from 1-2 years to 3-4 years. It is essential to keep the insulation dry, so the outer layer often consists of two or three sheets, a black outer one and heavy-gauge clear ones beneath to act as extra moisture barriers. This also permits changing of the outer black sheet, without disturbing the insulation.

Dark matt surfaces absorb more solar heat than light or reflective ones. Mushroom tunnels are often painted white during the summer when, despite the insulation, solar gain would heat the growing environment to above the desired temperature.

The insulation offers a considerable fuel saving potential over the single or twin skinned translucent structure. 50 mm of foamed plastic or 100 mm of glass fibre can reduce the potential heat loss from a single skin structure by 80-90 per cent.

3.5.3 Packhouses

Most packhouses are modifications of the types of clear span insulated structure used for box storage (section 3.5.1.2), the usual additions being

(a) Subdivision with insulated, dustproof walling to form separate working areas.
(b) Doors of rubber flaps or strip curtains to retain internal heat but allow forklift passage.
(c) Additional satellite units to form messrooms, offices etc.
(d) Because packing is often regarded as a 'factory' operation, better standards of lighting, heating, fire protection and emergency exit.
(e) Storage for packing materials, often as a loft over the office/messroom block, or as a mezzanine floor over the packing machinery.
(f) A flat, hard floor to allow operation of pallet trucks.
(g) Adequate drainage for 'wet' processing.
(h) 'Hygenic' internal finishes to walls, floor and roof, which are non-absorbent and easily cleaned.

4 FUELS AND HEAT PRODUCTION

Heat is an important input to most crops grown under protected cropping systems. The increasing cost of energy, from whatever source, means that the choice of fuel, combustion equipment, distribution systems and control must be carefully made. Most aspects of heating conform to the natural laws of chemistry or physics, thus it is possible to plan and predict performance with accuracy.

4.1 FUELS

4.1.1 Calorific value
This is the measure of potential heat energy present in a fuel.

4.1.1.1 Terminology
It is possible for two values of calorific value to be quoted, 'gross' and 'net'.

(a) Gross calorific value is the total energy contained in the fuel. However, during combustion of hydrocarbons the hydrogen fraction combines with atmospheric oxygen to form water, in the form of vapour, in the hot gases evolved. The energy contained in this vapour can be recovered only by condensing it to liquid, which for most situations is impractical. This system is, however, the one used in the U.K.
(b) Net calorific value is of more practical use. This is a measure of the energy that can be liberated as sensible (real) heat, and ignores that in the form of water vapour in the combustion products. Many European countries use net calorific values.

4.1.1.2 Fuel calorific values and relative energies
The calorific values of the most often used fuels are shown in table 4.1.

It is often useful to be able to compare the relative costs of the different fuels. This is not easy because the fuels are marketed in different

Table 4.1

Calorific values

Fuel	Gross calorific value (MJ/kg)	Unit of sale	Calorific value of sale unit
Coal	26.7–29.1	tonne	26700–29100 MJ/t
Anthracite	29.6–32.1	tonne	29600–32100 MJ/t
Class C oil	46.4	litre	36.7 MJ/l
Class D oil	45.5	litre	38.0 MJ/l
Class E oil	43.5	litre	40.5 MJ/l
Class F oil	43.0	litre	40.8 MJ/l
Class G oil	42.8	litre	41.1 MJ/l
Natural (mains) gas	58.1	therm or m^3	105.5 MJ/therm 41.9 MJ/m^3
L.P. gas (propane)	50.0	litre of liquid	25.7 MJ/litre

unit quantities, their calorific values differ, and the combustion efficiencies of the relevant equipment will vary. The nomogram in figure 4.1 allows such comparisons to be made. By using it the following can be found:

(a) Direct comparison on a gross calorific basis, by comparing vertically between the horizontal scales.
(b) The net energy cost of a fuel over a range of plant efficiencies.
(c) Comparisons between fuel costs at their relative efficiencies.

Some typical boiler efficiencies are given in table 4.4.

For example, the equivalent cost of coal to class D oil at 20 p/litre, if the oil boiler efficiency is 80 per cent and the coal boiler is 75 per cent, will be found by tracing vertically from the 20 p oil scale to the 80 per cent line, moving horizontally from this point to the 75 per cent line and descending vertically to the coal scale. Thus oil at 20 p/l, 80 per cent efficiency, will be equivalent to coal at £160/t, 75 per cent efficiency.

Note that fuel cost comparisons do not give the full picture of the overall cost comparison of a fuel change (see section 4.3.4).

4.1.2 Characteristics of fuels

4.1.2.1 Solid fuel
(a) Quality. Coal can be obtained in a range of qualities, hence the range of calorific values in table 4.1. The two factors of coal quality

Net energy
cost
(p/MJ)

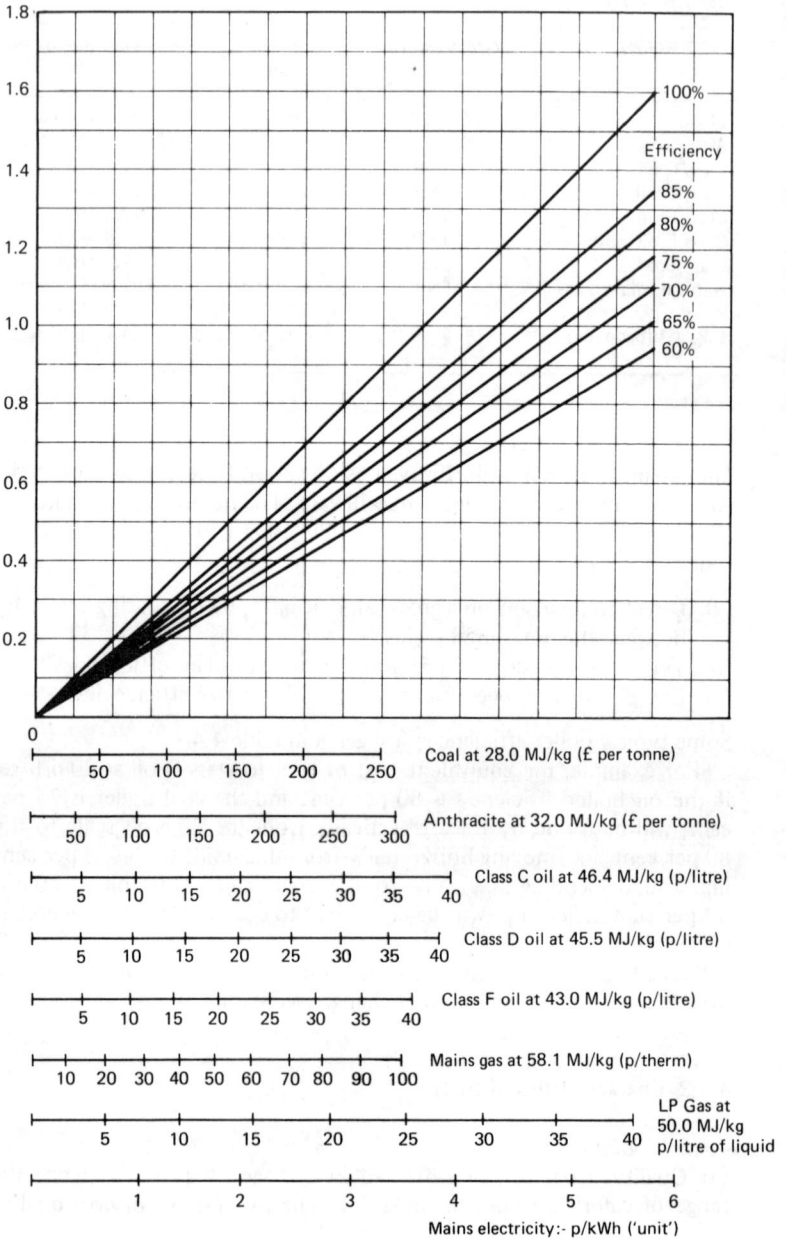

Coal at 28.0 MJ/kg (£ per tonne)

Anthracite at 32.0 MJ/kg (£ per tonne)

Class C oil at 46.4 MJ/kg (p/litre)

Class D oil at 45.5 MJ/kg (p/litre)

Class F oil at 43.0 MJ/kg (p/litre)

Mains gas at 58.1 MJ/kg (p/therm)

LP Gas at
50.0 MJ/kg
p/litre of liquid

Mains electricity:- p/kWh ('unit')

Figure 4.1   Fuel cost comparison nomogram.

affecting choice of combustion system are volatiles and caking. Volatiles refer to the part of the fuel that is liberated as combustible gases when the fuel is heated in the furnace. The volatile fraction can range from under 10 per cent for anthracite to over 35 per cent for bituminous coals. Caking results from the coal particles swelling and coalescing on heating. The resulting 'cake' tends to obstruct combustion air flow through the mass of fuel in the grate. Bituminous coals with even a small tendency to cake require the positive airflow from a fan to maintain adequate combustion. Most small, naturally draughted, furnaces require either anthracite with low volatiles and caking properties, or coal that has undergone processing to remove these, like coke or proprietary smokeless fuel.

The National Coal Board (NCB) has formulated a numerical classification system for coals according to their volatile fraction and tendency to cake. This runs from 100 for anthracite to 900 for highly volatile bituminous coals; caking properties are superimposed on these classes in a non-linear manner, so that medium caking coals run between 180 and 700. The solid fuels for most effective combustion on horticultural boilers are either 101 (anthracite) or 701 (medium caking).

(b) Ash. Both ash content and fusion temperature are important to the operation of stokers. While it might seem desirable for a fuel to produce as little ash as possible, some types of stoker rely on a layer of ash to protect grate parts from excessive temperature. For example, the drop tube stoker requires an ash content of 2–3 per cent, and the chain grate 6–8 per cent; in the latter case it is possible to recirculate ash to supplement low ash fuels.

Some ash will fuse (liquefy) at temperatures between 650 and 1000°C; if the fusion temperature is below the firebed temperature, the liquefied ash can coalesce in the burning fuel and affect combustion airflow.

(c) Moisture level. The amount of moisture that the surface of fuel particles can hold can affect stoker performance. Moisture level is governed largely by the fuel particle size, 'doubles' can hold 3 per cent, while 'smalls' can hold 20 per cent.

(d) Grading. Solid fuels for use in furnaces are normally supplied washed and closely graded. The common grades are shown in table 4.2.

'Singles' is by far the most common grade for nursery boilers, as it is easily handled by mechanical and pneumatic conveyors and suits the simpler stokers used.

4.1.2.2 Oils
This exists in several forms from kerosene or paraffin to heavy oils.

(a) Classification. Oil fuel is classified according to its kinematic viscosity, in centistokes (cSt) at a given temperature. Kinematic viscosity

Table 4.2

Coal and solid-fuel grades

Name	Passing a screen of (mm)	Retained by a screen of (mm)	Designation
Large cobbles	150	75	Graded coals
Cobbles	100–150	50–100	Graded coals
Trebles	63–100	38–63	Graded coals
Doubles	38–63	25–38	Graded coals
Singles	25–38	12.5–18	Graded coals
Smalls	12.5	–	–

is a measure of the force needed to shear a unit cube at unit speed and is expressed in units of m^2/s, the sub-multiple of this cm^2/s being equivalent to 1 Stoke (St); oil viscosity might alternatively be quoted in cm^2/s and can be compared by the relationship $cm^2/s \times 100 = cSt$. For convenience the viscosity bands are also denoted by a British standard (BS) letter grade and a colloquial name; these are shown in table 4.3.

Table 4.3

Viscosity classification of fuel oils

BS class	Viscosity (cSt) at temperature (°C)	Colloquial name	Temperature for flow (°C)	Pressure jet combustion temperature (°C)
+C1, C2	2.0 at 16	Kerosene or paraffin	ambient	ambient
D	3.0 at 38	Diesel or gas oil	ambient*	ambient
E	12.5 at 82	Light fuel oil	10	82
F	30 at 82	Medium fuel oil	30	104
G	70 at 82	Heavy or residual fuel oil	45	127

+Sub-class C1 is a paraffin-type fuel which has been refined further, to minimise the level of impurities, to render it suitable for direct combustion in domestic heaters.
*With additives for winter use.

The light and medium oils are blends of classes D and G. Class G was traditionally the residue from the refining process, and retains many of the impurities from the crude oil; this is in contrast to classes C and D, which are free from physical impurities. The heavier oils tend to be cheaper but some energy is consumed in heating them, and the greater impurities entail more burner servicing.

(b) Temperature requirements. Table 4.3 also shows the temperature of heavier oils, both to ensure flow along pipework, and to flow through the nozzle of a burner. Class D fuel can be problematical in severe U.K. winter conditions, because at temperatures much below $0°C$ waxes normally held in suspension congeal sufficiently to prevent its flow through filters and narrow pipes. To prevent this, class D oil supplied between October and March has a low-temperature additive, which effectively reduces its waxing temperature to $-10°C$.

(c) Contaminants. The main contaminant of most fuel oils is sulphur. This forms sulphur dioxide (SO_2) when burnt, which is highly toxic to plants. Where oil is to be burnt directly into the house atmosphere, fuels with less than 0.03 per cent sulphur content by weight are suitable. Although paraffin-type fuels contain very low levels of these impurities, some might be too high for direct combustion in plant houses. Only certain grades, commonly known as 'premium paraffin' contain less than the 0.03 per cent level.

4.1.2.3 Gaseous fuels

These are either natural (mains) gas or liquefied petroleum gas (lpg). Natural gas contains around 90 per cent methane, while lpg has varying proportions of butane and propane.

Methane cannot be liquefied at ambient temperatures whilst lpg can be held under pressure in the liquid form. Thus natural gas is available only by direct pipeline from the point of supply (public gas mains), while lpg is supplied in pressurised cylinders and tanks, and can be used in places remote from the public mains.

Both gases contain few impurities that are harmful to plant life when burnt, but the unburnt gas can prove toxic to plants. The absence of sulphur removes the problems of low-temperature corrosion (see section 4.6.5) in the boiler and chimney; also the gas burns cleanly and does not produce soot.

The older form of mains gas produced from coal (commonly called 'town gas') retained many of the impurities of coal, and was unsuitable for burning directly in a plant environment.

As main natural gas is supplied from a public utility, it is subject to supply interruptions occurring in the mains system. Where high-risk crops are being heated by mains gas, an alternative standby fuel and combustion system should be provided.

4.1.3 Fuel storage

4.1.3.1 Solid fuel
In all but very small installations the fuel will be supplied in loose bulk
rather than bags. It is possible to store solid fuel heaped on any level,
hard surface, and this simple 'stockpile' system is suited to delivery by
tipper or conveyor bodied truck. The latter type often has an extension
elevator at the rear to heap coal to 2.5–3 m. Flat sites suffer the disadvantage of exposure to weather; the wet coal may bridge in burner
hoppers and its effective calorific value is reduced, and the heap may
freeze solid in very cold weather. The coal has to be handled to the
burner, and often a tractor loader is used. The flat site has one advantage in freedom from constraint in capacity posed by any type of
bunker or silo.

Mechanical handling to the burner is possible only if the fuel is
stored in a bunker or silo having auger-conveying facilities from its base
to the boiler house. Traditionally bunkers were square or rectangular in
section, with sloping walls at the base to move the coal to the auger.
The slope needs to be 50–70° to ensure that no coal remains. Many
bunkers will hold only a few days' supply and are recharged by tractor
loader from a stockpile. A more recent development in coal handling
uses cylindrical tower silos made of vitreous enamelled steel; these are
beginning to be used on U.K. nurseries. The silos are 6–8 m diameter,
and can be up to 20 m high. They are loaded by pneumatic conveyor
from a specially built truck or, exceptionally, by elevator and belt
conveyor, and unloaded by the same 'flat base' augering systems used
for grain. The enamelled inner surface allows coal to slide freely without
bridging. As these silos depend on pneumatic conveyor filling, they
require to be serviced by the special truck, and cannot be recharged
from the stockpile; also a handling charge is added to the coal price to
cover the cost of this service.

It is recommended that the bunker or silo holds a minimum of 100
hours' firing, or 12 tonnes (1 truck load), whichever is smaller. Coal has
a bulk density of 1.2–1.4 m^3/tonne.

4.1.3.2 Oil storage
Oil fuels are stored in tanks constructed of welded mild steel; other
materials such as reinforced concrete and glass fibre reinforced plastics
are also suitable, but rarely used in U.K. nurseries. Steel should not be
galvanised, as oil can react with the zinc to cause a waxy byproduct
which clogs filters and burners.

Storage capacity should be based on at least 3 weeks' consumption
during the period of maximum heat demand. Small installations should
have sufficient tank capacity to accept the minimum tanker delivery

required, to avoid 'small delivery' cost penalties, this being normally 3000 litres. It is more prudent to allow for at least 6 weeks' consumption to minimise the effects of transport disruption.

The tank should be fitted with a lidded manhole, to facilitate entry for cleaning, and a vent pipe; this latter is normally one size of pipe larger than the filling pipe. The filling pipe is normally 50 mm BSP for kerosene, gas or light oil, and 80 mm BSP for medium or heavy oil; the tankers have flexible hoses, with couplings to screw on to these sizes. The filling pipe must be positioned for easy access by road tanker. Kerosene, gas and light oils can be pumped as far as 100 m, but medium and heavy oils need to be discharged near the tank. Tank contents can be gauged by dipstick, sight glass, float indicator or hydrostatic pressure indicator (see section 4.6.2). These should be clear to read. A contents gauge should be placed so that the tanker driver can see it and avoid overflowing the contents during filling. The tank should be placed within a walled compound (bund), sized to catch the whole tank contents should it leak.　Bunded　tenks

Oils other than kerosene or gas require to be heated (see table 4.3) before flowing or burning. It is normally sufficient to heat the oil to flow temperature at the tank outlet for light and medium oils, and the whole contents for heavy oils; in the former case tank insulation is desirable and in the latter case imperative. Heat is supplied by an electric immersion heater, but this should not have a surface temperature greater than $175°C$, to avoid localised breakdown of the oil. The supply pipe should be insulated and, if at any distance, be heated also. Pipes can be warmed by 'tracer tape', a ribbon of electric heating element which can be wound around the pipe, filters and valves; this is also useful for preventing gas oil waxing in very cold weather. As electric heating is expensive, many large installations have secondary heaters powered by the hot water or steam produced, the electric units being used only during starting.

All tanks should be sloped away from the outlet at 20 mm per metre length, so that contaminants like dirt and water can be held in the opposite end instead of being carried to the outlet. A drain valve at the lower end enables contaminants to be drawn off at intervals.

4.1.3.3 Gas storage

Only lpg is stored. This is held in the delivery cylinders on small installations, or in permanent tanks on larger installations. The larger tanks are normally made to hold ½, 1, 2 or 12 tonnes of liquefied gas, and are recharged from mobile pressurised tankers. Strict regulations govern siting of these tanks to avoid fire hazard, and also the siting must allow access by the delivery truck.

The gas must be vaporised from its liquid form before use, and this requires the absorption of latent heat. In most systems the latent heat is absorbed from the air through the tank walls; only a few installations use liquid offtake and a separate flow-line vaporiser. There is a limit to the heat absorption through the tank or cylinder walls, and this is normally quoted as 'maximum gas offtake' capability. Higher offtakes are possible if multiple tanks are used (two 1 tonne tanks have a larger surface area than one 2 tonne). This can give rise to installations with high peak demands having gas tankage capacity to last for several weeks, simply to provide the vaporising surface area.

4.2 COMBUSTION PRINCIPLES

4.2.1 Basic chemical reaction

The fuels listed in table 4.1 consist largely of either carbon or a mixture of hydrogen and carbon (hydrocarbon). During combustion the fuel combines with atmospheric oxygen, the hydrogen forming water (H_2O) and the carbon forming carbon dioxide (CO_2). Usually the carbon reaction occurs in two stages; firstly, it combines with a single molecule of oxygen to form carbon monoxide (CO), a flammable gas, which combines with a further oxygen molecule when it burns, to form CO_2.

Many types of combustion equipment intentionally separate the two parts of the carbon reaction. In the first stage, only sufficient combustion air (primary air) is introduced to convert the carbon to CO. The remaining combustion air (secondary air) is introduced where it can most effectively mix with the CO gas.

The solid fuel combustion reaction is often further divided because coals contains both carbon and volatile matter. In many systems the coal is first heated to release the volatiles, which being gaseous burn readily, and the remaining carbon is then burnt by the $C–CO–CO_2$ process outlined above.

With solid fuel the primary air is introduced through the grate; in the oil burner, it is mixed with the oil droplet spray; in the gas system it is mixed with the gas issuing from the supply jet. Secondary air is introduced across the top of the burning coal pile, around the inner burner tube of the oil burner, and around the combustion jets of the gas burner.

There are further problems in oil burners because the oil droplets have to burn in flight through the combustion chamber, and any oil remaining unburnt is lost as smuts or smoke. It is therefore essential that the oil is finely divided and the droplets are evenly mixed into the combustion airstream.

4.2.2 Air requirements

The theoretical amount of air required for fuel combustion can be calculated from the chemical reaction equation. This assumes that every oxygen molecule is able to combine with a carbon or hydrogen molecule in the fuel. This is impossible to achieve in practice as the combustion air is not intimately mixed with each fuel particle; therefore to ensure complete combustion, burners are supplied with air in excess of requirements. The percentage of excess air will vary between fuel types and combustion equipment, but it is likely to range from 30 per cent for oil and forced draught gas burners to 50 per cent for solid fuel and naturally draughted gas burners.

Oil and gas fuels must be evenly mixed with the combustion air, as any concentration of fuel will use only the oxygen in its vicinity and the unburnt portion will be carried away, enveloped in the CO_2 produced.

If insufficient air is supplied to complete fuel combustion, some unoxidised carbon particles could be liberated, causing smoke. A more serious consequence could be unburnt carbon monoxide being emitted. This gas is highly toxic to humans but carries neither smell nor colour; it can be dangerous where burners discharge combustion products directly into the building environment.

Too much excess air will result in high flue gas velocity and dilute the flue gases, thereby reducing their temperature. In any system where the flue gas has to transmit its heat to another medium, the hot gas will pass over the heat exchange surfaces too quickly to transfer all its heat energy, and a significant amount will be wasted.

In some burner systems a great excess of air can lead to nitrogen from the air combining with the surplus oxygen to form oxides of nitrogen, which are highly toxic to plants.

4.2.3 Combustion air measurement

The air supply to a burner is a compromise between wasting unburnt fuel (too little air) and high flue gas velocity (too much air). The most significant aspect of air starvation is smoke; in the U.K. the density and duration of smoke emission is strictly controlled under Clean Air legislation.

The optimum combustion air requirement for any heater or boiler is determined by measurement of three parameters in the flue gas

Carbon dioxide or oxygen level
Temperature
Smoke density.

(a) The most common method for CO_2 measurement is to place a volume of flue gas in a sealed vessel containing an absorptive fluid. The CO_2 is absorbed and causes a reduction in gas pressure; this is recorded by an integral manometer directly calibrated in per cent CO_2. Oxygen is measured with an electronic cell, the CO_2 level being inferred by the reduction in the normal atmospheric oxygen level of 20 per cent. CO_2 can also be measured electronically. Electronic measurement permits continuous monitoring, whereas the fluid absorption method involves manual sampling.

(b) Temperature is measured by a suitable thermometer. The required value is the level of flue gas temperature above that of the boilerhouse.

(c) Smoke is measured by drawing the flue gas through a filter paper and comparing the darkness of the stain against a standard. The darkness of the standard is graduated in 10 steps from 0 (no stain) to 10 (totally black); the smoke intensity is often termed 'smoke number', using one of the foregoing values.

(d) In addition to the three foregoing properties, CO level might also be measured. This is essential for a heater burning directly into the atmosphere. It also gives a more accurate indication of fuel wastage as unburnt CO.

The apparatus is a glass tube containing a chemical reagent, through which a known volume of gas is drawn. CO causes a colour change in the reagent, which progresses along the tube; the length of the coloured portion gives an accurate indication of the CO content.

These readings must be representative of burner conditions. It is essential to take these close to the flue exit from the heater or boiler, and certainly upstream of any flue draught balance damper.

The readings are used to choose the optimum setting for the air inlet control. In most cases the manufacturer of a burner or heater will quote the CO_2 level and smoke number best suited to his equipment.

4.2.4 Efficiency and flue loss

The flue gas conditions can also indicate the percentage of the fuel being wasted in the flue. The calculations are:

For coal: flue loss by volume (per cent)

$$= \frac{0.63 \times \text{net flue gas temp. } (^\circ C)}{CO_2 + CO} + 5$$

For oil: flue loss by volume (per cent)

$$= \frac{0.56 \times \text{net flue gas temp. } (^\circ C)}{CO_2 + CO} + 5$$

The combustion efficiency is 100 per cent – flue losses. An indication of efficiency for some types of boiler and heater is given in table 4.4.

Table 4.4

Efficiency of boiler types

		Combustion efficiency	Overall efficiency
Cast iron sectional	(hand-fired)	65	58 or less
	(auto-stoke)	75	68
	(oil-fired)	77	71
2-Pass Shell tube		79	73
3-Pass Shell tube		82	76
Welded steel sectional		77	71
Indirect air heater		78	75

A low-efficiency factor can indicate three possible burner or heater defects.

(a) Air inlet control setting, as mentioned in section 4.2.2.
(b) An impediment to heat flow across the heat exchanger walls, commonly caused by a build-up of soot and scale. Normally this is indicated by a high flue temperature when CO_2 and smoke are correct.
(c) Burner malfunction, manifested in oil or gas systems as poor air/fuel mixing and in all types by poor primary or secondary airflow. This is normally indicated by high smoke number, with correct or even low CO_2 and temperature.

4.2.5 Fuel contaminants

Any sulphur in the fuel combines with atmospheric oxygen to form sulphur dioxide (SO_2). This is toxic to plants when the fuel is burnt directly in the house environment. Its effect is characterised by white spots or total bleaching of leaves.

The SO_2 also combines with more oxygen and the water produced during combustion, to form sulphuric acid (H_2SO_4). This is highly corrosive to the internal surfaces of heaters and chimneys. Other acidic flue gases can result from chlorides in the fuel forming hydrochloric acid (HCl).

Acid damage is prevented by maintaining the susceptible surfaces above the acid's condensation temperature, so that it is expelled from the system as a vapour. The most serious corrosion occurs when the surface is below 65°C (150°F), and boilers and heaters burning sulphurous fuels should be operated above this temperature (see section 4.6.5), and chimneys and flues should be insulated to maintain the flue gases above condensation temperature.

4.2.6 Smut emission

A further consequence of condensation in the chimney is soot formation. The carbon particles in the smoke combine with the water droplets to form small agglomerations of soot. These do not firmly adhere to the chimney, and either collect in the base or are dislodged by the next updraught of flue gas when the heating system fires up. Soot ejected in this manner often falls on to the roofs of surrounding production buildings, seriously reducing the light transmission.

4.2.7 Turndown ratio

This is the term describing output variation of a combustion system. The ratio shows the smallest fraction of full output which is possible, thus 4:1 represents a variation potential of full to ¼ of full output.

4.3 COMBUSTION EQUIPMENT

The essential requirement of any burner or stoker is thoroughly to admix the correct quantities of fuel and air, so that the maximum energy in the fuel is released as heat.

4.3.1 Solid fuel

The essential requirement of any burner or stoker is thoroughly to butes and limitations; some are only suitable for certain types of solid fuel, others are not suited for the size of boiler used on most nurseries.

4.3.1.1 Gravity feed or magazine (figure 4.2(a))

Normally these can use only non-caking, low volatile fuels, such as anthracite and smokeless fuel, which flow easily. The fuel is held in a hopper above the grate and flows by gravity beneath a feed plate to replace that consumed by the fire. A fan supplies combustion air when the full fire is needed, and sufficient air is naturally induced to keep the fire smouldering, when the heat load is satisfied. The ash formed collects on the grate and is ejected at regular intervals by a hand or automatic pusher.

One gravity-feed system developed for bituminous coal has a sloping grate fitted with transverse louvres. A thin layer of fuel slowly descends the slope, the volatiles are liberated and burnt at the upper end, and the solid carbon, resembling coke, burns at the lower end. As fuel feed is governed by burning rate, the combustion air can be varied to suit heat demand, and the boiler automatically adjusted to the load.

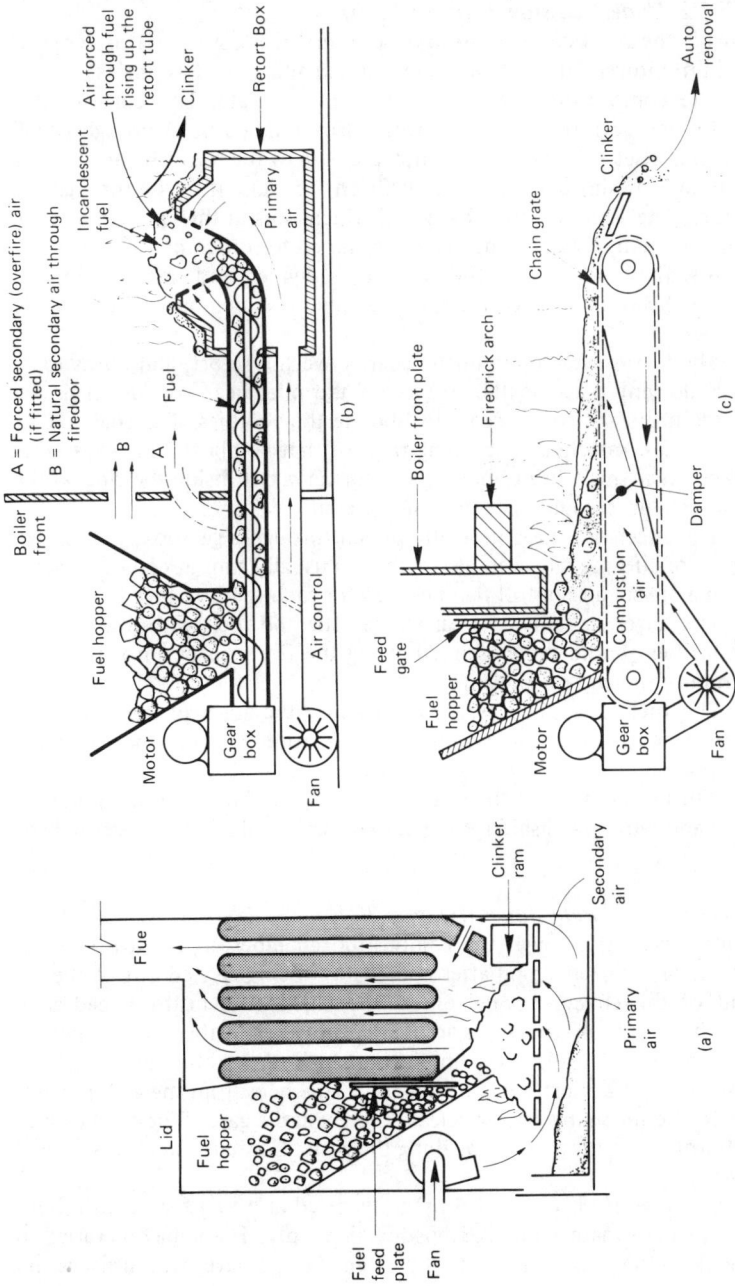

Figure 4.2 (a) Gravity feed stoker. (b) Underfeed stoker. (c) Chain grate stoker.

4.3.1.2 Underfeed stoker (figure 4.2(b))

This is the most common form of solid-fuel firing system. It is designed to burn bituminous coal, normally washed and graded as singles. The combustion takes place on a retort grate. This consists of a perforated cast iron air supply ring, surrounding a hole through which the coal rises. The coal is fed into the base of the retort by an auger or ram, and the injection force is sufficient to cause it to rise through the retort. The air is supplied by a fan, which runs at the same time as the auger or ram, its air output being regulated to suit combustion requirements. In some systems the air flow is divided and some is supplied above the retort (overfire air) to complete the combustion of volatile gases.

The fire is established in the coal above the retort, and burns to an incandescent mass on the surface of the pile; heat conducted downwards heats the lower coals to liberate the volatiles. The coal and air in-feed are matched to burning rate, so that combustion always takes place on a small heap above the retort and not inside the ring, as the heat produced could melt the ring material.

The auger or ram is normally driven through a gearbox, so that two or more burning rates can be set; the fan usually runs at constant speed, with a pre-set air control flap position for each gearbox speed.

The auger or ram can wear in the tube and fuels with low abrasive impurities should be chosen. Allowing the fire to drop into the retort can burn the end off the auger.

The fuel is supplied by a hopper above the auger or ram inlet, and this system can be linked to a bunker supply screw for automatic supply.

Ash gathers around the retort and is removed periodically, normally by hand, although ash augering systems are available for larger boilers.

4.3.1.3 Chain grate stoker (figure 4.2(c))

Fuel is carried through the combustion chamber on a cast iron chain conveyor, ash remaining after combustion being carried out of the far end of the chamber. Fuel enters the chamber beneath a feed gate, which spreads an even layer across the conveyor. It then passes beneath a firebrick arch which is maintained at high temperature by burning of the volatile gases just inside the chamber; the heat from the arch radiates on to the incoming coal to release these volatile gases. The solid carbon is burnt as the mass proceeds along the grate. Combustion air is supplied by a fan.

Burning rate is controlled by grate speed and fuel feed depth, both of which are matched by combustion air supply. These may be varied to give turndown ratios of up to 4:1. Some boilers have twin furnaces and stokers, allowing one or both to be used, which gives an effective turndown of 8:1.

Heat is kept away from the chain links by upward airflow at the start of the chamber and a layer of ash. It is desirable to have a fuel ash content of at least 6 per cent to form a satisfactory insulating ash layer.

4.3.1.4 Drop tube stoker

In this type of boiler the coal is conveyed to the top and allowed to fall on to the grate. Because this involves installing the coal drop tube through the boiler crown, it is available only as an integral part of a packaged boiler. Some combustion air can be supplied with the coal, and the remainder by a fan from the front of the furnace. This stoker will burn a wide range of coal ranks, although an ash content of 2–3 per cent is needed to protect the fire bars. De-ashing is, at present, manually done, so high ash level fuels can be a disadvantage.

This stoker type is available for boilers above 600 kW output. It can offer a turndown ratio of up to 3:1 and can respond rapidly to load fluctuations. One manufacturer has adapted the drop tube system to burn wood and solid waste.

4.3.1.5 Coking stoker

In this type the volatile fractions are released on entry to the combustion chamber, and the coal reaches the grate as 'coke'. The coal is fed from the hopper, through a firebrick arch, in a deep layer, flowing over a pair of stepped plates (coking plates) in the process. Primary ignition of the lower coals occurs in the zone between the two plates, and at the same time the upper layer is ignited by the heat from the firebrick arch. The layer thus approaches the grate burning at the top and bottom, with a wedge of unburnt fuel between. Heat produced in the primary zone releases the volatiles, which burn within the brick arch.

The grate consists of longitudinal bars, reciprocated by a cam mechanism such that the burning mass is 'walked' towards the ash discharge end. Combustion air is introduced through the grate to complete the carbon (coke) burning reaction.

This stoker does not require a 'coking' class of coal, rather it is able to burn a wide range of graded coals and washed smalls. The coal, however, should be free of fine materials which might be readily lost through the bars. A moderately caking fuel will minimise losses through the bars of coal broken down by the reciprocating action.

It is common for steam to be blown under the grate, to cool the bars and condition the clinker, thus few coking stokers are fitted to hot water boilers.

4.3.1.6 Fluidised bed

This uses a bed of sand or similar inert material, through which strong air currents are blown to cause the whole bed to 'boil'. The sand temperature is first raised to 700°C by heating the fluidising air with oil or gas and the coal is fed on, the hot bed igniting the coal. The 'boiling' sand bed keeps the coal in suspension so that the combustion air can reach all the fuel surfaces; the burning coal maintains bed temperature. The combustion creates finely divided ash, which is blown out of the boiler, but the sand bed needs periodic cleaning to remove heavier impurities and large ash pieces. The bed is held below ash fusion temperature to avoid formation of hard clinker.

4.3.1.7 Selection of stoker

There are often specific reasons why a certain type of stoker is chosen for a particular application, the predominant factors being boiler/heater compatability, fuel specification and the type of heat load. These factors are summarised in table 4.5.

4.3.1.8 Maintaining combustion

Solid-fuel stokers are not capable of instant re-ignition, therefore a small fire has to be maintained even after the boiler heat demand is satisfied. This process is often termed 'kindling', and the burner system controls incorporate a kindling setting, by means of a timer which injects fresh coal and combustion air periodically during periods of non-operation. In some systems the heat loss from the 'heat sink' (see section 4.6.7) calls the burner system into action sufficiently often to maintain the kindling fire.

4.3.2 Oil fuel burners

4.3.2.1 Pot burner

These are suitable only for class C (kerosene) fuels. There are normally no mechanical parts to cause fuel atomisation, instead the flame is established on the surface of hot oil in a special pot. The pot has a refractory brick lining which is heated by the flame; heat is conducted down the lining to the oil and raises its temperature to combustion point. A float valve maintains a set level of oil in the pot.

   (a) On simple burners the flame burns continually, inducing the necessary combustion air. The float is adjusted manually to increase or decrease the flame size.

   (b) Larger burners use a fan to supply combustion air and the flame size is fixed. There is no natural induction, so the flame dies when the

Table 4.5

Comparison of solid-fuel combustion systems

Type	Boiler size (kW)	Coal types	Preferred sizes	Turndown	Remarks
Gravity feed	15–275	Anthracite	Grains, beans	High	Controlled by forced draught fan
Underfeed	40–1750	Wide range but not strongly caking or abrasive	Singles	Up to 4:1	Turndown on most cannot be altered while running. Avoid strongly swelling coals
Chain grate	200–over 7500	Wide range but ash at least 6 per cent; not strongly caking	Singles and washed smalls	Up to 4:1; 8:1 by twin furnace	Can burn low-grade fuels efficiently
Drop tube	600–8500	Wide, ash at least 2 per cent	Singles	Up to 3:1	Highly responsive to load fluctuations
Coking	300–over 7500 normally steam	Wide	Wide plus washed smalls		Fine particles lost through grate; moderately caking coals preferred
Fluidised bed	1500–7500+	Wide		Poor	High turndown possible only by subdividing bed

fan is switched off by the thermostat. An electric re-ignition system relights the fuel.

Other oil fuels are not suitable, as they do not become sufficiently volatile at the temperatures in the pot.

4.3.2.2 Pressure jet (figure 4.3(a))

These are the most common type of burner used in horticulture, handling oil fuels from class C to class F, and in some instances class G. The oil is forced through a hydraulic nozzle at a pressure of 300–700 kPa, to break it into droplets sufficiently small for combustion. Oils in classes E, F and G require also to be heated (see table 4.3) in order to lower their viscosity sufficiently for atomisation. A fan blows the combustion air past the nozzle which causes the spray from the nozzle to form a fine mist, which burns just beyond the burner nozzle. In simple direct-fired air heaters, the combustion air might be diverted from the main airflow. This is done with a forward-facing funnel surrounding the burner tube. The air/oil droplet mixing is improved by a 'quorl plate', a finned ring around the nozzles which causes the correct air turbulence to shear the droplet emission into small fragments.

The oil pump is normally a positive displacement vane or gear type. It is designed to produce an oil flow in excess of demand, the surplus being bled away through a pressure relief valve. This return is either led back to the tank or into the in-feed fuel line.

The pump is driven by the air fan motor. However, when the burner starts, there is a period of 20–30 s when the fan runs to purge the combustion chamber of any explosive gases. The oil is held back from the nozzle during purging by a solenoid valve, the entire pump output being exhausted through the relief.

The flame is maintained only when heat is demanded; when the thermostat is satisfied the oil pump and fan are switched off. The flame is re-ignited by a high-voltage spark from electrodes placed either side of the nozzle.

Most burner oil pumps are manufactured to high tolerance and maintain oil tightness by metal to metal contact of moving surfaces. All fuel oils, except kerosene, contain sufficient waxes to lubricate these sliding surfaces, and prolonged use of kerosene in these pumps can cause high wear.

Combustion temperatures are shown in table 4.3. The combustion temperature heater is fitted into the in-feed line immediately ahead of the burner, so that the oil does not cool significantly between it and the nozzle. The heater normally uses electric elements, although larger systems switch to an alternative hot water or steam exchanger once the boiler is up to temperature. Oil returned from the relief valve is introduced to the in-feed before the heater.

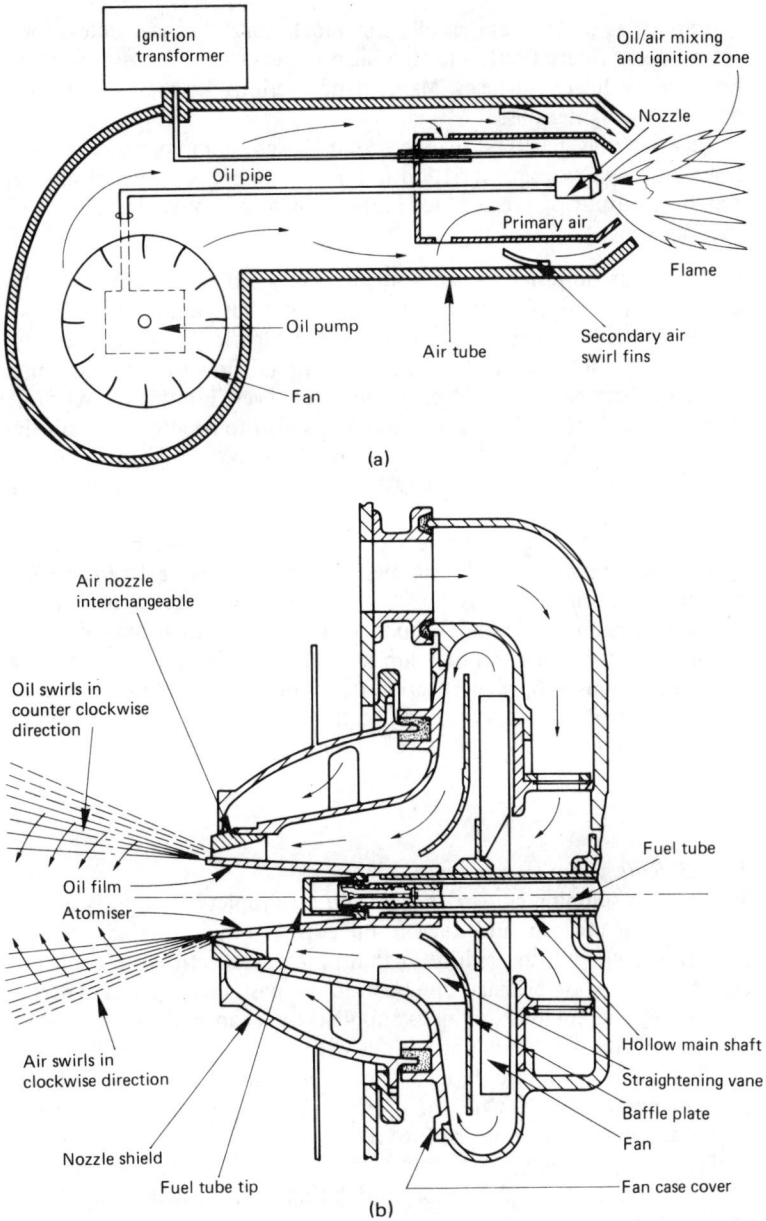

Figure 4.3 (a) Pressure jet oil burner. (b) Rotary cup oil burner (*courtesy of Hamworthy Engineering Ltd, Poole*).

Impurities in the heavier oils can block nozzle orifices unless they are properly filtered out, and they also increase soot deposition in the boiler or on heater surfaces. Maintenance periods for these oils are less than for the lighter oils.

Flame size is governed by the nozzle design, pump pressure and air-flow, although extreme variation in any will result in flame instability. The heat output of pressure jet burners might be controlled by one of the following.

(a) The heat output of small and medium sized burners can only be controlled by on/off switching; it cannot be adjusted during operation.
(b) Some medium sized burners, known as high/low type, incorporate two nozzles. Both run to full heat, then the oil flow to one is switched off as the heat demand reduces, to limit the severe hunting of an on/off burner on a light load. The air supply has also to be altered to suit the number of nozzles operating. This is usually done with a solenoid flap linked to the oil valve, which restricts the fan output when on single flame.
(c) Modulating of larger burners offers limited automatic adjustment of both oil pressure and air volume, to suit a varying heat demand. Oil pressure is normally altered by a motorised pressure control valve, although because flow rate is proportional to the square root of pressure change, the turndown ratio is limited. The valve motor also rotates a cam which adjusts the air restriction flap. The cam has a flexible surface with a series of adjusters beneath, so that its profile can be changed to match air requirements at all stages of oil flow.

4.3.2.3 Rotary cup (figure 4.3(b))

These use a spinning cup to atomise the oil droplets. The oil is fed to the centre of the cup, and flows to the edge in a thin film under centri-fugal force, where it shears into small droplets. Vanes fitted to the rotor create the flow of primary combustion air past the cup rim. The re-mainder of the combustion air is supplied by a fan in the normal way. The rotary cup will handle heavy oils with some impurities as there are no fine nozzle holes to block. The oil will atomise satisfactorily at lower temperatures than for the pressure jet, class G oil only requiring to be heated to 80°C and class F to 57°C.

The rotary cup will handle most oils with minimal adjustment, and can be designed for high/low or modulating control, with a turndown of 4:1.

The burner is ignited via a gas jet, as normal electrode sparks do not create sufficient heat to start combustion.

4.2.3.4 Air atomising burner
With this system, atomisation is carried out by a blast of compressed air mixing with the oil as it leaves the nozzle. Because the oil is not being atomised by hydraulic pressure creating a finely divided spray, the nozzle orifice can be relatively large, and hence less prone to blockage than the pressure jet nozzle.

There are two basic types of air atomising burner, low pressure and medium pressure. The low-pressure type operates with air at 1.5–2.0 kPa and often incorporates an air-driven rotary cup to aid atomisation. The air can be supplied by a fan and the volume delivered accounts for around 20 per cent of combustion air needs. The medium-pressure type operates at 25–100 kPa, with air supplied by a rotary vane compressor. The air volume accounts for only 10 per cent of the combustion air needs.

These types of burner do not require heavier oils to be heated to the same level as for the pressure jet, and can offer relatively high efficiencies. Large, medium-pressure burners can offer turndown ratios of 5:1. These burners are more expensive to purchase and to run than the pressure jet, and can prove more noisy.

4.3.2.5 Selection of burner
As in the case of stokers, there are certain factors to consider when selecting a burner for a particular application; the main ones are summarised in table 4.6.

4.3.3 Gaseous fuel burners
Mains gas is supplied at a pressure of 2.75–3 kPa. Most small gas burners operate on fuel at this pressure; larger burners require higher pressures, which are achieved by passing the incoming gas through a mechanical compressor (often termed a 'booster'). Lpg is supplied at high pressure and can be used in burners designed for natural gas, if the pressure is reduced to 3.5 kPa and the metering jets are changed to suit the different calorific value. The pressure reduction is normally done in two stages, dropping from tank pressure of 1400 kPa to 75 kPa in the supply pipe and the remaining reduction being done in the burner train.

Some gas burners are termed 'high pressure' and operate at a fuel supply pressure of up to 200 kPa. These can be run on lpg with lesser pressure reduction or mains gas with pressure boosting.

Three types of burner are used.

4.3.3.1 Natural aspirated jet
In these the gas flows through a nozzle within a venturi, and this induces a small amount of air to mix with it. The gas/air mixture then passes

Table 4.6

Comparison of oil burner systems

Type	Boiler size (kW)	Oil class	Atomising temp. (°C)	Turndown	Remarks
Pot	10–50	C	Ambient	High/low	The low flame might be just sufficient to maintain combustion
Pressure jet	15–2000	D	Ambient	High/low	Most common types
		E	80		
		F	105	2:1	
		G	125	7:1	Special nozzle types only
Rotary cup	1500–7500	D	Ambient	High/low	Small burners only
		E	24		
		F	55	4:1	
		G	80		Medium/large burners
Air atomising	50–2500 (low pressure) 100–10000 (medium pressure)	D	Ambient	Up to 5:1	Higher turndown only on medium pressure types
		E	24		
		F	55		
		G	80		

through a series of jets where it burns on mixing with the remaining combustion air. These are used in small boilers, heaters and CO_2 producers, and have the advantage of simplicity. The main control method is simple on/off, with re-ignition from a pilot flame or electric spark. Finer control can be obtained by reducing the gas pressure, although this must be within the limits of flame stability, the normal turndown being only 2:1. Modulation can be done with a motorised restrictor valve.

A system with more flame stability uses a 'sponge' of stainless steel instead of a series of jets. The gas/air mixture is evenly spread across the whole surface, rather than from points, and any lateral wandering of the flame does not remove it beyond the gas source.

4.3.3.2 Pressure jet gas burner
This is similar to the oil pressure jet, in which gas issuing from a nozzle combines with a forced air flow, to form a combustible mixture, which burns just beyond the burner nozzle. These burners can modulate with a turndown of 15:1 in some cases. They produce a flame in the form of a directional tongue, rather than the vertically rising flow from a jet burner. This makes the pressure jet more suitable for fitting to boilers and heaters requiring horizontal or even downwards heat input.

4.3.3.3 Airstream aspiration (figure 4.4)
Where gas is used directly to heat a high volume air flow, the combustion air can be diverted from the main airflow. This diversion is caused by a louvred V-shaped shield enclosing the gas jet, air/gas mixing and combustion takes place within the shield. The louvre shape and size are designed to divert sufficient air for combustion, but not an excess since this would make the flame unstable.

Modulating versions of these burners can have a turndown as great as 30:1 by suitable adjustment of the supply gas pressure. The shield louvres are graduated so that only a small amount of air is entrained near the jet, with an increasing amount as the V widens. On very low gas pressure the flame sits close to the jet bar in the small air supply; as the supply increases, the flame fills more of the V where air entrainment is greater.

Most burners of this type require an airspeed past the shield of 12.5–17.5 m/s for correct entrainment, and this requires adjustable air throttling plates in systems where the airflow may vary.

4.3.4 Factors affecting choice of fuel
There is considerable variation between the unit energy costs of the fuels available to the horticulturist. It is, however, wrong to select a

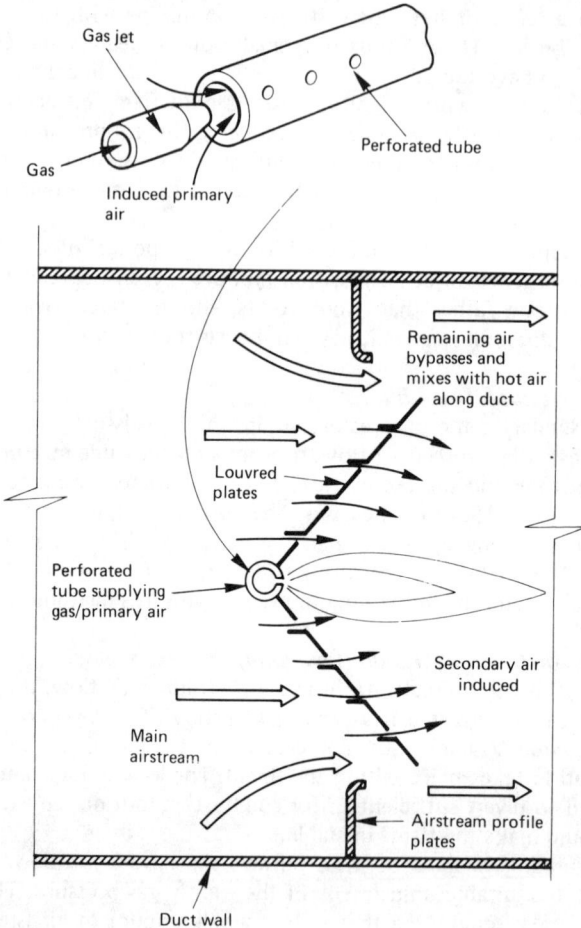

Figure 4.4   Airstream aspirated gas burner.

heating system purely on the basis of fuel costs, because both the equipment needed to handle and burn it, and its management, will considerably affect any cost benefit calculations. The two most common fuel choice decisions are the following.

4.3.4.1 Oil/coal
At the time of writing, coal is considerably cheaper than oil; however, the price differential will be influenced by the following considerations.

(a) The relative costs of stokers and burners.
(b) Most packaged shell boilers are designed specifically for either coal or oil. The coal boiler normally has a larger combustion chamber to allow for the stoker size and the burning coal mass; this is important when contemplating converting an existing system.
(c) As the flue gases from coal might contain a higher level of polutants than those from oil, a higher chimney could be required.
(d) Coal can be stored in simple bunkers, but if automated handling is required, the silo system might be relatively expensive and an extra delivery charge will be levied.
(e) Except for oil grades C and D, the storage tank will need to be heated and insulated.
(f) Automated coal and ash handling might require a larger boiler house.
(g) Heavy oils incur a cost for heating.
(h) Ash handling will either involve manual labour, or investment in automated equipment.
(i) Maintenance on a stoker can be more costly than on a burner. Routine servicing and cleaning frequency will be dictated by the fuel and combustion system.
(j) Stokers can offer similar turndown ratios to burners, but when loads fluctuate the stoker response will probably be slower. During long periods of low demand the stoker will continue to use some fuel to maintain a fire.

4.3.4.2 Choice between grades of oil

The main considerations involve the heating needed by the heavier grades, and the levels of impurities.

Normally lighter grades are more expensive, but as seen in table 4.3 grades E and above require heating for both tank outflow and atomisation; this involves extra equipment and adds to operating cost.

Impurities in the heavy grades lead to more frequent cleaning of the burner, or to using a more complex burner, and to increased boiler tube cleaning. The declared impurity level might influence the chimney design.

It is normally easy to convert heavy grade burners to use lighter grades, but changing in the opposite direction often involves modification or renewal of the burner. While a simple pressure jet burner will run on grades C or D, the poor lubrication properties of grade C can cause severe pump wear.

4.4 CHIMNEYS AND FLUES

The chimney not only conducts away the products of combustion, but also helps to create an airflow through the boiler or heater, even where an air supply fan is fitted to the burner or stoker.

4.4.1 Size requirements

Upwards gas flow is induced because the warm flue gases are less dense than atmospheric air at ambient temperatures. The strength of the updraught is dependent on chimney height, and most systems are designed for a height of at least 6–9 m. Local authorities will often insist on much greater chimney heights, to ensure dispersal of the flue gas above surrounding properties.

4.4.1.1 Cross-section area

The gas flow rate up the flue is governed by the internal size of the chimney. If this is too small flow will be restricted, but if too large the gas flow will be inadequate to prevent downdraughts and internal circulation. Flue and chimney cross-sections are often suggested by the manufacturers of the heating plant, but should be calculated for each installation, because cross-sectional area is very much influenced by updraught height and internal surfaces. Methods for this can be found in heating engineering manuals, such as the Chartered Institute of Buildings Services Guide Book, section B 13.

Chimney cross-sectional area should be based on a minimum design velocity of 6 m/s and many modern systems will cope with velocities of 12–15 m/s. The minimum velocity should ensure prevention of downwash due to wind, but if a chimney has been sized for this velocity when the plant is at full capacity, it will be much reduced when the system is 'turned down' or on 'kindling combustion'. To prevent downwash in these situations the top of the chimney can be narrowed to provide a suitable minimum exit velocity on low load. If this is done with a short conical restrictor, its resistance effect at full load gas flow will be minimal. The cone should taper inwards at 15° for the best effect in both circumstances (figure 4.5).

4.4.1.2 Resistance

The flue and chimney will offer resistance to gas flow, this is largely governed by gas velocity, internal roughness and any turbulence induced.

(a) Velocity is dependent on gas volume flow and cross-sectional area. In some poorly designed systems the cross-sectional area will be less than the size in the design, as accumulations of soot in bends or horizontal sections will effectively constrict the section.

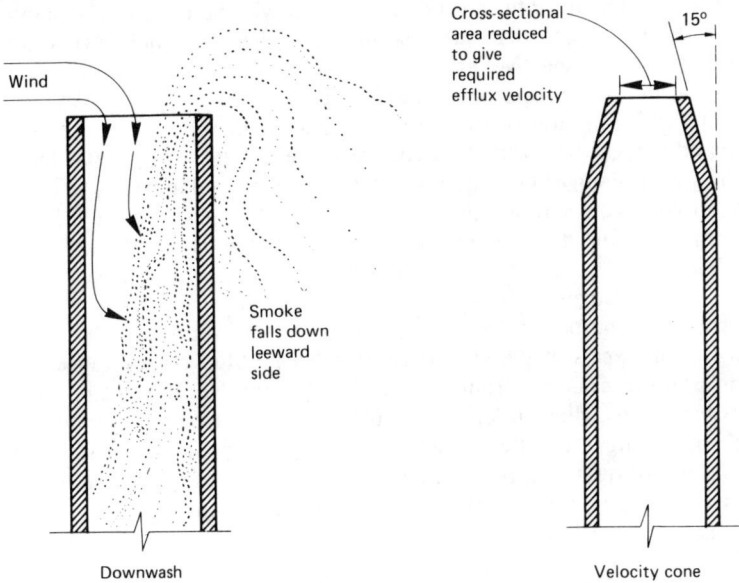

Figure 4.5 Discharge from chimneys.

(b) The internal finish is important; a smooth metal chimney could require a smaller cross-section than one lined with firebrick.

(c) Turbulence is created where gases change direction or two flows merge. Careful design should ensure smooth, shallow bends or that the two gas flows are travelling in the same direction before merging, rather than one being injected into the other at a sharp angle. Ideally each boiler should have its own flue.

Resistance is calculated in the same way as for gas flow in ductwork, and for any situation the calculated resistance has to be balanced against the available draught and boiler requirements.

4.4.1.3 Heating plant draughting requirements

Most boilers and heaters require either a slight suction or atmospheric pressure at the flue outlet, and the chimney system should provide at least this. In many cases the available updraught will be much stronger, to a point where it can induce excess airflow through the burner, and this can be prevented by fitting a draught stabiliser. The latter is a hinged air inlet placed at the commencement of the chimney system; the lower end is weighted so that it remains closed when the draught pressure is correct, but any increase will cause it to open to feed the excess air directly into the flue, rather than via the burner. The stabi- liser should ensure that the heating plant draught requirements are maintained, irrespective of chimney draught changes due to wind changes in load or atmospheric temperature.

If the flue is too restrictive for natural draughting, a fan (termed 'forced draught fan') can be fitted, which overcomes the extra resistance. The forced draught fan requires a heavily constructed impeller, to with- stand corrosion and abrasive particles in the flue gas, and the drive is normally arranged to site the motor away from the flue gas heat.

The fan is sized to handle the greatest flue gas flow, and often incor- porates a draught stabiliser to prevent it inducing excessive airflow through the burner on light load. The fan operating pressure should be slightly in excess of the difference between the flue gas resistance and the pressure available from the natural draught. Net draught pressure at the heater flue outlet is measured with an accurate manometer (draught gauge); usually an inclined tube type is needed to permit the small pressures to be read. The manometer is direct reading and gives instant indication of the effects of adjustments or other chimney condi- tions.

4.4.2 Construction and installation

4.4.2.1 Construction materials
The most common construction materials are brickwork or steel, although certain plastics and cements are also used.

(a) Stainless steel tube types are fitted to air heaters and, occasion- ally, to small boilers. The single thickness does not maintain the flue gases above acid dewpoint, but corrosion is prevented by the stainless steel. The chimney also collects large quantities of liquid and soot, so provision should be made for these to drain from the base without interfering with heater performance.

(b) Larger metal chimneys are constructed from heavy steel plate, with 40–50 mm of insulation around the outside, the insulation being protected by a layer of sheet metal, normally aluminium. The plate material is either ordinary mild steel or an alloy of copper and steel called Corten, in which the initial rust scale protects the surface against further attack.

The inner steel core also forms the structural part of the chimney; the plate has to be sufficiently thick to support it, with due allowance for some thinning by corrosion.

The chimney might be self-supporting or held upright by guy wires. The 'self-supporting' chimney is mounted on a large block of concrete which acts as its sole means of withstanding the toppling action of side winds. Chimney wall thickness and design of the base block or the guys and anchors must be calculated for each case, to take account of soil conditions as well as height and wind velocity.

(c) Brick chimneys normally have an outer structural casing of brickwork, with an inner core of special bricks to provide both insulation and protect the structural bricks from heat and corrosion. The thickness of the outer wall depends on the height and likely wind loadings, but it will often taper – for example, being 3 or 4 bricks thick at the base and only 1 at the top. These chimneys are usually self-supporting, and use the downwards force from the weight of the brickwork as part of the restraint.

The inner lining is of fireclay in the form of blocks or an *in situ* concrete sleeve. In many cases the blocks have to be laid without mortar, and with space between them and the structural brickwork, to allow for their thermal movement as a result of flue gas temperature fluctuations.

4.4.2.2 Flue connection
The chimney is normally sited to one side of the heater flue outlet, with the connection made by a length of flue pipe. This prevents soot or liquor produced in the chimney from falling back into the boiler. A door at the base of the chimney, below the flue inlet, allows any accumulation to be removed before it builds up to flue level.

Flue pipes leading to the chimney should be sloped upwards or downwards, with large radius bends. This prevents soot accumulating in horizontal sections or sharp corners. The flue should run in the same direction of inclination over its entire length, because any change from a downslope to an upslope would act as a soot collector.

4.5 AIR HEATERS

The term 'boiler' is normally reserved for units that heat water or produce steam, and 'heater' to those that produce warm air.

4.5.1 Direct firing
This burns class C or D oil, or gas, and the products of combustion are mixed with air being warmed. Its application in a cropping building requires careful consideration of toxic contents in the products of combustion, oxygen depletion, CO_2 enrichment and water vapour production. Reference is made to toxic products in section 4.2.5.

Some CO_2 enrichment might be beneficial to actively photosynthesising plants but excess can have a growth retarding effect. The water vapour can increase the house humidity to a level that encourages disease, or accumulate on inside surfaces as condensation, and dripping causes erosion of small areas of plants. These problems can be avoided if the maximum size of direct heater is one that can hold the house 5°C above ambient, where there is no specific combustion air supply. or 11°C if a combustion air inlet duct is fitted.

In the direct fired heater a large volume of air is blown past the burner by a fan. Some of this air will be used for combustion, and the hot flue gases are re-introduced to the main volume of air. To ensure thorough mixing the heater duct work is in the form of a maze of concentric chambers, which both effectively treble the air path length and create turbulence at each turn (see figure 4.6(a)). The airflow apportionment is normally set to lift the total flow by 40°C with a flue gas temperature of 1500°C. In many heaters the main air fan can be used independently of the burner, to circulate cold air. It is also normal for this fan to run for a few minutes after the burner has switched off, to ensure that the inner ductwork has cooled.

4.5.2 Indirect heater (figure 4.6(b))

The burner heats the walls of a metal combustion chamber around which the air to be heated is blown. The combustion chamber is connected to the flue by a number of small tubes which also run through the heating air ducting to ensure that the maximum heat is extracted from the flue gases. (The unit comprising the combustion chamber and small flue tubes is normally termed the 'heat exchanger'.)

In all but the simplest heaters the burner will be a fan aspirated oil or gas unit. The simpler heaters draw combustion air from the main airflow, like their direct firing counterparts, but this air is exhausted rather than being returned. The heat exchanger surfaces, especially those nearest the air inlet, often operate at temperatures below acid dewpoint. Corrosion is reduced by making the chamber and tubes in stainless steel, although some manufacturers reduce costs by using stainless only in areas where maximum corrosion is likely. To prevent the heat exchanger operating at very low temperatures when the burner first starts (in heaters with a separate burner fan) and remaining hot when it stops, the main air fan is controlled by a thermostat, so that it runs only when the exchanger is above the correct temperature.

As there is a possibility of unburnt combustible gas gathering between firings, the heat exchanger is fitted with a sprung flap or 'explosion door' which allows any explosive pressure to exhaust safely.

Even when the combustion chamber is made of stainless steel the burner flame should not play directly on to the walls, otherwise severe distortion will result. In large units this is prevented by choosing a burner nozzle to give a flame length and spread within the chamber

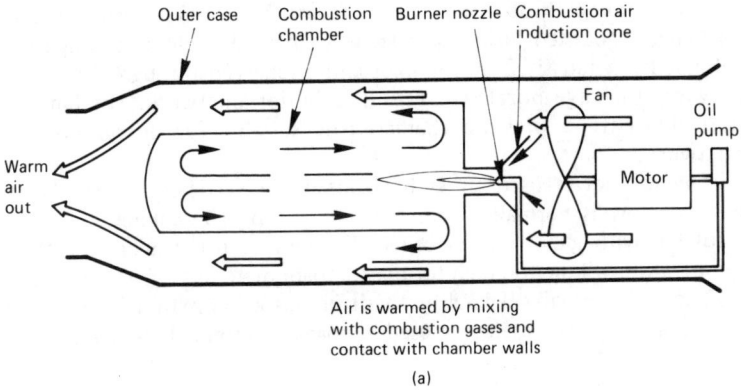

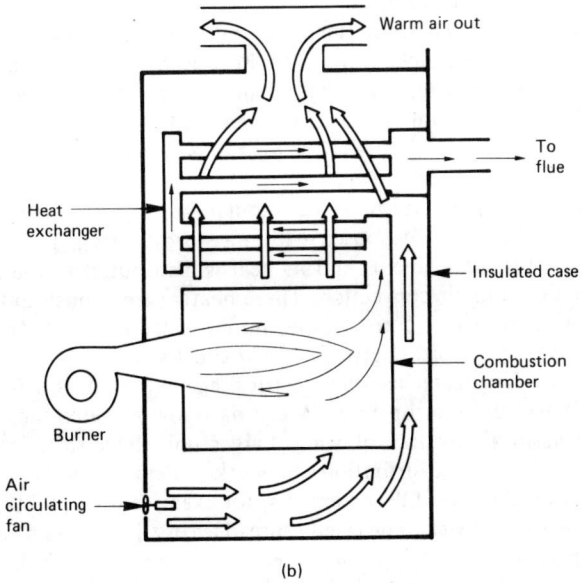

Figure 4.6 (a) Directly fired heater. (b) Indirectly fired heater.

dimensions. If this is not possible, the areas where flame can impinge on the walls are lined with firebrick, which takes the full force of the heat.

Most indirect heaters are in the form of a cabinet with the heat exchanger mounted inside. The air to be heated is blown through the cabinet by a fan sited on the inlet and discharged through either free blowing discharge nozzles or into distribution ductwork. The fan will normally have a pressure characteristic suitable for distribution by ductwork.

The cabinet is used either horizontally or vertically; in the latter case, airflow is normally from bottom to top. The cabinet walls are insulated with glass fibre or other high-temperature insulants, as their temperature will be too high for plastic foam materials.

There is normally a facility to fit air filtration materials in the air inlets, although these are not used in normal cropping building heating.

4.5.3 Electric heating

Heat is produced from electricity by the friction caused as electrons flow along resistance wire. The heat is free from contaminants and highly controllable, thus it is normally used directly, rather than through a transfer medium. Electric heating plant is cheap and simple when compared with other fuels. The heat is used in one of two ways.

(i) Heating the house air

(a) The simplest form is the tubular heater, in which the electrical restive elements are housed within a sturdy casing. The casing tube is heated by the element, and its heat is distributed to the house air by radiation and air convection. These heaters are robust and safe against water ingress if of correct type and correctly installed. They are normally available in sizes between 100 W and 1 kW.

(b) The fan heater uses an electrical element to heat a forced flow of air. Small units of up to 5 kW can have low powered fans to distribute the warm air by free blowing. Larger units have sufficient fan power to power an air distribution ductwork system. Large heaters are normally available in 3 kW increments, for example 6 kW, 9 kW, 12 kW; this enables the power to be evenly spread across the phases of a three-phase supply.

Owing to the cost of electricity and supply limitations, electric air heating is normally used only on small production houses or specialist propagation units. However, its versatility allows easy installation, and it is suitable for providing temporary heating for frost protection or other uses in a normally unheated house.

(ii) Direct soil heating
This uses cable pattern elements which are buried in the growing medium. The warming cable heat output is sufficiently low to warm the medium evenly, without localised overheating. This application is similar to buried warm water pipes and is described in section 5.5.

4.6 BOILERS

These provide both hot water and steam.

4.6.1 Types of boiler
The basic boiler layout consists of a combustion chamber (firebox) and a series of passages (flue ways) through which the hot gases pass to heat the water or steam. Boilers used in horticulture can be divided into three types.

4.6.1.1 Cast iron sectional
The cast iron sectional consists of a number of transverse sections clamped together. The front and rear sections are specially fitted with fire door and flue respectively, the intermediate ones having a basic horseshoe shape. The casting shape allows for a large lower combustion chamber with the flue ways cast into the upper parts (figure 4.7(a)). The water is contained in passages within the legs of the horseshoe and between each of the flue ways. In older solid-fuel boilers the fireside surfaces of the castings were smooth but modern versions and those designed for oil or gas are finned or heavily corrugated, to improve heat extraction from the hot gases. Fins are not suited to solid fuel, as they can become blocked with soot and light ash, which then acts as an insulant.

The sections are either clamped together by external bolts, with gaskets between each water joint, or by nipples screwed between the joints. The nipple has a right-hand thread at one end and a left-hand at the other, so that by rotating in one direction it screws into both sections simultaneously. The remainder of the mating surfaces have to be gas-tight but not waterproof and are packed with asbestos rope and fireclay.

The boiler output rating depends on the number of sections used; for example, a five-section unit might produce 150 kW and a ten-section, 300 kW. In theory, the boiler size can be increased by adding further intermediate sections; although in practice the disturbance caused to existing sections during such modifications can make them leak.

The sides of the boiler sit on a brick base. If the boiler is solid fuelled the stoker hearth is built into this base. An oil or gas burner is usually fitted through the lower fire door in the front section, although it can be fitted into the rear section or under the side brickwork if this is more convenient. The burner flame length should be shorter than the combustion chamber, and especially if the end section has no waterway across its width, firebricks are used to divert the hot gases upwards into the flue tubes.

The front section contains small doors which coincide with the flue-ways to allow access for cleaning. The solid-fuel boiler has a large lower door to allow for removal of clinker and ash; this door is normally replaced by a burner mounting plate for oil or gas firing.

4.6.1.2 Shell and tube

Tubular shell boilers are of unit construction and normally have a cylindrical barrel of welded steel (shell) encompassing the combustion chamber and tubes. The tubes of a shell boiler can be used in one of two ways.

A 'watertube' boiler has the combustion gases flowing within the shell, and the water to be heated is contained inside tubes.

In a 'firetube' boiler the water is contained with the shell, and the flue gases pass through the tubes from a combustion chamber also in the form of a large tube (see figure 4.7(b)).

The watertube boiler is normally best suited to high-pressure steam applications as the small tubes are stronger than an equivalent thickness outer shell of a firetube unit.

The firetube is the most common type now used on nurseries. It is often termed a 'packaged economic' unit, as these were its obvious attributes when compared with a cast iron sectional. The tubes are normally straight and run from front to back; they are fixed into a perforated plate across each end of the boiler. There is a space between the tube plate and the boiler ends to allow the flue gases to travel from one pass of tubes to the next. The boilers are normally built as 'three pass', to extract the maximum heat from the flue gases (figure 4.7(b)). The first pass is the single combustion chamber tube, the second is a few large diameter tubes which sends the gases back towards the burner end, and the third pass takes the gases back towards the chimney in a large number of smaller tubes.

In some boilers the back will also contain water between two closely spaced end plates (wetback), otherwise the back end plate will be a single sheet (dryback). The wetback is more efficient as this increases the heat transfer surface, but the strength required to withstand pressure makes the boiler more expensive. The pressure tries to force the two flat end plates apart and this is resisted by 'staying'; this uses a

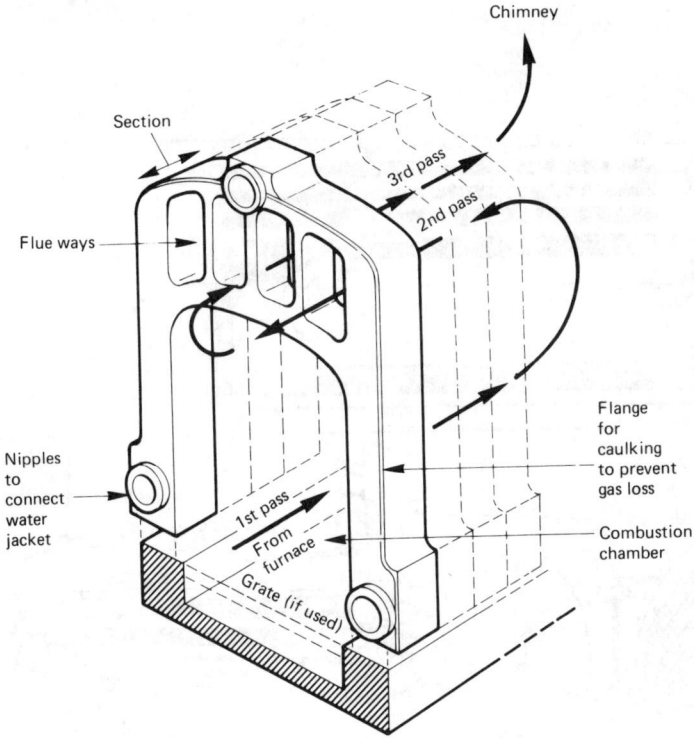

Chimney

Section

3rd pass

2nd pass

Flue ways

Nipples
to
connect
water
jacket

1st pass

From
furnace

Grate (if used)

Flange
for
caulking
to prevent
gas loss

Combustion
chamber

(a)

Caulking

Caulking
flanges
machined flat

Nipple

Water
jacket

Section   Section

Fireside (inside boiler) surfaces

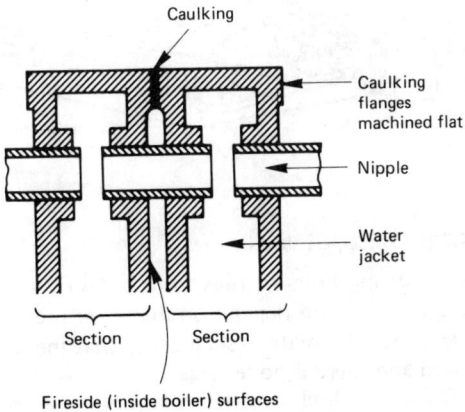

DETAIL SECTION OF NIPPLE CONNECTOR

Figure 4.7   (a) Cast iron sectional boiler.

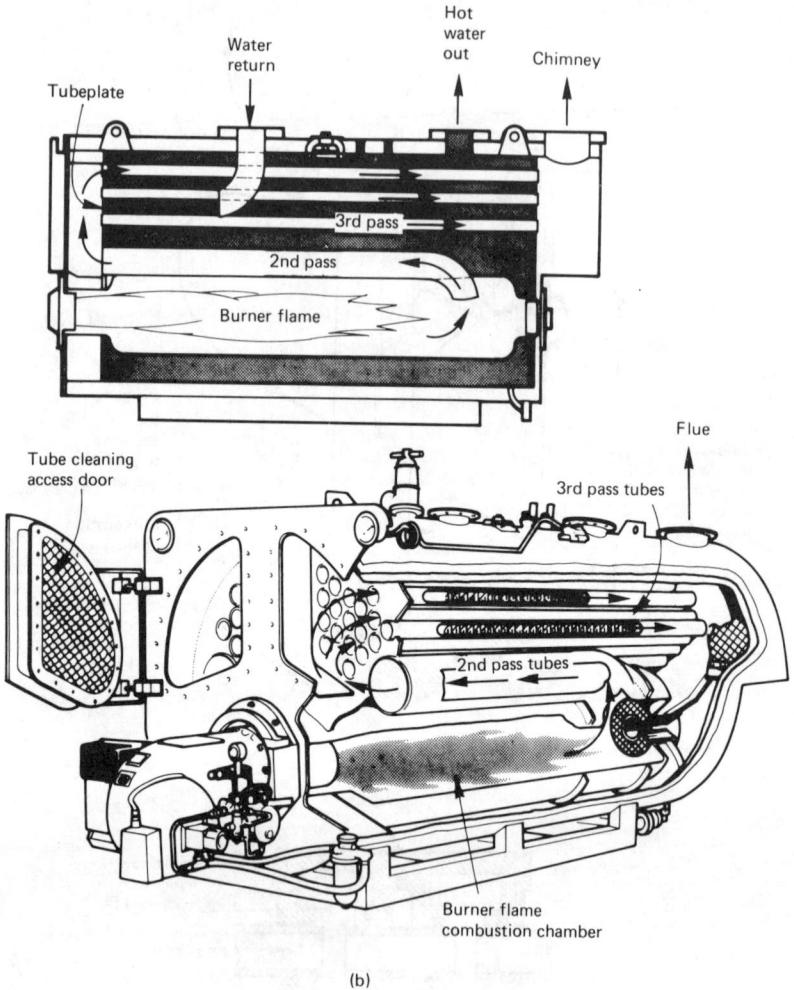

Figure 4.7 (b) Three-pass shell boiler.

number of strong bolts or pins to link the two surfaces. The strength
and siting of stays will depend on the boiler pressure rating. Stays have
to be fixed into the plate in such a way that the full restraining force is
transmitted and there is no leakage.

The front of a boiler fuelled by oil or gas is in the form of a large
single door, with the burner mounted on. Solid-fuel systems require
doors both above and below the stoker inlet. The main purpose of this
door is to expose the flue tubes for cleaning.

4.6.1.3 Flash steam boiler

The flash steam is a special type of watertube boiler which uses a single length of pipe formed into a coil inside an insulated combustion chamber. Water is pumped into the bottom of the coil, and is converted to steam as it passes along.

4.6.2 Working pressure

A boiler might be used to provide hot water at atmospheric pressure (commonly termed low pressure hot water), hot water for a system operating at elevated pressures (commonly termed medium or high pressure hot water) or to produce steam. The latter two pressures can cause dangerous explosions, therefore any boiler to be used for these applications must be tested for safe working pressure (SWP). The pressure relief valve is set to operate at SWP. These tests are initially carried out before installation and periodically during use; the later ones include physical examination for corrosion or other forms of weakening.

The pressure test is carried out by the hydrostatic method. In this the boiler is completely filled with water which is then pressurised by the injection of a small amount of extra water. Water is nearly incompressible, so a small volume change produces a high pressure. As there is no highly compressed gas within the boiler, any failure does not produce a dangerous rupture, instead the hydrostatic pressure is relieved by loss of few ml of water, and small failures like leaking rivets or welds can be repaired.

To ensure a margin of safety the test pressure is usually at least 50 per cent above its normal working pressure. Where corrosive weakening is shown during a physical examination or hydrostatic test, the boiler can be derated — that is, it is certified for working at a lower pressure.

The cast iron sectional boiler is not usually suitable for pressurised applications, although some will produce medium pressure hot water or low pressure steam up to around 100 kPa gauge. When used to produce steam the boiler is normally run full of water, to ensure that all the flue ways are water cooled and the steam produced is stored in a drum mounted above.

The majority of shell boilers will produce hot water at all pressures or steam. The safe working pressure will depend somewhat on design and specification, but it is usual for nursery boilers to be designed for 500 kPa gauge. It is possible to use a steam boiler to produce hot water by running it flooded (totally full of water) if there is sufficient provision for water to flow both in and out. This sometimes requires enlarged inlet and outlet tappings, as the volume flow of hot water will be approximately 50 times larger than the water volume flow to move the same heat as steam. Sometimes low pressure shell boilers are installed for the main purpose of providing hot water for heating, but are converted for short periods to produce steam for soil sterilising.

4.6.3 Feed water quality and treatment

Most water supplies contain dissolved substances which can have harmful effects on the boiler or other heating components. The main problems are caused by dissolved minerals, oxygen and carbon dioxide, in certain areas the water might be acidic also.

4.6.3.1 Dissolved minerals

These are normally salts of calcium or magnesium, and exist in two forms. The bicarbonate form is unstable and can be converted to an insoluble carbonate precipitate if the water is heated above $70°C$ and carbon dioxide is released. This form is normally called 'temporary hardness', and is responsible for lime deposits (furring) on heating surfaces. 'Permanent hardness' is caused by insoluble sulphates or chlorides of calcium or magnesium which are not precipitated by heating. These compounds do not cause furring in hot water systems but are left behind when water is evaporated in a steam boiler.

Hardness is expressed as the equivalent concentration of calcium carbonate in the water, either in 'parts per million' (ppm) or 'degrees of hardness' on the Clark scale. One Clark's degree is equivalent to 14 ppm.

Treatment requirements will depend on the type of boiler; for hot water it is sufficient to remove temporary hardness; for steam, all hardness must be treated. Treatment can be either external, using a softener, or internal, using chemicals.

(a) External softening is usually by the soda-lime process or the base exchange process.

Soda-lime is suitable for carbonate treatment only, and cannot removal all the hardness. This can be suitable for a hot water system, but in a steam system the remaining solids will still accrue, if only at a very reduced rate.

Base exchange uses a zeolite sand in which the compounds causing hardness exchange their bases (calcium or magnesium) with sodium from the zeolite; the sodium salts are not precipitated by heating. When the sodium has been exhausted from the zeolite it is 'regenerated' with sodium chloride (common salt); in this process the attached calcium and magnesium are exchanged for sodium and the resulting magnesium or calcium chloride is flushed from the system. Regeneration is carried out after a pre-determined quantity of water has been treated (the actual quantity will depend on the water hardness and softener capacity), and is often automated using a water meter. Because the softener is out of action while regenerating, the treated water side of the system should contain a buffer tank.

Hardness can be tested by chemical analysis; testing for 'softness' is possible using a soap solution and observing bubble stability.

(b) Chemical treatment involves injecting compounds into the boiler water which combine with the temporary hardness and prevent its deposition on heating. Some compounds render the scale-forming minerals harmless, while others prevent the growth of scale crystals; most treatment chemicals also contain corrosion inhibitors.

The method of softening depends on the potential usage pattern; external softeners are expensive to install but cheap to run, while chemical methods require little additional equipment but can prove relatively expensive. Closed systems require most of the treatment during initial fill, and only small amounts of feed water to replace that lost by leaks or evaporation thereafter, so chemical methods might be appropriate. Where water is lost from the system, as in sterilisation (see section 6.2.3), an external softener will be more economic.

It must be recognised that the above treatments might still leave products in the water which will remain when the water is evaporated for steam. These must be removed from the boiler before they affect its performance. In a properly designed boiler and treatment system the salt deposits will accumulate in the bottom of the boiler, from where they can be easily removed. In most boilers the sludge of solid matter is forced out of a valve at the base by steam pressure; this operation is known as 'blowing down', and is either done at regular intervals or as a continuous bleed.

4.6.3.2 Dissolved gases

These can cause corrosion to internal surfaces of both the boiler and the associated system; unlike solid matter, gases pass around the system with the steam. The main problems are corrosion pitting, caused by the oxygen, and dissolution by the weak carbonic acid formed from the carbon dioxide.

Dissolved gases can be combated by chemical inhibitors; these either absorb the gases or coat the internal surfaces and protect them against corrosion. In both cases the chemical has to be added continually because its effects diminish as a result of gas saturation or erosion of the protective coating by water flow. In most cases the chemical is injected by a dosing pump, set in accordance with chemical analysis of the boiler water.

Treated water can also re-absorb gases, so feed tanks and condensate sumps should be covered to minimise atmospheric contact.

Note that, if an existing system is being treated for the first time, or the treatment is being changed, there is a risk that scale deposits will be loosened and block the system, or foul mechanical equipment.

4.6.4 Water feed to steam boilers

Feed water must be forced into a steam boiler against its working pressure; on modern boilers this is done with a piston or multiple-stage centrifugal pump. Older boilers used injectors in which a partial vacuum, caused by a combination of steam condensation and a venturi effect, produced by running some of the boiler output through a set of conical nozzles, drew in the feed water.

The pump is controlled by a pair of float or probe switches, the 'low level' one maintaining the water level above the tubes, and the 'high level' one ensuring that the steam space is maintained in the top of the boiler.

Water level within the boiler is checked visually by a 'sight glass', which is a clear glass tube connected at each end into the boiler water jacket, and placed to span the highest and lowest desirable levels. Injectors are manually controlled by reference to the 'sight glass'.

The final safeguard against low water level is a 'fusible plug' in the crown of the combustion chamber. This is made of a lead compound which is solid at the normal operating temperatures, but melts if the temperature rises to a dangerous level. On failing, the water and steam are released into the combustion chamber, to be vented to atmosphere, extinguishing the fire in the process.

4.6.5 Low-temperature corrosion

Cold water returning to the boiler from the system will have two effects, it will cool the fireside surfaces below the acid dewpoint, and the thermal shock can cause leakage by contracting the joints. This latter problem is serious in tubular boilers, where thermal shock loosens the joints where the tubes are swaged into the tubeplate.

These problems can be avoided if the return water temperature is maintained above a certain minimum. There are two ways of doing this:

(a) A small pump (shunt pump) is installed to pump hot water directly from the flow outlet to the return (see figure 4.8). This pump should move at least 15 per cent of the main circulating pump flow. A shunt pump also keeps the boiler contents mixed when the main pump is off; this prevents hot water gathering at the crown and cold in the base.

(b) A full flow bypass, which connects the flow and return pipes, is controlled by a three-port diverter valve, with a control sensor on the boiler return pipe. The valve can operate in any position between diverting all the flow water back into the boiler and allowing it all to run round the heating circuit. The thermostat controls the valve position so that sufficient hot water is admixed into the return to maintain the minimum temperature. Because the boiler

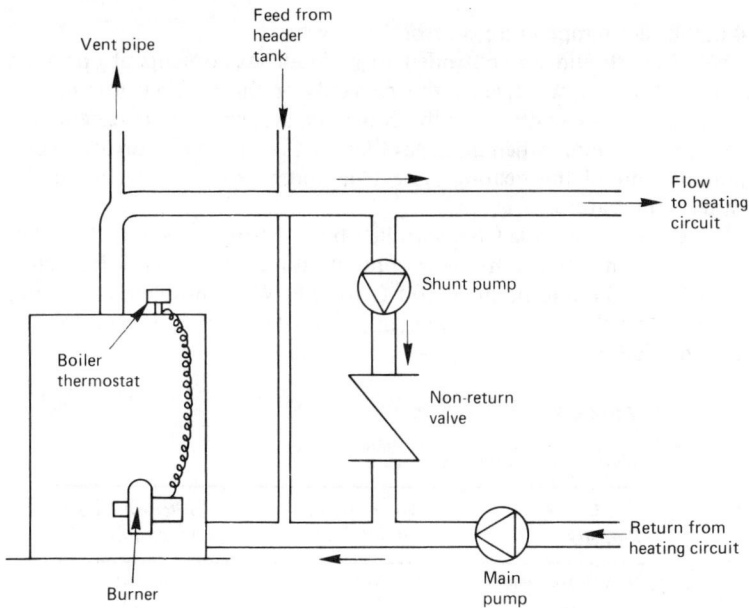

Figure 4.8 Shunt pump boiler return water temperature control.

return temperature has priority by this method, the flow main temperatures will vary.

4.6.6 Feed and expansion connections

The LPHW boiler has two connections to its water supply tank. The 'feed' pipe runs from the tank base to the boiler in-feed to allow water to flow into it. The 'expansion' or vent pipe runs from the crown of the boiler to terminate above the tank. Its purpose is to vent air and steam. It is terminated over the tank so that any water ejected in the process is not lost to the system; in effect any 'expansion' occurs as a backflow up the feed pipe. The vent must never be obstructed, as it is the main protection against build-up of explosive pressures within the boiler.

Both pipes should be fitted to the boiler in such a way that the pump pressure is the same on each. The vent pipe is always under positive pressure when the pump is fitted to the return pipe; the feed pipe should be fitted between the pump and the boiler, where it will experience the same pressure. If it is fitted to the suction side of the pump, the resistance of the heating circuits, especially when some valves are closed, will be greater than the resistance of the feed and vent pipes, so water will be driven up the vent and drawn down the feed in preference to flowing around the circuit.

4.6.7 Boiler temperature control

The boiler should be controlled to maintain its contents at operating temperature, irrespective of the demands of the heating system. This requires separate controls for the boiler and system. Only in exceptional cases, for example when using gas that does not produce corrosive compounds, should the heating system be controlled by adjusting boiler water temperature.

The burner or stoker is controlled by a thermostat set in the boiler crown. This maintains the water contents at least $10°C$ below its boiling point. This boiling point is $100°C$ for LPHW (atmospheric pressure) system, but the benefits of pressurising on operating temperatures are shown in table 4.7.

Table 4.7

Water boiling temperatures

Gauge pressure (kPa)	Water boiling point (°C)	Boiler running temperature (°C)
0 (atmospheric)	100	90
50	110	100
100	120	110
170	130	120
360	140	130
475	150	140
620	160	150
790	170	160

Problems can arise in controlling solid-fuelled boilers because of the residual heat in the fire after the combustion system is switched off. If this coincides with the heating system controls shutting down the hot water offtake, the boiler contents will boil. This is undesirable because

(a) the vibration caused can damage the boiler or its fittings
(b) steam pockets forming against the heating surfaces can lead to localised overheating and buckling
(c) hot water will be ejected from the expansion pipe and this both wastes treatment and poses a danger to staff in the vicinity.

This problem can be alleviated by installing a small non-controlled heating circuit which acts as a 'heat sink'. In large systems this can sometimes be achieved by fitting a small connection between the flow and return mains, at the opposite end of their run to the boiler, and using mains heat loss as the heat sink.

5 HEAT DISTRIBUTION

5.1 BASIC LAYOUT CONSIDERATIONS

5.1.1 Heat input requirements
All heating systems must fulfil the following needs:

(a) Provision of the desired environmental temperatures during periods of the coldest weather that can reasonably be expected. This requirement covers the capacity of both the heat production and distribution systems.

(b) The capability of close control; this will usually involve automatic control on all but the smallest greenhouse.

(c) Rapid response to changes in external conditions. This criterion is more easily met by modern low-inertia systems, based on high-speed hot water, steam or blown warm air suppliers.

Modern protected crop production demands precise temperatures; in some crops, a divergence of 2–3°C from the optimum will seriously affect performance and returns. The production systems of some crops, such as tomatoes, can involve day and night temperatures at different levels.

5.1.2 Temperature distribution
A well-designed system should provide as near uniform a house temperature as possible, both horizontally and vertically. This will involve attention to the following details.

(a) The heat input should be distributed according to the potential losses from each part of the structure; in simple terms, this involves a uniform heat input throughout the house to account for roof losses, and additional heating at the sides and ends to cover losses from these areas.

(b) Convection within the house will result in warm air rising towards the roof. This effect can be countered by high heat output piping, which induces powerful convective vertical circulation, or the use of positive vertical air-mixing methods. On a sloping site the lateral distribution will be affected by warm air percolating towards the 'high' end.

(c) Where low-level heating is important, it is preferable to install the pipe or duct at low level also, otherwise additional heat will be needed to achieve the desired effect by convective circulation. If soil temperature is important, undersoil heating should be considered.

(d) Heat distribution pipes/ducts can be placed to fit the cropping layout, for example, one loop of pipe per raised bed or double tomato row.

(e) Lateral temperature uniformity is possibly only if the heat is distributed throughout the house.

5.1.3 Versatility

Often the house will grow a range of crops, each with its own temperature requirement and cropping pattern. The system can be designed for this by including the following considerations.

(a) The heating capacity must cater for the crop with the highest demand.

(b) A permanent pipe/duct layout might not be possible; for example, the floor loop layout for tomatoes might be removed totally to allow the preparatory soil cultivation, or moved into the roof to protect a mechanically planted lettuce crop against frost.

(c) The installation must accommodate other components, such as thermal screens.

(d) It might be possible to use the heating pipe layout for other purposes, such as rolling bench supports or a transport monorail.

5.1.4 Reliability

Because heating is of such importance to the success of the crop, the possibility of its failure must be minimised. The important considerations at the design stage are as follows.

(a) Arranging for manual bypassing of controllers.

(b) Installing the higher risk components (pumps, warm air fan motors) so that they can easily be changed.

(c) Duplicating the high risk components.

(d) Installing stand-by electric power.

(e) Fitting suitable alarms to warn of component malfunction or conditions deviating from those desired.

5.2 WARM AIR

This is normally produced by direct or indirectly fired oil and gas units in commercial glasshouses and tunnels, and electric heaters in small houses. In some situations the warm air is produced by hot water or steam powered air heater batteries.

The heater battery is a simple radiator connected to the steam or hot water supply; a fan blows the air to be warmed through the matrix. This offers a cheaper system for heat distribution than that provided by pipes. It is easier to control air temperature to suit heat demand than is possible using oil or some gas fired units, by controlling the battery temperature.

The hot air can be distributed within the house as freely blown jets or through ducting.

5.2.1 Free air blowing

These sytems have the advantage of absence of ductwork, which can hinder operations and reduce light transmission, and so installation is relatively cheap and easy. However, temperature distribution can be poor owing to the warm air jets being deflected by the crop and the house structure, or by being overcome by vertical convection currents. Because the cabinet types discharge heat at a high level, the house floor can remain several degrees colder, than the rest of the structure, as convectional heat rise will keep the warm and cold air in their relative positions.

Small direct fired heaters of the portable 'torpedo' type discharge air in one direction only. Larger units of the 'cabinet' type have a number of adjustable outlets on the top, so that the efflux can be spread in several directions.

5.2.2 Ducted warm air

A correctly designed duct system can distribute the heat evenly within the growing house. The ducts running through the house are usually tubes of clear polyethylene film, inflated by the air pressure from the heater fan and having a number of air outlet holes along their length. Tubes of this material are cheap and easy to install, and do not produce the patches of heavy shading that a metal or timber system would. When the heater fan stops the tube deflates, which gives rise to its common name of 'layflat' ducting. The size of this ducting is often quoted as the 'layflat' width of the strip, which in effect is half the inflated circumference. Thus a 500 mm 'layflat' will inflate to a tube of only 320 mm diameter.

The duct perforations should be designed to produce an even heat output, which is not necessarily an even air output, as the duct walls also emit heat by conduction and radiation. The air discharge rate from each hole will be influenced by the pressure variation along the duct, caused by its air flow resistance and static pressure build-up towards the blank end. These factors combine to require a non-uniform perforation pattern for even heat distribution; because this involves complex calculations, ADAS have developed computer programs which can design the correct pattern and hole size.

Layflat ducts can operate only in a straight line. Any significant curves or bends crease the duct, so creating air turbulence which can cause the duct to flap and eventually tear. Any changes of direction, therefore, are done using rigid materials, normally a matching tube of galvanised sheet. It is possible to construct the main (header) duct in layflat with rigid tees to the lateral layflats, but owing to the close spacing of most duct layouts it is normally simpler to make the whole header duct in rigid materials.

The ducts are sometimes installed at high level, with holes pointing downwards to counteract natural convective heat rise. The layflat is normally threaded over a catenary wire stretched along the house, although some installers prefer to fit wire support hoops at intervals along the house. Alternatively the ducts are placed at floor level between crop rows to improve heat utilisation at root zone level. The air inlet temperature of the ducts is normally 50°C above the house temperature. This means that the air in the ducts will be at 65–70°C, which can be too hot for some plants; temperatures can be reduced by increasing the fan output together with the number or size of ducts. The ducts are normally designed for an airspeed of 4–5 m/s. Speeds much in excess of these complicate air distribution problems and cause excessive rippling and tearing of the fabric.

Air-heating equipment can also be used to circulate cold air where it is beneficial to prevent humidity building up, or to supplement ventilation.

5.3 PIPED HOT WATER

5.3.1 Pipes for air heating
The pipes are normally steel, with plain (conventional) walls or with walls fitted with fins (gills). Modern heating systems are based on 'small bore' pipes with pumped circulation. The pipe sizes used are normally 32 mm, 38 mm or 50 mm nominal bore. Older systems relying on

gravity flow used 100 mm nominal bore pipes, normally of cast iron with caulked socket joints. The small bore systems are much more responsive to control than the large bore.

5.3.1.1 Plain wall pipe

Plain pipe should have a 'black iron' finish, as this emits more heat than a galvanised finish; despite its lack of corrosion protection, the pipe should have a life of several years. Black iron pipes can be protected from some corrosion by painting but bituminous or oil-based paints must be avoided, as the solvents can harm plants; one suitable material is a mixture of lamp black (a form of carbon) and linseed oil.

5.3.1.2 Extended surface (gilled) pipe

The fins on a gilled pipe greatly increase the surface area for heat emission. It is normal for a gilled pipe to emit 4–7 times more heat than the equivalent diameter of plain pipe. Because the heat transfer from the pipe to its fin depends on the closeness of fit between the two (fins are seldom welded to the pipe). horticultural gilled pipe should be galvanised to prevent corrosion causing loosening of the bond.

5.3.2 Heat emission

Heat emission from a pipe depends on its surface area, and the temperature difference between the water and the house temperature. For a plain pipe the linear surface area $(m^2/m$ run) depends solely on pipe external diameter; for gilled pipe the linear surface area depends on the number of gills per metre and their diameter. Pipe heat emissions are usually tabulated or presented in graphical form.

Table 5.1 shows the heat output from a single, horizontal plain wall pipe in still air, at a range of pipe/house temperature differences. The

Table 5.1

Heat emission from plain pipe

Nominal bore (mm)	Heat emission (W/linear metre) for temperature difference (°C) between water and house of								
	40	45	50	55	60	70	90	100	120
25	58	68	78	88	98	120	160	190	240
32	70	82	93	110	130	150	200	230	300
40	80	90	105	120	150	160	230	260	330
50	95	110	130	150	170	200	270	320	410
65	120	140	160	180	200	240	330	390	500
80	140	160	180	210	230	280	380	450	580

outputs of gilled pipe in still air at a pipe/house temperature difference of 55°C are shown in table 5.2.

Table 5.2

Heat emission from gilled pipe

Nominal bore of base pipe (mm)	Gills/m	Outside diameter of gills (mm)	Heat emission (W/linear metre)
32	85 100 110	78	380 390 410
	85 100 110	88	430 460 470
40	85 100 110	95	480 500 530

The gilled pipe emission at other temperature differences can be calculated from the relationship

$$\frac{\text{actual temperature difference (°C)}}{\text{quoted temperature difference (°C)}}^{1.2} \times \text{quoted emission} \qquad (5.1)$$

For example, a 32 mm n.b. pipe having 100 gills/m of 88 mm O.D. running at 75°C would have an emission of

$$\frac{(75)^{1.2}}{(55)} \times 460 \text{ W/m} = 1.36^{1.2} \times 460 = 665 \text{ W/m}$$

The effect of one pipe above another is to reduce the heat output of each pipe. Table 5.3 shows the emission from vertically banked plain pipes.

Table 5.3

Effect of banked pipes on heat output

Number of pipes	Percentage of emission from one pipe
2	170
3	230
4	280
5	335
6	385

5.3.3 Pipe layout

The pipework layout (see figure 5.1) is a compromise between the cropping pattern and the areas of heat loss from the structure. To satisfy

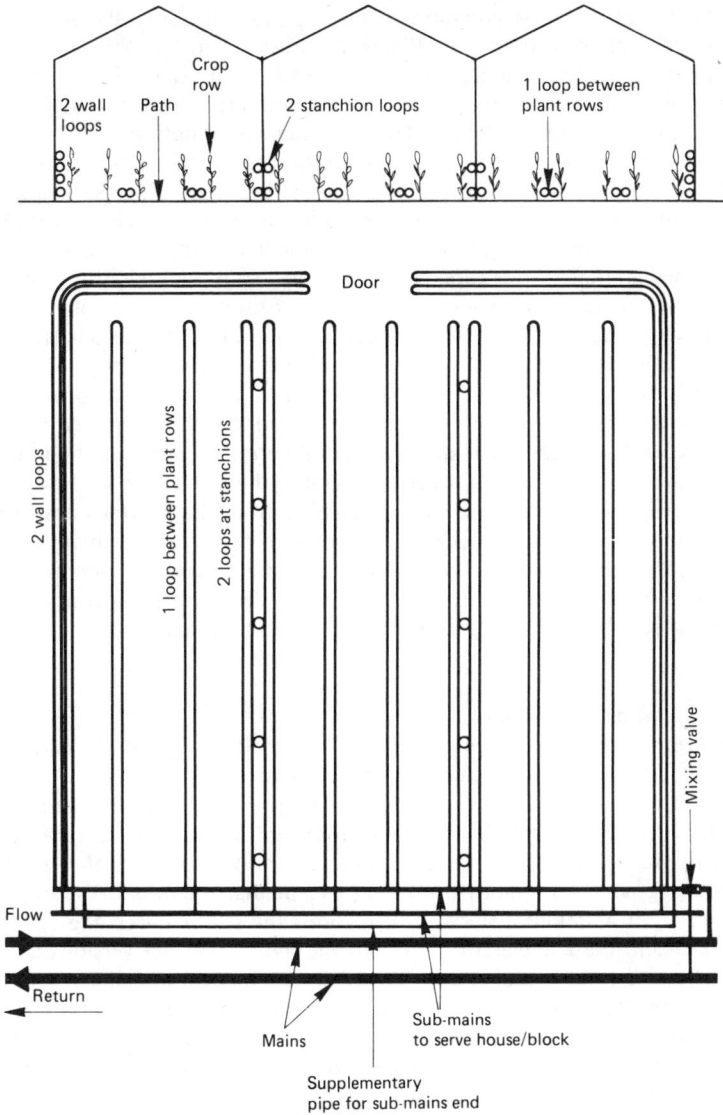

Figure 5.1 Heating pipe layout.

heat-loss criteria, some of the pipes will be mounted against the walls, to compensate for heat lost through them. The remaining pipework satisfies the heat lost through the roof, and it is these that are positioned according to cropping. For crops that require heat at root zone level, like tomatoes, it is common to place pipes just above the soil level beside each row of plants. Where the heat is most beneficial to the upper parts of the plants, for example in tall flower crops, it is common for these pipes to be placed in the roof, although this can lead to bad vertical temperature gradients and extra fuel consumption.

The pipework has to be installed to form complete circuits for water flow. The boiler is connected to the house by a pair of pipes (mains) — one to carry water away (flow), the other to bring it back (return). In order that both mains are at one end of the house, the heating pipes are 'looped' — that is, one pipe of a pair connects to the flow, the other to the return and they are joined together at the opposite end. Most loops, therefore, consist of two pipes, but in cases where the installation of two loops (four pipes) would be excessive, asymmetrical loops of three pipes can be used; these will have one flow joined into two returns, although this latter is not good practice and should be avoided where possible. Each loop normally has one valve for the purpose of controlling water flow; these valves are adjusted so that the emissions from the longer loops are in balance with emissions from the shorter ones. It is common for a floor loop to be fitted with a valve on both flow and return so that it can be removed when required without draining the whole system. These loops are fitted to the valves with easily dismantled screw couplings or strong hose and clips, to facilitate removal.

5.3.4 Water circulation

Except in the case of small houses with simple pipework, the water is pumped around the system. As the system resistance is low and the water volume flow high, single-stage centrifugal pumps are common. Many modern pumps have induced rotation rotors, to avoid problems with gland leaks. In these the stator motor coils surround the central rotating coil in the normal manner, except that the two are separated by a thin aluminium sleeve, which forms the seal between the system water and the live electrical parts of the motor. Smaller versions use a flat coil behind a sealing disc, which directly induces impellor rotation. The impellor is normally mounted in ceramic sleeve bearings, lubricated by the system water. These have no means of axial location, and the pump must be mounted with its impellor shaft horizontal, so that it does not bind against the case.

The rate at which the water is pumped around the system will determine the temperature that it gives up between flow and return. In atmospheric pressure (LPHW) systems it is usual to design for a 10°C drop, and in pressurised (MPHW and HPHW) systems for a 30°C difference. The water temperature against which pipe heat emission is calculated is the mean of the flow and the return temperatures. For example, in a LPHW system water will enter the loop at 85°C and leave at 75°C, so the mean water temperature will be 70°C; for MPHW the temperatures will be 125°C, 95°C and 110°C respectively. The pump output calculations are shown in section 5.8.4.

5.3.5 Steam/hot water conversion

On large nurseries it is common for the heat to be conveyed from the boiler to each house in the form of steam. The heat-carrying capacity of a pipe conveying steam is considerably greater than if it were conveying hot water, owing to the latent heat contained within the steam. Also, the steam system requires only one large pipe to convey the steam, with a smaller one for its condensate to return to the boiler; the hot water system requires large diameter pipe for both flow and return.

In modern installations the steam heats the house system water in a heat exchanger, or calorifier. Other methods have been tried, such as directly injecting the live steam into the water, but although the installation was cheaper to install than the calorifier, it proved more difficult to operate and was noisy.

A calorifier consists of a cylindrical steel shell, with a number of small tubes inside. The house system water is pumped through the outer shell and the steam flows through the small tubes. The water flow within the shell is arranged to mix intimately with the hot tube surfaces for maximum heat transfer efficiency. Calorifier heat output is based on the surface area of the steam tubes, the flow capacity for the water and the pressure at which the steam is supplied.

The temperature of the system water is easily varied to suit the heat requirements of the house, by controlling steam flow.

The specialist pipework fittings to control steam and remove condensate are described in section 5.4.

5.3.6 Pressurised hot water

Pressurising allows the system to operate at temperatures above normal water boiling point (100°C). The pressures and temperatures are shown in table 4.7.

It is possible to increase system pressure by raising the header tank supplying water to the system, but this is impractical for true medium and high pressure applications, as the tank would need to be raised by

10 m for every atmosphere (101 kPa) required. The common methods used are as follows.

5.3.6.1 Expansion pipe backpumping

A simple system, which pressurises sufficiently to allow water to run at 100–110°C, is to apply pump pressure to the boiler feed pipe. This uses one or two heating circulator pumps, circulating water in a closed circuit attached to the feed pipe. The circuit also contains an orifice plate, which creates the pressure by water flow resistance through it (figure 5.2). The system pressure is raised by up to 1 atmosphere (110 kPa), which allows a boiler thermostat setting of 105–110°C. This system is useful where the pipe heat output at atmospheric-pressure water tem-

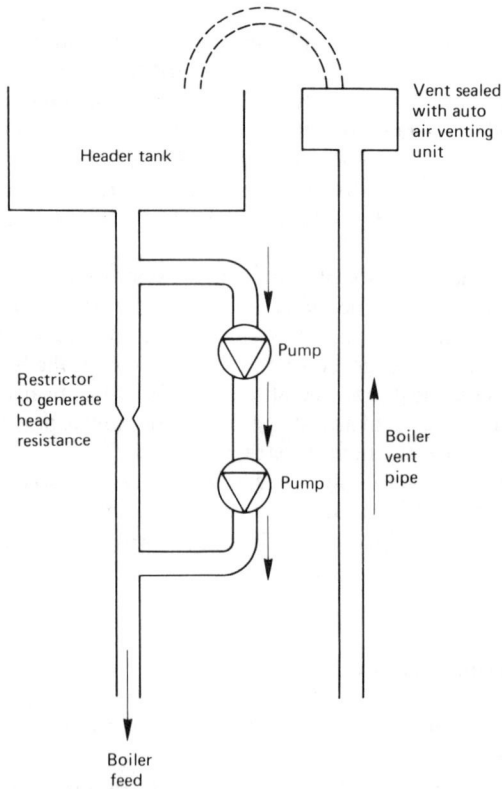

Figure 5.2 Backpumping pressurising.

peratures limits the house temperature, as it can be added without much pipework modification and switched off to revert to normal pressure running.

5.3.6.2 Inert gas closed system

Medium and high pressure systems use a sealed expansion tank, installed so that the water enters the base and traps a layer of gas or air above it. The simplest method uses the thermal expansion of the system water to create the pressure, whereby the surplus water is pushed into the base of the pressure vessel, reducing the air volume and thereby compressing it.

In larger systems the pressure vessel is divided by a strong rubber diaphragm, with an inert gas such as carbon dioxide or nitrogen above it. These systems are brought to the necessary pressure when cold, by a combination of initial gas pressurisation and pumping in water against it. As the system heats, expansion water is first pushed into the tank until system running pressure is achieved, and the surplus is then passed out through a pressure relief valve to an open holding tank. As the system cools, the pressure is maintained by re-introducing this water through an automatically controlled pump. This system overcomes the need for a very large pressure vessel to take the expansion from large heating systems.

5.4 STEAM

5.4.1 Live steam heating

This, as the name implies, uses the steam directly in the heating pipe. The pipework has to be constructed with screwed, welded or bolted flange joints to withstand the pressures involved; temporary attachments or plastic pipes are unsuitable. All the heating pipes must slope evenly towards steam traps, to allow the condensate to drain by gravity.

The heat output of pipes in a live steam system is considerably greater than that with low pressure hot water, resulting in fewer runs of pipe being needed. Where only a few runs of high output are used, there can be problems with uneven heating in times of low heat demand. As the steam heats the pipe progressively from the in-feed end, it is possible for the house heat demand to be satisfied by the output from the first few metres of pipe, although this will heat the crop only in this area. The problem is reduced by feeding steam through a smaller bore plain pipe, running parallel to the high output pipe and introducing steam into it at regular intervals along its length.

5.4.2 Steam characteristics

Steam differs from hot water in that it carries latent heat of evaporation
in addition to the sensible (apparent) heat. For example, 1 kilogram of
pressurised hot water at $130°C$ cooling to $80°C$ will produce 0.206 MJ;
1 kilogram of steam at $130°C$ cooling to $80°C$ will produce 0.206 MJ as
sensible heat, *plus* 2.260 MJ as latent heat.

The latent heat of evaporation is shown in table 5.4. The temperature
of saturated steam is related to its absolute pressure, and this relationship is also shown in table 5.4.

Table 5.4

Properties of saturated steam

Pressure (kPa abs.)	Temperature (°C)	Latent heat of evaporation (kJ/kg)
10	45.83	2392.2
20	60.09	2357.7
30	69.13	2335.4
40	75.89	2318.6
50	81.35	2304.9
60	85.95	2293.2
70	89.96	2282.9
80	93.51	2273.7
90	90.71	2265.4
101*	99.63	2257.7
151	111.37	2226.3
202	120.23	2201.9
252	127.43	2181.6
303	133.54	2163.9
353	138.88	2148.2
404	143.63	2133.9
454	147.92	2120.8

*1 atmosphere.

It is important that absolute pressure is used in these tables, rather
than the pressure that a gauge would indicate. Gauge pressure includes
the pressure of the atmosphere (101.3 kPa at standard air conditions),
so that when a gauge indicates zero it is actually reading the pressure of
the atmosphere. For ease of identification it is common to add the
words 'gauge' or 'absolute' (sometimes 'abs.') after the pressure unit.
The relationship between these two pressures is

$$\text{Pressure kPa abs.} = \text{Pressure kPa gauge} + 101.3 \qquad (5.2)$$

The table refers to the temperatures of 'saturated' steam — that is, steam in contact with the water from which it has evaporated. Saturated steam can be subdivided into two types:

(a) Wet steam, which contains small globules of moisture carried over from the boiler or caused by partial condensation.
(b) Dry saturated steam, which does not contain entrained moisture.

If the steam is heated further, out of contact with the water from which it has evaporated, it becomes 'superheated'. The level of temperature over saturation temperature is termed the 'degree of superheat'.

Steam is superheated by bringing it into contact with boiler heating surfaces above the water level; this part of the boiler is termed the superheater.

5.4.3 Pipework sizing

This involves separate calculations for the steam main and the condensate return pipe.

Steam pipes are sized from a set of tables, which are first used to find a pressure drop factor from the initial steam pressure and the acceptable pressure drop; this factor is then used in a second table to correlate steam flow with pipe size.

A further table gives condensate pipe sizes for a range of flow rates and installation conditions. The data in this table are based on flow resistance levels which allow correct trap operation.

5.4.4 Steam traps

The condensate produced as the steam gives up its heat must be removed from the system; this is done by means of 'steam trap'. The condensate can be returned to the boiler house by gravity, or pumped back if the site slopes are adverse or the pipe lengths are excessive. It is possible to force the condensate back using the incoming steam pressure, although since this requires special traps and adds to the inefficiencies of the system, it should be avoided where possible. Traps are placed at all low points in the pipework, because the liquid will run to these points under gravity; the steam-heating coil or calorifier must also be arranged to allow condensate to drain to the trapping point. The trap is designed to allow water to flow freely but to block the passage of steam.

5.4.4.1 Types of steam trap

Float types operate in a similar manner to a ballcock. Condensate collects in a chamber ahead of the valve, and a float in the chamber is

136   *Horticultural Engineering Technology*

lifted by the rising water level to open the valve. The true 'float trap' involves a separate float operating the valve through a linkage (figure 5.3(a)). The 'inverted bucket' trap is a more compact unit and contains fewer moving parts; in this the float is a small inverted pot, relying on air trapped in the base to provide buoyancy. The bucket presses upwards against the valve linkage built into the top of the chamber (figure 5.3(b)).

Thermostatic types rely on the fact that the condensate is cooler than the steam. In the bimetallic type a strip bends on heating, and straightens on 'cooling'. One end of this strip is linked to the valve. The strip opens the valve when it is immersed in condensate, but as soon as hotter steam starts to flow through, it bends and closes the valve. Other methods of operation rely on bellows filled with a temperature responsive liquid or gas (figure 5.3(c)).

Thermodynamic types incorporate a small disc resting over an orifice (figure 5.3(d)). The disc does not form a seal when immersed in condensate, so allowing it to run under through the orifice. When steam begins to flow, its velocity in the gap between the disc and the orifice sucks it down on to the face of the orifice. This trap is compact and has one moving part, but loses the small amount of steam needed to draw the disc down. The disc reacts rapidly to steam flow and this can cause water hammer.

5.4.4.2 Choice and operation of traps
The choice of trap type will depend on several factors, the main ones being as follows.

(a) Water hammer — a trap might either create this by opening or closing suddenly, or it might be damaged by water hammer produced in other parts of the system.
(b) Air venting — some traps will vent entrapped air into the condensate line or incorporate separate air vents.
(c) Locking — this can occur to some traps if steam or entrapped air is caught above the condensate layer.
(d) Response to load — some traps discharge condensate as it forms, while others require a certain build-up of liquid or for the condensate to cool before operation. The trap might also be slow to respond to load variation, so that flooding occurs on increasing load, and steam is lost as it decreases.
(e) Freezing — traps that do not empty all the condensate can suffer damage from the liquid remaining, if located in exposed areas and operating intermittently.

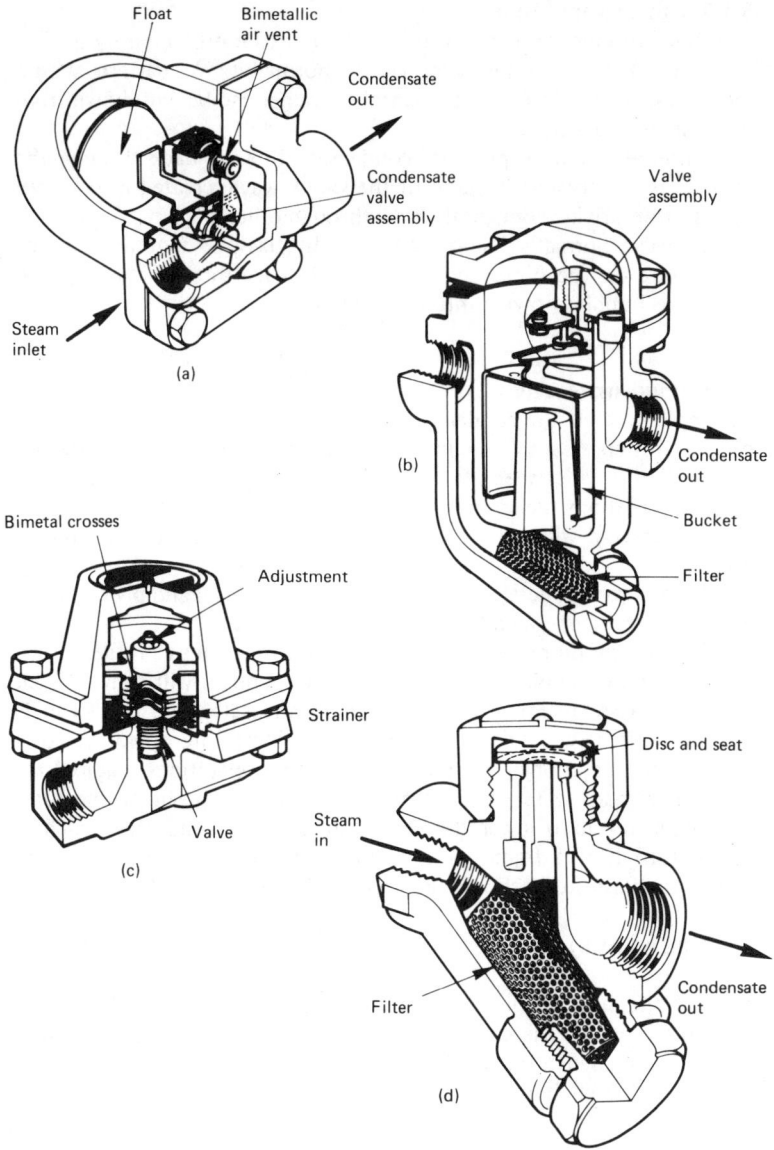

Figure 5.3 (a) Float steam trap. (b) Inverted bucket steam trap. (c) Bimetallic (thermostatic) steam trap. (d) Thermodynamic steam trap (*all courtesy of Spirax – Sarco Ltd, Cheltenham*).

5.4.5 Other steam fittings

The fine working faces of the trap valve must be protected by a filter from debris in the condensate. This is normally a 'Y' pattern, with a mesh strainer basket in the branch; the strainer can be withdrawn from the branch for cleaning.

A non-return valve prevents condensate flowing back through the trap. This is necessary to prevent the shock wave, created as one trap opens, from driving condensate back through other traps.

The valve normally incorporates a sight glass, so that the flow of condensate can be observed. Any steam leakage through the trap will be seen as bubbles flowing through the liquid.

5.4.6 Condensate return

In simple systems the condensate is driven back to the boiler feed tank by the steam pressure. If the installation is extensive, the steam pressure required to drive condensate will seriously affect system performance. In these situations the condensate will be collected in tanks at low level, so that gravity will aid flow, and pumped into a condensate return main.

The pumps can be electrically powered centrifugal and piston types, or a piston type operated by steam pressure.

The condensate released from high-pressure systems can still be considerably above ambient boiling temperature, and so will convert back to steam (flash steam) as it runs into the condensate tank. This steam is normally discharged to the atmosphere, so increasing operating costs through the additional treatment and heating operations required for the replacement water. If flash steam is a serious problem, measures should be taken to lower the temperature of the condensate, such as using it to heat a frame yard, to lower its temperature sufficiently, or else the flash steam should be tapped off and recondensed.

5.5 SOIL WARMING

Part of the heat requirement can be applied directly to the soil or compost in which the crop is growing. The heat is normally introduced to the soil or bench on which the crop stands, or in some cases to the borders in which it is growing, by hot water pipes or electric heating cable.

5.5.1 Soil warming system design

The spacing and depth of the cable or pipe runs depend on soil depth, its heat conductivity and the required heat emission.

In glasshouse soil the cables or pipes are usually placed 250-500 mm deep and spaced 300-600 mm apart; often the minimum depth is dictated by cultivation.

On benches with about 100 mm depth of sand, they are laid at about half depth. A very thin sand layer or even just a capillary matting cover is possible where the pipe or cable systems are built into a heavily insulated base panel. Bench system spacings will be between 50 and 100 mm, depending on the required heat loading, where a sand cover is used. The matting cover requires closer spacings for even distribution, and some electric systems are based on a plastic sheet with a matrix of heating elements printed on the surface.

The heat input is usually 60-100 W/m^2 for deep soil systems, and 80-160 W/m^2 for propagating benches. Electric systems can be based on the rated linear heat emission of the cable, 10-15 W/m being common. Heat emission from buried water pipes is not accurately known, thus most of these systems are designed empirically from the experience of earlier successful installations. For example, a layout of 20 mm n.b. polyethylene pipe, at 500 mm spacings and with water at $50°C$, appears to give 60-80 W/m^2 on most soils.

Soil warming will provide only 25-35 per cent of the heat requirement of a propagating house; the rest is obtained from conventional air heating.

5.5.2 Electric systems

Electric cables can operate either at mains voltage or at low voltage. Mains voltage systems require to be heavily protected against moisture ingress for operator safety. These cables normally have the heating element mounted inside a screen of earthed braiding, so that any electrical leakage should run to earth and operate the circuit protection breaker.

The low-voltage system operates at 6-24 V and can use bare wire, as the voltage will not promote short-circuits between the cables or be harmful to the operator. The printed sheet elements also operate at low voltage. Power is supplied through a mains transformer; the low-voltage windings should be fully isolated from the mains to increase safety. Although the wire is cheaper than special mains cable, a transformer is required, which can make the system more expensive than mains cable.

5.5.3 Hot water systems

Most systems use polyethylene water pipe of 20 mm nominal bore, and class B or C wall thickness. In benches the pipe is laid in the sand, in glasshouse borders it is inserted into narrow slots dug by a small powered trenching machine.

The water in the pipe should not exceed 60°C, or it will soften the walls and soil pressure could collapse it; also extreme heat can dry out the soil surrounding the pipe, to form a heat insulating layer. As the water temperature is relatively low, it is normal to install a high pump capacity to limit the temperature drop between flow and return to 5°C. The system can be directly connected to a LPHW system through a thermostatic valve or mixing system, to limit the water temperature but plastic pipe must be protected from overheating in the event of mixer valve malfunction. One method consists of a 'normally closed' solenoid valve on the flow, held open by a thermostat on the pipe if the water is below a certain temperature. Alternatively a suitably designed mixing system should prevent the plastic circuit becoming overheated.

The plastic pipe is unsuitable for direct connection to a pressurised hot water or steam system; it should be totally isolated from the pressure effects by a calorifier.

In both the hot water and electric systems, the underside of the heated area should be insulated against downward heat flow. The bench can have a base of sheet polystyrene 30–50 mm thick. It is impossible to install a complete sheet beneath the glasshouse border, but some growers have installed strips of expanded polystyrene in the base of the pipe trench, in an attempt to reduce downwards heat flow. The strip width is limited to the trench width (typically 50–100 mm), and little information exists on its efficacy.

The temperature control of these sytems cannot be precise, owing to the thermal inertia of the soil or sand. In the bench system the thermostat is normally placed 15–20 mm beneath the surface of the sand. In border soil, the thermostat is placed up to 200 mm into the soil. In both cases the final thermostat setting should be decided by temperature measurements of the surface over a period of time and the actual plant response.

5.6 MAINS AND ANCILLARIES

5.6.1 Insulation
In most cases the mains do not form part of the heat-emitting part of the system; it is, therefore, strongly advised that they be insulated, both to conserve fuel and to ensure that the heating circuits are able to receive water as near as possible to boiler temperature.

The current practice on insulation is for 25 mm thickness on LPHW and 50 mm on pressurised hot water and steam.

The materials used have to withstand the pipe temperature, which precludes most foamed plastics. The normal materials are mineral based, the common ones being glass fibre, mineral wools, foamed glass and vermiculite (expanded mica). The first three are produced in blanket form or pre-formed shapes to fit pipes; vermiculite is normally in the form of loose grains, which are used to fill pipe ducts. Most of these materials absorb water, and this can totally ruin their insulating properties; therefore, to be fully effective, the insulation must be waterproofed after installation. The traditional method is to wrap roofing felt tightly around the insulation, secure it with closely spaced wire bands or a complete wrap of wire netting, and finally seal it with a coat of bitumastic solution. This treatment must also include the ends of the insulation. More recently, water-proofing in the form of thin aluminium sheeting has become available. This normally forms the outer surface of a pre-formed insulation sleeve, enabling both insulant and waterproofing to be fitted in one operation, with mastic or riveted banding to cover the joints between each piece.

It is normal for the pipe joints (other than welded) and fittings to be left uninsulated. This enables any leaks to be seen, and prevents escaping water from saturating the insulation inside the water-proofing.

5.6.2 Thermal expansion
Pipework expands and contracts as it heats and cools. The expansion coefficient for steel is 0.0113 mm/m per °C temperature change; this means that 100 m of pipe will lengthen by 57 mm when heated through 50°C.

It is not practical to attempt to restrain this movement, so all mains systems should have allowance for thermal expansion. It is also important that the expansion forces are not transmitted to connected equipment, otherwise serious damage can occur.

Thermal movement is accommodated by expansion loops or legs (figure 5.4), in which the pipe is able to bend. The leg is simpler to construct, and can often use part of the pipe layout; the loop can be placed in any position along the pipe run. In either case each end of the pipe is fixed so that it does not put strain on to the connected equipment.

The pipe supports must also allow movement, and this is made possible by either laying the pipe on flat bar supports, laying it on roller supports or suspending it by means of a strap which can accommodate lateral movement. In the case of the roller or sliding support, the area of contact is left uninsulated.

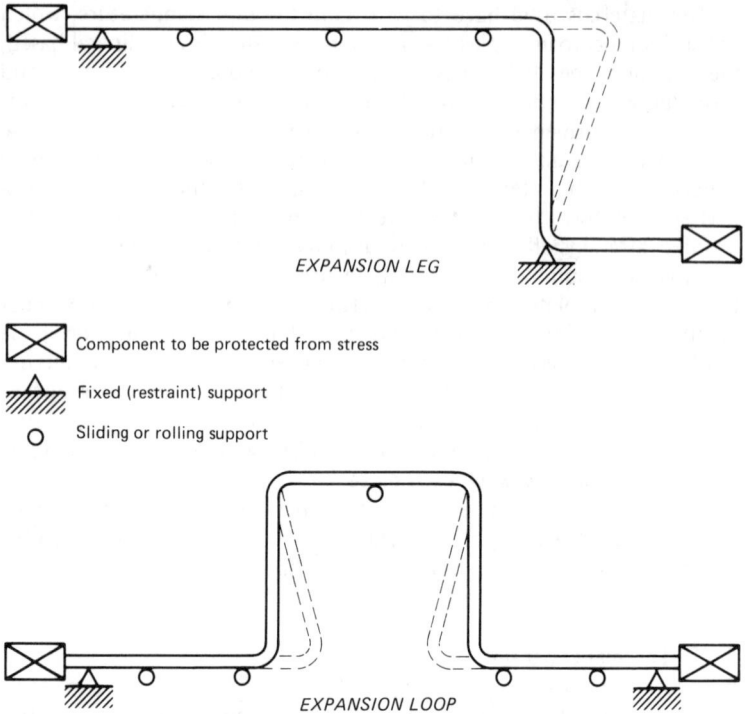

EXPANSION LEG

⊠ Component to be protected from stress

🔺 Fixed (restraint) support

○ Sliding or rolling support

EXPANSION LOOP

Figure 5.4 Expansion of pipework.

5.7 SYSTEM CONTROL

5.7.1 Warm air

In most warm air systems the house thermostat controls the heat source (burner or electric element). The air-circulating fan either runs continuously or runs to suit the heating and cooling requirements of the heat source. Only a few types of gas burner and electric element allow modulation (heat output variation); the majority use simple on/off control.

5.7.2 Hot water

Because the boiler should always be maintained above acid dewpoint temperature, house temperature control operates only on the circulating water; the boiler is controlled by a thermostat in its water jacket.

5.7.2.1 On/off control

Small layouts, where the boiler and heating system serve only one cropping area, are controlled by switching the circulating pump directly from the house thermostat.

In multi-house layouts, where one pump supplies hot water to all the houses, the flow to each house is controlled by a power-driven valve on its mains junction. The valve can be solenoid operated or a motorised butterfly type, but normally the solenoid is used only on pipework under 50 mm n.b. Both types are controlled to be either fully open or fully closed. The valves work independently of one another, but there are times when all the valves are switched off and the pump is running against a total resistance to flow. This can cause overheating in a direct coupled motor, it its rating is based on it being 'cooled' by water flow. Also, if the boiler feed and expansion pipes are not installed in the correct positions in the system, water will be circulated through them instead. This problem can be avoided in two ways:

(a) Most motorised valves contain a set of electrical contacts which are opened (switched off) when the valve is closed; if the pump power supply is linked to all these contacts in parallel, it will stop when all valves are fully shut, but restart when one opens.

(b) The alternative is to install an 'escape' between flow and return; this is a piece of small bore pipe which creates a permanent short-circuit. It passes sufficient water when the valves are shut to keep the pump resistance at an acceptable level, but does not noticeably reduce water flow to the heating circuits.

5.7.2.2 Proportional (mixing) systems

Better temperature control of the house is possible if the water temperature in the pipes is varied to suit the prevailing heat demand. By this method, when the house is close to its desired temperature, the pipes run with only lukewarm water, but if it is significantly cooler the pipes run with hot water. This is acheived with a flow mixing system (figure 5.5). The house is regarded as a self-containing circuit with its own pump, which circulates water continuously within this circuit only. A three-way mixing valve is used to divert sufficient hot water from the flow main to raise the circuit water to the desired temperature. The cool water displaced by the incoming hot water flows into the return main. This system ensures that the heating effect is fully distributed through the house, irrespective of demand. The mixing valve can be fitted with further controls to control return water temperature or to ensure that each circuit gets a share of hot water in times of high demand. These will operate to over-ride the demands from the house controller and inhibit full valve opening.

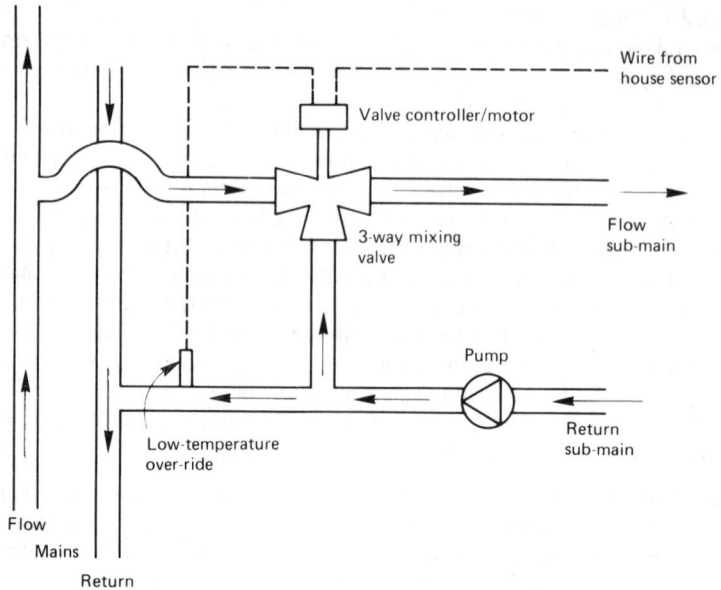

Figure 5.5 Mixing valve circuit.

5.7.3 Steam systems
The valve can be either a solenoid or modulating variable orifice type.
As a smaller volume of steam than hot water is required for a given
heat output, the steam valves are smaller but are made to a higher specification to withstand the pressure. Steam systems are more responsive
to control than hot water, so on/off control is often sufficient to provide an even temperature response. Modulating steam valves are often
powered by vapour or wax expansion, rather than by electric motor
systems, but as the sensor is connected to the valve head by capillary
tube, the distance between them is limited.

5.8 HEATING SYSTEM DESIGN

5.8.1 Heat loss from the structure
The theory of structural heat losses is explained in chapter 3 (sections
3.2 and 3.3). Glasshouse* heat loss calculations have been simplified by
the use of a combined heat loss factor of $8.0 \text{ W/m}^2 \text{ }^\circ\text{C}$. This includes

*The terms 'glasshouse' and 'glass' are used generically and include all translucent
protected cropping buildings.

floor transmission loss and a nominal air leakage loss, so the total losses can be calculated by

$$\text{Glass* surface area (m}^2) \times 8 = W/°C \text{ temperature difference} \quad (5.3)$$

If the house has a brick or concrete block dwarf wall, it is normal to assume that it has one-third the heat loss of glass, and therefore to add one-third of its height to the glass in the wall when calculating its surface area.

Equation (5.3) can be expanded as shown:

Side walls: Length (m) × Height (m) × No. of walls   = m²
Roof: Length (m) × Width of one slope (m) × No. of slopes = m²
Ends: Width (m) × Average height (m) × No. of ends   = m²

$$\text{TOTAL SURFACE AREA} = m^2$$

$$\text{Heat loss per °C temperature difference (W/°C)} = \text{Total surface area} \times 8$$
$$(5.3a)$$

The temperature difference beween inside and outside will depend on the internal regime and the time of year; temperature difference is sometimes called 'temperature lift', because the inside temperature is required to be above the external temperature during the time for which the heating system is being designed.

The design external temperatures can be obtained from meterological data, for the locality of the glasshouse; table 5.5 shows these data for the Lea Valley area of the U.K. (25 km north of London)

Table 5.5

External design temperatures for the Lea Valley

	Jan.	Feb.	March	April	May	June
2%	−6.6	−6.6	−4.6	−0.3	1.8	5.7
5%	−4.6	−4.5	−2.5	1.2	3.8	7.5
	July	August	Sept.	Oct.	Nov.	Dec.
2%	8.7	8.2	4.2	−1.5	−3.8	−5.6
5%	10.0	9.5	6.2	1.0	−1.6	−3.3

It will be seen that two values are given for each month, prefaced by a percentage figure. These are the probabilities that the temperature might be exceeded; thus at 5 per cent there is a 95 per cent chance that the external temperatures will not fail below those stated, and at 2 per cent, that probability will be 98 per cent.

*See footnote on opposite page.

Therefore the design house heat loss will be

$$\text{kW heat loss} = \frac{\text{W/}^\circ\text{C (from equation (5.3a))} \times \text{design external temp. } (^\circ\text{C})}{1000}$$

$$(5.4)$$

5.8.2 Heater or boiler rating

This is calculated from equation (5.4) with a margin added to cover unexpected cold periods and the slight falling off of performance between services. In normal circumstances the margin will be 25 per cent, thus the required rating will be

$$\text{Rating (kW)} = \text{House loss from equation (5.4)} \times 1.25 \qquad (5.5)$$

Note that this 'rating' is the quoted heater output, not the gross energy input.

5.8.3 Heating pipework

The total lengths of pipe needed to cover the losses calculated in equation (5.4) can be found from table 5.1 (plain pipe) or 5.2 (gilled pipe).

$$\text{Length of pipe} = \frac{\text{Heat loss (kW)} \times 1000}{\text{Heat output (W/m)}} \qquad (5.6)$$

(i) Pipe layout
This is dictated both by house design and cropping pattern. The following basic points apply to most situations.

(a) The perimeter (wall) pipes should supply the heat being lost through the walls.

(b) The heat loss through the roof should be mostly supplied by the pipes among the crops and at high level. The wall pipes might supply some of the roof loss in single span houses.

(c) Certain cropping patterns require a loop of 32 mm or single run of 50 mm pipe between each pair of rows or on either side of each bed.

(d) The sub-mains supplying the heating pipes will be unlagged beyond the control valve and can be counted as contributing to the heat input.

(e) The floor and roof pipes will normally run the full length (or width) of the house.

(f) The wall pipes will run the perimeter of the house, except for door-ways and the side where the sub-mains are positioned.

Table 5.6

Heating pipe layout calculation

Circuit position	A Pipe size (mm)	B Length (m)	C Heat output from one run of pipe (kW)	D Heat loss to be met by that circuit (kW)	E Number of whole runs to satisfy D	F Heat output of whole number of runs in E (kW)	G Balance remaining when F is subtracted from previous G figure
Starting balance = house heat loss (equation (5.4)) =							kW
Sides							kW
Floor							
Roof							
Sub-mains							
Supplement to sub-mains						Final balance	kW

(ii) Calculation of pipe requirements

Having decided the approximate layout, use equation (5.6) to determine the length or size of pipe for each part. It is best to arrange the calculations for each part as in table 5.6, using a system of subtractive balancing until the full heat requirements are met.

The final balance should be negative by a small amount; this indicates that there is a slight excess of pipe to satisfy the design heat requirements. If it is positive or greatly negative the calculations should be redone with different amounts or sizes of pipe. If using gilled pipe, the quantity and density of gills can also be reconsidered. If the chosen layout is generally inadequate, the effects of raising water temperature should be investigated. A wide difference between the values in columns D and F will indicate those circuits that need to be amended.

5.8.4 Pump requirements

(i) Flow rate

The water flow rate is calculated using the house heat loss in equation (5.4)

$$\text{Flow (kg/s)} = \frac{\text{Heat loss (kW)}}{\text{Flow/return water temp. drop (}^\circ\text{C)} \times \text{Specific heat of water}}$$

(5.7)

The recommended water temperature drop is 10°C for LPHW systems and 30°C for pressurised ones.
The specific heat of water is 4.2 kJ/kg $^\circ$C.
Water has a specific gravity close to 1, so that 1 litre weighs close to 1 kg.

The foregoing points can be used to change equation (5.7) to

$$\text{Flow (litre/s)} = \frac{\text{kW}}{10 \times 4.2} \text{ (LPHW)}$$

or

$$\text{Flow (litre/s)} = \frac{\text{kW}}{30 \times 4.2} \text{ (pressurised water)}$$

(5.8)

(ii) Resistance or head

The pump head is taken from the resistance of the water flowing to the furthest point in the system, and this is often termed the 'indicator circuit'. Pipe resistance to water flow is found from tables or a graph, as shown in figure 5.6. The resistance for each part will vary with the water flow it needs to carry; this can be full pump output in the main, partially reduced flow in the sub-main, and a small portion of flow in

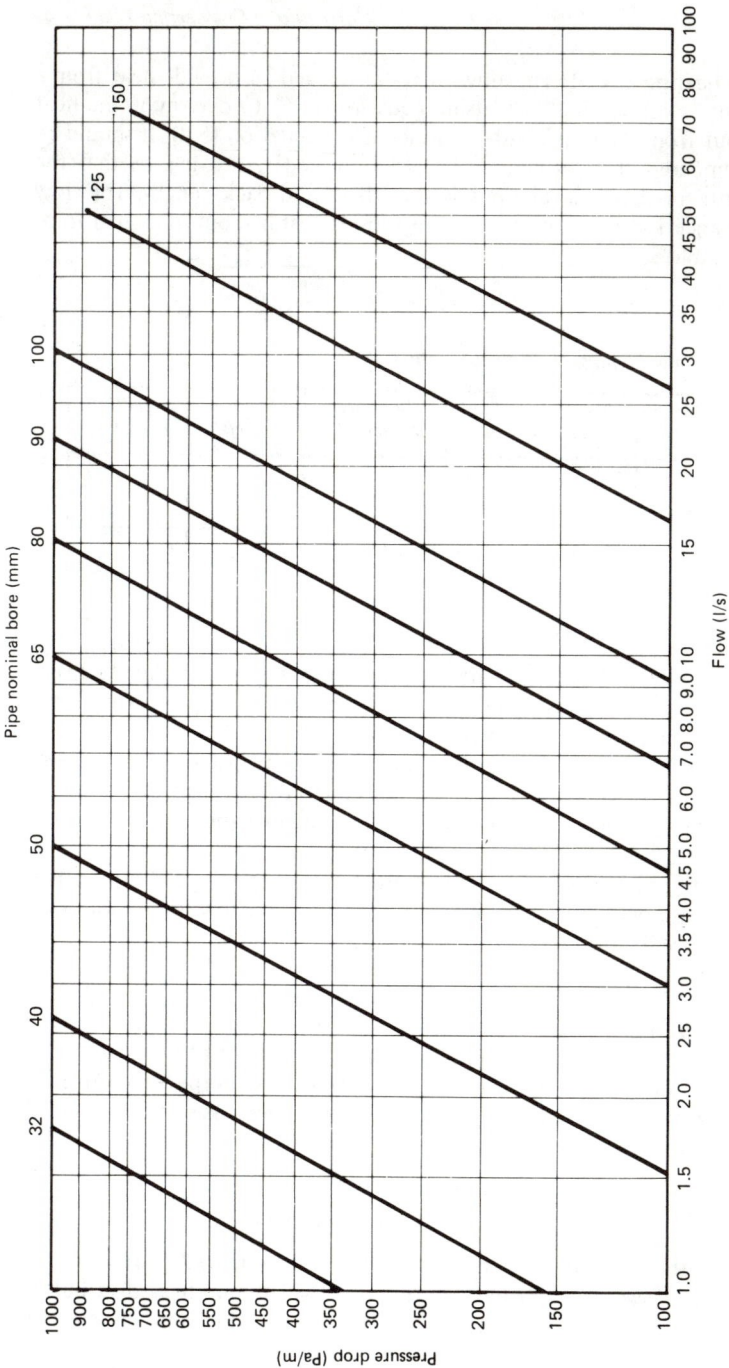

Figure 5.6 Pipe friction loss chart.

each heating circuit. The flow of water needed to provide heat from a circuit is found firstly by using equation (5.6) to determine the heat output from its total length, and then using equation (5.8). It should be remembered that all circuits have a flow and return leg, so that the 'length' in these calculations is the 'there and back' length. The flow resistance for a complete indicator loop is best laid out in tabular form as in table 5.7.

Table 5.7

Pipework pressure drop calculation

Run section	Water flow	Pipe size	Loss per unit length	Section length	Section head loss
			Total head loss		

The tabular form highlights any section that is contributing to a very high or low head loss, and this can be changed for a pipe of different size if such a change does not affect the heat output.

In a long run of gilled pipe, the pipe might not be able to carry sufficient water for the heat output; this problem can be solved by running a plain pipe in parallel with the gilled one and feeding into it at intervals.

The head loss factors are for straight pipe runs only, and it is normal to add 30 per cent on to the calculated head to allow for bends, valves and other fittings.

5.8.5 Warm air ducts

In most warm air systems the fan is an integral part of the heater, thus there is little point in calculating an airflow. The output from this fan will dictate duct sizes; it is normal to base the cross-sectional area on a duct airspeed of 5 m/s.

$$\text{Cross-sectional area } (m^2) = \frac{\text{Airflow } (m^3/s)}{\text{Duct airspeed } (m/s)} \tag{5.9}$$

At the beginning of the system the main duct will carry the full volume flow of the heater fan, but this will diminish as distribution ducts branch off. The cross-section can be reduced in steps corresponding to each branch, by recalculating it for the diminished flow. Likewise, the airspeed or cross-section of each distribution duct will be calculated from the portion of main airflow that it carries.

5.8.6 Predicting fuel consumption

The calculations for this are based on degree-hour figures, which have been obtained from past meteorological data. The degree-hour is the sum of the temperature difference between the inside and the outside of the house (when the outside is cooler), multiplied by the number of hours for which each temperature difference lasts. For example, if a house is kept at 20°C for 24 hours, and the outside temperatures are 5°C for 2 hours, 7°C for 12 hours, 10°C for 7 hours and 15°C for 3 hours, the accumulated degree-hours are

$$
\begin{array}{ll}
(20 - 5) \times 2 = & 30 \\
(20 - 7) \times 12 = & 156 \\
(20 - 10) \times 7 = & 70 \\
(20 - 15) \times 3 = & \underline{15}
\end{array}
$$

Total degree C-hours = $\underline{271}$

It is normal for these to be converted to degree-days by dividing by 24. For example

$$\frac{271}{24} = 11.3 \text{ degree C-days} \tag{5.10}$$

The degree-days accumulated each month for a range of base (house) temperatures are given in table 5.8, for the Lea Valley, north of London.

The heat energy consumption in MegaJoules (MJ) for any heating season is given by

$$MJ = \frac{\text{heat loss/}°C \text{ (equation (5.3a))} \times 86\,400^* \times \text{degree C-days for season}}{1\,000\,000}$$

$$\tag{5.11}$$

The net fuel consumption is calculated using the calorific values in table 4.1.

$$\frac{\text{Heat consumption (MJ)}}{\text{Fuel calorific value (MJ/kg)}} = kg \tag{5.12}$$

*Number of seconds per day = 24 × 60 × 60.

Table 5.8

Accumulated degree-days for the Lea Valley

			Base temperature (°C)						
	8	*10*	*12*	*14*	*16*	*18*	*20*	*21*	*Month*
	117	180	240	303	367	427	490	520	January
	100	157	210	267	323	380	437	463	February
	77	120	183	247	307	367	427	457	March
	37	70	117	173	230	290	350	377	April
	3	17	43	80	127	180	240	270	May
'24 hour'	—	3	17	40	67	110	160	187	June
degree-day	—	—	3	17	37	70	113	133	July
	—	—	10	23	47	80	127	153	August
	—	7	20	43	73	120	173	200	September
	13	33	67	120	177	237	300	333	October
	60	107	167	227	287	347	407	437	November
	110	173	240	297	360	420	483	513	December
	517	867	1317	1837	2402	3028	3707	4043	Total

This gives the fuel consumption at 100 per cent heater efficiency. For a true indication, it should be increased by the efficiency factors quoted in table 4.4 or, better, from the actual heater efficiency.

$$\text{Gross fuel consumption} = \frac{\text{Net fuel consumption} \times 100}{\text{Efficiency}} \qquad (5.13)$$

As the degree-day figures are historic and averaged over 20 years, and the insulation values from equation (5.3) are an average for all types of house construction, the gross fuel figures are for guidance in planning, and will not reflect accurately one particular season or house construction.

6 EQUIPMENT FOR PROTECTED CROPPING STRUCTURES

Protected cropping buildings need to be ventilated to remove excess heat, humidity and any undesirable gases. One of two systems can be used: natural or powered.

6.1.1 Natural ventilation

Glasshouses and a few specialised tunnels use upwards opening ventilator windows (vents) along the roof close to the ridge. Ventilation is partly caused by the wind blowing into the windward vents and out of the leeward ones, and partly by the 'stack effect' of warm air rising through the upper parts of the vent and being replaced with cooler air entering through the lower part of the roof vent or through sidewall vent openings (figure 6.1). This type of ventilation is normally limited to rigid (that is, glass) structures, rather than polyethylene tunnels, owing to the sheet-joining problems. Most tunnels are ventilated through open ends, or an opening strip along the base of each wall.

It is recommended that the roof vents of a house are equal to 15 per cent of its floor area for normal circumstances, where some air can be admitted through side vents, but in still, hot conditions, or where there is no side ventilation, the roof vent area should be 33 per cent of the floor area.

6.1.1.1 Vent opening mechanisms

Ventilators can be mechanically powered and automated to suit the house environment. The main systems are as follows.

(i) Wax expansion
A pellet of wax is placed at the base of a ram, and expands when heated to drive the piston outwards. The small, but powerful, motion of the

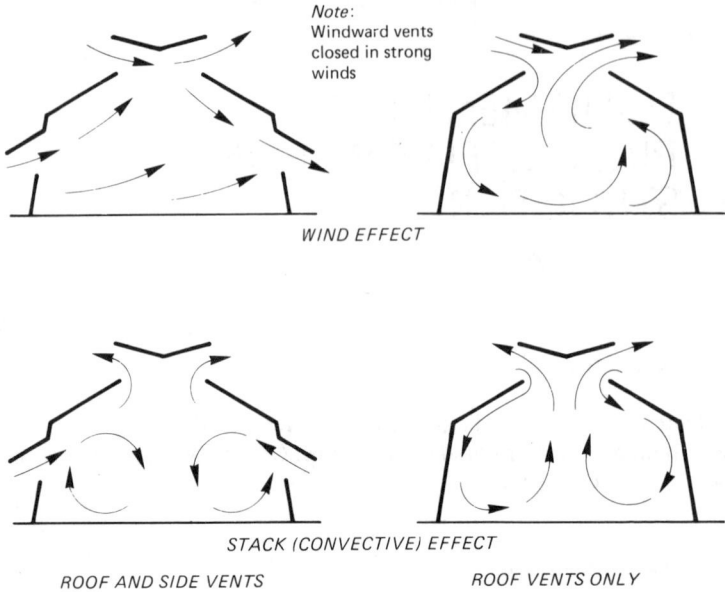

WIND EFFECT

STACK (CONVECTIVE) EFFECT

ROOF AND SIDE VENTS   *ROOF VENTS ONLY*

Figure 6.1   Natural ventilation.

wax expansion is magnified by a series of levers, to provide sufficient movement to open the vent. One of these units is normally fitted to each vent. The cost and lack of co-ordinated adjustment limit their fitting to small houses with few vents.

(ii) Mechanically powered systems
On larger houses the vents are worked simultaneously by a single activator unit, through a variety of mechanisms.

(a) A horizontal winch wire passes beneath each row of vents; its horizontal motion is converted to lifting motion by means of an L-shaped lever or a short length of cable passing over a pulley, so that it lifts the vent by pulling on a downward projecting 'pram handle'.
(b) Instead of the winch wire, a light-weight metal rod or tube is used to pull on the L lever or pram handle cable.
(c) The rack and pinion uses a rotating shaft (torque tube) fitted with a gear wheel (pinion) at each vent. A toothed rack hanging from the vent engages with this pinion, so that the vent is raised and lowered by shaft rotation.

6.1.1.2 Vent mechanism drives

(a) The cable is pulled in by the retraction force of a large water ram. This is a very simple method, using mains water power, with an in-feed valve to open it and an exhaust valve to allow water to leave to close it. This system was designed to directly replace the manually operated levers on old glasshouses, and therefore it is not common on modern types of house.

(b) The cable is wound around a drum turned by an electric motor. In multispan houses all the drums are mounted on a common torque tube running across the full width of one end of the house. This allows all runs of vent to be operated from one source.

(c) The rod system is usually worked by a horizontal rack and pinion driven by an electric motor. It is possible to fit the rack at any convenient point along the rod, as there is sufficient stiffness in the rod and its mountings to push open those vents ahead of the drive. Multispan rod systems use a torque tube to drive the pinions from one source.

(d) Rack and pinion systems use a geared electric motor to turn the torque tube. In large multispan glasshouse blocks one motor will drive several torque tubes through a system of gearing.

(e) The load on the motor, and hence its size, can be reduced if part of the weight of the vents is counterbalanced. On cable systems this is simply done by adding weight to the motor end of the cable. Systems using a torque tube have a counterweight on a length of cable, wound so that it unwinds as the shaft rotates to open. Modern designs of vent and operating systems have reduced the need for this.

(f) Any automatic system must have protection against the motor overwinding the vents. This might be simply provided by limit switches on the cable, rod or one vent to stop the motor at the extremities of travel. Alternatively, some drive motors are mounted on a sprung base, so that any resistance to normal movement causes the motor to move against the spring and activate a small switch in the base. This system protects against vents jamming at any angle of opening, in addition to sensing the limit of travel.

6.1.1.3 Synchronisation of vent opening

The main problem with systems using rigid means of power transfer, such as the rod and the rack and pinion, is to ensure that all the vents seat simultaneously on closing; leaving some vents projecting can lose heat or lead to gale damage. It is not normally sufficient to adjust each vent at installation, as there can be subsequent movement in the house frame and vent gear. Some form of free linkage is needed on to each vent to ensure that it seats independently; the free linkage travel must, however, be limited to prevent wind lifting the vents. The winch system does not suffer this problem, as the cable is allowed to slacken completely and each vent seats by gravitational force.

6.1.1.4 Choice of mechanism
The linkage of some systems projects downwards when the vents are closed, and this can be a problem in low houses, especially where thermal screens are installed. The rack of rack and pinion units, and the pram handle of cable systems, prove the biggest problem, whereas the L levers on cable and rod systems can be angled so that they do not project below eaves level when the vents are closed.

The rack and pinion and cable/pram handle types are better suited for fully opening large vents, as the lifting force is constant over the full travel, compared with the lever where the force diminishes with the increasing lift.

6.1.2 Powered ventilation
This is used on both rigid (glass) and plastic structures. The fan produces a horizontal current of air, flowing either from end to end on small houses or crosswise on larger ones.

6.1.2.1 Fan type
The fans are sized according to an airflow per unit of floor area. The recommended rates are

Glasshouse: 0.03–0.04 m^3/s per m^2 of floor area
Plastic: 0.02–0.03 m^3/s per m^2 of floor area

The exact rates will depend on the crop and its state of development. The fans are usually low-pressure axial flow or propellor types, as operating resistance is only around 25 Pa. They are usually mounted along one wall close to floor level, and the air inlet vents are placed in the opposite wall. On some tunnels the fan is placed at the end, and the inlet is in the form of a perforated skirt along the bottom edge of both sides. It is normal for the fan to draw the air from the house. This ensures that the temerpature of the incoming air is not raised by the fan motor or blade friction, and any in-leakage through the structure, away from the vents, is used to good effect.

Where it is necessary to control the state of the air being used for ventilation, the air should be blown into the house by the fan; this system is often termed 'pressurised ventilation'.

The width of house that can be fan ventilated is governed by the maximum airspeed that the crop can tolerate. This is because the volume flow is based on floor area, and is hence proportional to width, while the velocity is determined by the height beneath the gutters. In practice, a maximum air velocity of 1.5 m/s will limit a 2 m gutter height house to 75 m, and a 3 m gutter height to 130 m.

6.1.2.2 Control of ventilation rate
The ventilation rate must be capable of some form of adjustment to suit the ventilation requirement of the crop. A system is installed to allow maximum ventilation rate and can be reduced by one of the following methods.

(a) Reducing the impeller speed by motor speed control or drive pulley ratio variation.

(b) In systems that use a number of fans, it is possible to vary the number running; this is commonly termed 'cascade control'.

(c) The inlet vent area might also be varied and, if done in conjunction with fan output control, will provide a constant inlet airspeed which is more proof against wind.

6.1.2.3 Air inlet design
The inlet should be designed to avoid excessive draughts at crop level, as well as to avoid high resistance to the fan. The latter can be satisfied by keeping the air velocity below 5 m/s, but the recommended velocity for the crop is only 1.5 m/s. Therefore this latter figure must be used when the air is being drawn into the house, although 5 m/s might be acceptable where the air is being discharged from a 'pressurised' ventilation system. The vent size can be calculated from

$$\text{Vent area } (m^2) = \frac{\text{Airflow rate } (m^3/s)}{\text{Recommended velocity } (m/s)}$$

Where louvre blades or flaps control the vent opening, the 'vent area' must be measured as the free area of the hole and not the overall dimensions.

On most glass structures the inlet is provided by high-level wall vents, opposite the fans, while on tunnels the cladding usually dictates a strip vent at the base of the wall (sometimes on both walls if the fan is fitted in the end of the tunnel). Some multispan blocks use the ridge vents of the span opposite to the fan as air inlets, either in entirety, or to supplement the wall vents of a low block.

Vent openings can be closed by the wall vent windows in the glass structure, or by a weighted flap in the tunnel; the fan is normally fitted with self-actuating louvre blades.

6.1.2.4 Wet pad cooling
In some hot, dry countries a layer of wetted fabric is placed across the air inlets to cool the incoming air by evaporation. Because this tech-

nique works only if the ambient relative humidity is low, it is seldom practised in the U.K.

The effects of evaporative cooling can be calculated using the psychrometric chart discussed in section 7.8.1.

6.1.2.5 Ventilation of mushroom sheds
Mushroom production involves four distinct phases, and each requires a specific environment, as follows.

(i) Peak heating — compost preparation (see section 6.2.4)
The shed temperature is 54°C and, because the compost is producing heat, a ventilation rate of up to $0.014 \, m^3/s$ per tonne of compost is required to remove the excess. An internal air movement of 30 empty shed volumes/h is recommended to maintain an even internal environment. Even where the ventilation is not required for heat removal, a minimum rate of $0.006 \, m^3/s$ per tonne is needed to maintain oxygen levels above 16 per cent.

(ii) Peak heating — pasteurisation
Ventilation is reduced to the minimum to allow heat rise to 60°C; at the end of this stage, maximum ventilation is used to cool the compost to 25°C.

(iii) Spawn running
The temperature must be in the 18–26°C range, with an optimum of 21°C; above 26°C will encourage development of competitive fungi. Ventilation might be required for heat removal, but it should be at a minimum rate of $0.00025 \, m^3/s$ per tonne for oxygen replacement. The optimum relative humidity is 90 per cent or above.

(iv) Growing
The optimum temperature is 16–18°C, as high temperatures depress yield. During the pre-cropping stage a CO_2 level of at least 0.1 per cent is needed to promote fruiting; this requires a maximum ventilation rate of $0.022 \, m^3/s$ per tonne, which might not be sufficient for heat removal, and thus artificial cooling could be needed.

During cropping the temperature requirement is the same, but the CO_2 level has to be below 0.06 per cent. The relative humidity has to be 70–95 per cent. The ventilation level will need to be at least $0.036 \, m^3/s$ per tonne for CO_2 removal, but this might cause a reduction of relative humidity in winter, so artificial humidification should be installed.

The internal air circulation will need to be 10–15 empty volumes per hour, with the distrubution ducting arranged to provide an airspeed of 0.03–0.05 m/s over the beds.

The ventilation system for modern intensive mushroom sheds will incorporate air mixing, to ensure the correct combination of internal circulation and ventilation, heating, and refrigeration and humidification. In addition, the incoming air should be filtered to prevent re-infestation of the compost; this requires a filter capable of removing 95 per cent of all particles over 2 micrometres.

6.2 STERILISATION OF SOILS AND COMPOSTS*

This involves raising the soil to a temperature that will kill weed seed and pests, but not so high as to affect nutrients and structure. In most situations this temperature is near the boiling point of water (82°C or above). Because of the increasing use of 'bought in' composts and chemical sterilisation, on-site heat sterilising is becoming less common in the U.K.

6.2.1 Batch treatment
For small lots a batch 'oven' can be used. This consists of an insulated cabinet, inside which is a series of vertical electrically heated panels. The soil is loaded from the top and lies between the plates to be heated, and the bottom of the cabinet is removed to empty the batch of treated soil.

6.2.2 Continuous flow treatment
This involves conveying a thin layer of soil through hot flue gases produced by an oil burner. Most systems use a rotating drum, inclined downwards so that the soil flows along by a tumbling action. A variant uses a flat plate which is vibrated horizontally to cause the soil to move along; the hot gases play on to the base plate. If the soil is sufficiently dry, both types can produce a reasonably fine crumb structure as a result of the conveyor action. Treatment temperature is controlled by a combination of flue gas temperature and the speed at which the compost passes through. The hot soil should be heaped after leaving the steriliser to allow the heat to penetrate any large particles.

6.2.3 In situ treatment
Soils in greenhouse borders and frames can be sterilised with steam. Steam has a number of advantages: it is an effective way of transferring

---

*Note that other aspects of compost preparation are described in the companion volume: *Horticultural Engineering Technology – Field Machinery*.

heat, it cannot raise the soil above 100°C, it does not leave toxic residues and it can be carried out with the crop in other parts of the house.

6.2.3.1 Methods
There are two basic methods for introducing steam.

(a) Sheet steaming
This is normally used for shallow sterilisation and involves introducing the steam beneath a heavy sheet laid over the soil surface. The soil has to be well cultivated to below the required sterilising depth, to allow the incoming steam to replace the air among the soil particles. Because the sheet is anchored by weighting at the edges, the steam pressure is only slightly above atmospheric; for example, if a 3 m x 3 m sheet has an anchored weight of 250 kg, steam over 275 Pa (gauge) will lift it. Steam is distributed beneath the sheet by perforated pipes.

(b) Deep injection
This was formerly done with perforated pipes (Hoddesden pipe) buried by hand, 350–400 mm deep and 450 mm apart. The act of digging loosens the soil sufficiently for steam penetration. To increase work rate two sets were used, one being dug in while the other was steaming.

The spiked pipe grid consists of a series of vertical pipes which are pushed into pre-cultivated ground. The tip of each pipe has a closed, pointed end, with steam escape holes just behind the tip. Lateral steam spread is poorer than for a Hoddesden pipe or plough, but less effort is needed to install it.

The steam plough is a winch-hauled cultivator with hollow tines through which the steam flows (figure 6.2). The tine forms a 'mole' for the steam to run along beneath the surface, and a trailed plug prevents it from travelling too far. A sheet trails to contain any steam that might escape up the loosened areas behind the tines. The plough is towed by a winch at the house end, but has to be dug in at the start of the run, so long runs of bed offer the best labour utilisation.

6.2.3.2 Steam requirements
The sheet system requires an initial flow of 30–35 kg/h* per m², reducing to 10–15 kg/h as the soil warms up. Control is manual, the operator seeking to maintain a ballooned sheet without losing steam beneath the edges. It takes several hours for the steam to penetrate to the required depth.

The deep injection systems require 70–80 kg/h per m², but it will take only 30–45 minutes to complete a 'cook'. The steam plough speed

---

*1 kW of boiler rating will produce 1.6 kg/h of steam.

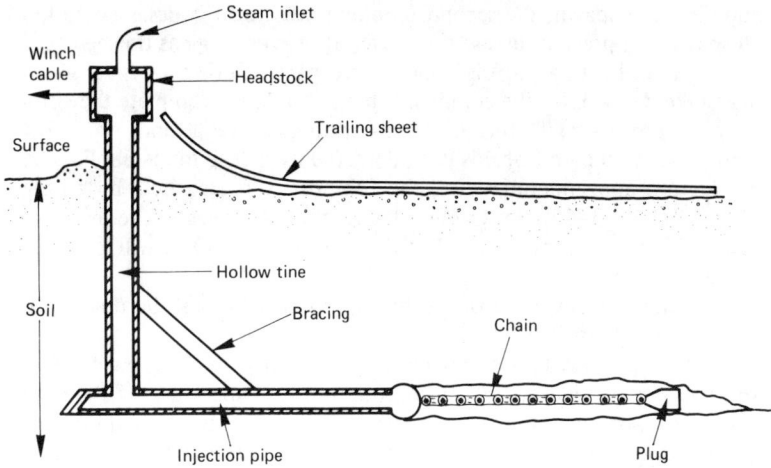

Figure 6.2 Steam plough.

is related to the time taken for the treating effect (sheet and mole plug length) to pass any spot.

Steam pressures at the application point will be less than 15 kPa (gauge), which is considerably lower than normal boiler operating pressures. In some circumstances the boiler pressure can be reduced to 25-30 kPa (this allows for frictional head loss in the supply pipe) but normally steam is supplied at full pressure and reduced at the steaming site. It is also feasible to use an old boiler which has been derated below normal working pressure.

The steam is totally lost from the system, so the boiler will need a continuous supply of treated feed water (see section 4.6.3).

For good performance the steam must be 'dry'; any droplets of moisture caused by condensation in the supply pipe can be removed by a cyclonic separator. The separator, if one is being used, must be placed upstream of the regulator.

The progress of the heat front can be monitored using a soil thermometer. The recommended minimum temperature is 82°C and the target heat front rate for deep injection systems is 15 mm/minute.

6.2.4 Mushroom compost

This undergoes two stages of sterilisation. The first (peak heating stage) is to kill pests and stabilise compost fermentation organisms before applying the spawn; the second (cooking out stage) is designed to kill all spawn and prevent disease carry-over after cropping has finished.

The peak heating stage is done in two parts. During the first, which may take 3-10 days, the compost is held at 54°C to complete the composting process, kill the nitrogen-forming bacteria and drive off ammonia. At the end of this part, detected by a drop in metabolic heat production and ammonia level, the compost is 'pasteurised' by raising it to 60°C for 3-4 hours to kill eelworm and other pests. The temperature has to be controlled closely, as exceeding 60°C will produce undesirable changes.

Cooking out is carried out at 80°C, but this can also be done with chemical sterilants if the heat required is too expensive.

Both stages can be done while the compost is in the growing tray, and they are carried out by raising the house temperature. If the farm has a steam-based heating system, heat can be directly injected into the house atmosphere, otherwise a gas or oil burner discharging directly into the house atmosphere must be used. Previously, coke braziers placed in the house were used. Some farms are able to sterilise in any production house, by having the heating facilities available for each one. Others have specially designed peak heating rooms through which the trays pass between filling and spawning.

Much of the heat required for peak heating is produced by the compost itself; a good compost should produce 4.5-6 kW/t. The externally sourced heat is mainly used for a few hours after loading, to ensure that the process starts uniformly and predictably. Ventilation is also important at both parts of peak heating; this has already been discussed in section 6.1.2.5.

6.3 CARBON DIOXIDE ENRICHMENT

Growing plants extract carbon dioxide from the air during photosynthesis. The rate of growth of some crops is increased if the level of atmospheric CO_2 is increased; this is possible within the enclosure of a glasshouse or polyethylene tunnel. The atmospheric concentration of CO_2 is measured as a ratio between the gas and the total air volume, termed either as 'parts per million' (ppm), or as 'volumes per million' (vpm), the latter being the preferred unit terminology. The normal atmospheric CO_2 level is 300 vpm. Crops like lettuce show a positive response at concentrations as high as 2000 vpm.

6.3.1 Methods of CO_2 enrichment

6.3.1.1 Pure gas

This is obtainable in two forms: compressed gas or as a frozen solid (dry ice). In these forms it is easily applied but is relatively expensive to purchase and to store; gas requires a pressure tank and dry ice a heavily refrigerated container. The storage and handling problems of dry ice have limited its use in the U.K.

Gaseous CO_2 is distributed within the glasshouse by a system of distribution tubes placed 2-3 m apart, each tube having very small discharge holes at intervals. Dry ice can be placed in a sealed container and its gas distributed as above, or the blocks can be broken up into chips and placed in small open containers at regular intervals through the house. Dry ice must be handled with care as its intense coldness can cause severe 'burns' to unprotected hands.

6.3.1.2 Products of combustion

Carbon dioxide can be manufactured 'on site' by burning hydrocarbon fuels

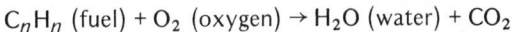

$$C_nH_n \text{ (fuel)} + O_2 \text{ (oxygen)} \rightarrow H_2O \text{ (water)} + CO_2$$

Only fuels free of harmful by-products such as sulphur can be used for burning directly within the house. The normal fuels for this are mains (natural) gas, liquefied petroleum gas, (LPG) or premium-grade paraffin (see section 4.2.5). These are burnt in direct fired space heaters or, if gas, simple ring or ribbon burners. These units can also be used for a limited amount of heating for frost protection in 'cold cropping' houses. Sufficient ventilation for complete combustion must be provided, otherwise carbon monoxide (CO), which is dangerous to personnel, will be formed. LPG can form ethylene type products which are toxic to plants. Poor combustion can also result in some of the atmospheric nitrogen being oxidised, and these products are also a serious hazard to plants. In countries where the above 'premium' fuels are scarce or expensive, attempts have been made to extract the CO_2 from heater flue gases or to produce them by burning charcoal. Both of these methods require the gas to be passed through a scrubber to remove SO_2 and other harmful by-products. Because the heat demand periods might nct coincide with the maximum photosynthetic activity, heater flue extraction systems must incorporate storage for either the CO_2 produced or the excess heat resulting from running the heater for the CO_2. CO_2 is denser (heavier) than air at the same temperature, although when it is produced by these means it is warmer and hence less dense than the house air. The relative change in CO_2 density as it is cooled by the house air aids its mixing.

Gas distribution is also aided by the natural tendency for gas molecules to diffuse throughout the atmosphere and, where used, by the convection currents produced by the heating system.

6.3.2 Quantity of gas
1 m^3 of CO_2 will be provided by 1 m^3 of mains gas, 0.67 kg of LPG, 0.77 litres of paraffin, or 2 kg of dry ice or pressurised gas. 1000 vpm are equivalent to a concentration of 1000/1 000 000 or 1/1000, so 1 m^3 of CO_2 will increase the level in each 1000 m^3 house volume by 1000 vpm. The quantity of fuel or pure CO_2 calculated from this will be the least amount required each day, although the actual amount can be 25-50 per cent greater to account for losses by draughts. As a guide, 25-30 m^3/h per ha will maintain 1000 vpm in a reasonably air-tight house.

6.3.3 Control and monitoring
Carbon dioxide levels can be detected by electronic analysis or chemical reagent tubes (Dreager or Kittigowa, for example). These latter are not automatic but are inexpensive to buy, and easy to use for spot checks on the CO_2 level. The electronic systems use CO_2 sensing cells, calculate from the depletion in normal oxygen levels as measured by oxygen sensing cells or measure by infra-red gas detection methods. The monitoring is continuous, and with some systems dosing can be directly controlled. The normal method of control is to set the running rate of the burner or gas discharge, following spot check analysis of the house atmosphere with reagent tubes. This method does not take into account gas losses due to draughts in high winds or the plant response to other factors, such as heat or photosynthetic active radiation (PAR). Most systems link the burner or gas discharge to the vent controller, so that it does not waste gas by running when the vents are open.

Carbon dioxide is absorbed by the plant only during daylight, thus any enrichment should not be carried out between sunset and sunrise. It is recommended that any enrichment be carried out during the period between 1 hour after dawn, for direct CO_2, or ½ hour after dawn, for combustion-based CO_2, and 1½ hours before sunset. These times might need to be exceeded during winter daylight hours. Because of potential losses in warm weather, when the vents are open for long periods in the day, operators of manually controlled systems often abandon enrichment after April. Computer-based glasshouse controllers can monitor CO_2 levels and integrate gas application periods with vent operation — for example, shutting the supply off when the windward vents are open beyond a certain position. This allows the enrichment periods to continue throughout the season.

The problems of abandoning summertime enrichment are further complicated by results of recent work at the Glasshouse Crops Research Institute (U.K.) and the Naaldwijk Research Station (The Netherlands), which has demonstrated a serious depletion in the atmospheric CO_2 within the glasshouse during periods of high photosynthetic activity, even though the vents are fully open. Trials at the above centres have shown it is economically viable to add CO_2 to restore the atmosphere to ambient levels and, for some crops, to enrich it further. As a guide, 12.5–15 m^3/h of CO_2 per ha will avoid summer depletion when vents are open.

Research at the Australian National University, Canberra, has indicated that enrichment benefits can decline as the plant adapts to its new atmsophere. It is postulated that supplying the CO_2 in a series of pulses, rather than as a single daily dose, can prevent this acclimatisation.

6.4 IRRIGATION

Crops within a protected environment rely totally on water provided artificially. Traditionally, water was applied by hand but this is no longer practical or economic on most nurseries, therefore most now use fixed pipe systems, applying the water either overhead or directly to the roots at low level.

6.4.1 Overhead systems

6.4.1.1 Spray nozzles
(a) Static hydraulic nozzle
This is similar to a crop spray nozzle. It is installed to spray upwards, and produces a fan or cone of fine droplets which fall on to the crops. The droplet size and spectrum is not as critical as for crop spraying, thus this nozzle can be formed from moulded plastic rather than being precision engineered.
(b) Pin nozzles
These consist of a single-hole jet discharging on to a conical deflector. The deflector is fixed on to the head of a pin protruding from the jet hole. The clearance between the pin and the jet hole, together with the deflector shape, govern the spread pattern and water output. The nozzle head and pin are normally colour coded, each colour relating to an output rate and droplet spread diameter.
(c) Anvil jets
A high-pressure jet of water, created by a nozzle with a cylindrical bore, hits a metal disc (anvil) a few millimetres away. The anvil can be

flat or cone shaped with its apex pointing towards the nozzle. The water jet is deflected into a circular spray of droplets by the anvil. This jet is always used with the anvil horizontal, to produce a lateral droplet discharge, but may be positioned with the nozzle discharging upwards or downwards. There are conflicting views as to which gives the best results. If the jets are downwards, they drip when the water is switched off and the line is draining, and they are also more prone to blockage. If the jets are upwards, the droplets landing on the pipe coalesce and drip from any low points in the line.

The spread and droplet pattern is governed by the velocity of the water stream leaving the nozzle, not the clearance between it and the anvil.

These systems usually apply water at a heavier rate than outdoor systems, a precipitation rate of 40–50 mm/h being common.

Many overhead systems suffer from problems of drip when the water flow is shut off, as the water in the line empties through the nozzles by gravity. Even when the nozzles are mounted into the top of the pipe, those in any part of the pipe that has sagged will drip. This can be prevented by either flow check valves in each nozzle, which open only under pressure, or a solenoid valve at the end of the pipe, which opens when the water flow is shut off and allows the pipeline to drain. This latter method will not drain the line completely if sections have sagged.

6.4.1.2 Travelling boom distribution

The circular distribution pattern of most nozzles causes uneven watering. This can be tolerated in many crops, but is serious when watering, for example, compost modules where, to ensure that all have sufficient water, over-application directly beneath the nozzles can wash away the modules in that area.

The Agricultural Development and Advisory Service (ADAS) have designed a system using hydraulic crop-spraying nozzles, mounted on a mobile boom which traverses the whole house area. The boom is suspended from a track running the length of the house, and is propelled by a small winch. The supply hose is suspended at intervals from the track, so that it folds concertina-wise as the boom approaches the water supply end (figure 6.3). The nozzle output and winch speed are normally chosen to apply 6 mm precipitation at each pass. Some systems can be used to apply pesticides to the crop, but as a 6 mm precipitation rate is equivalent to 60 000 l/ha, about 50 times normal 'high volume' spraying rate, the boom speed has to be increased and nozzle output decreased to use normal dilutions.

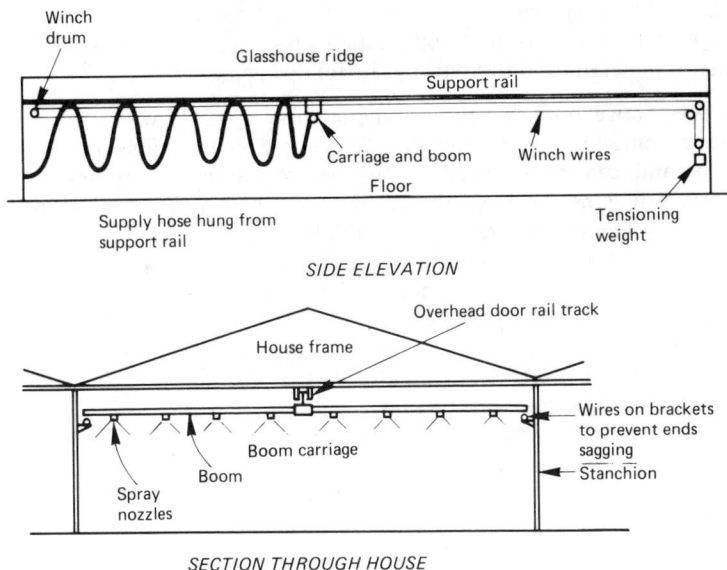

Figure 6.3   Travelling overhead irrigation boom.

6.4.1.3 Misting

Special anvil nozzles working at pressures of 175–350 kPa are used to supply the fine mist needed to prevent transpiration when establishing cuttings. The mist nozzle is placed on top of a vertical pipe projecting above the cuttings bench. The pipes are placed at suitable spacings to ensure even coverage.

The mist unit is controlled by an 'electronic leaf'. This is a piece of insulating material with two electrodes let into the surface about 5 mm apart, placed among the cuttings. The mist landing on the 'leaf' deposits a layer of water which completes an electric circuit between the electrodes, and this operates a relay to close the water valve. As the 'leaf' dries, the circuit is broken and the valve opens.

6.4.2 Low-level systems

These systems apply water to the area around the plant roots, without wetting the plant foliage. The water might be applied as a trickle or as a low-level spray.

6.4.2.1 Trickle systems

These systems require the supply pipe to pass close to each root. The water is metered from this pipe by the following means.

(a) Restrictive nozzles — the commonest use a nozzle with a loosely screwed plug to restrict water flow. The screw plug permits rate adjustment, and can be removed completely for cleaning purposes. The nozzle can either be fixed directly into the pipe wall or via a small length of 3 mm plastic feeder tube, the latter giving greater versatility in plant position. The system works at low pressure, so that the water discharges in a fast stream of drips rather than a high-pressure jet. The nozzle output is 1–2 l/h. Normally the nozzle spacing will depend on crop requirements, but in some cases soil type can also influence this; for example, in overall watering a spacing of 400 mm is suggested for heavy soils, and a closer one on sand.

(b) The microbore system uses a length of 0.8 mm bore capillary tube between each watering point and the supply pipe. The bore of this pipe restricts water flow predictably, the output being correlated with the length of tube used, so that the progressive supply pipe pressure drop can be compensated by adjusting tube length. The water feed into the supply pipe passes through a restrictor tube also, to drop its pressure to about 120 kPa; the length of this restrictor tube can also be varied to compensate for pressure drops along the supply main. Each capillary normally delivers 0.9 l/h. An additional advantage is the ability to water pots which have to be progressively spaced as plants grow.

An alternative system uses a 3 mm bore drip tube with restriction to flow by a grooved stick pushed into the end, the distance of penetration governing flow rate. Typical outputs are 2–4.5 l/h.

(c) Seep tubes — these emit water along their entire length. The two common types are thin-walled plastic strip, loosely stitched into a tube, or a tube of porous material. The water in the tube is at low pressure, about 20 kPa, and seeps, rather than being forced, out. The local discharge rate can be affected by undulations in the bed.

A system which reduces the effects of undulation uses a seep tube bonded to a supply tube. The supply tube carries water at 50–150 kPa, and this is bled into the seep tubes through a series of metering holes.

The normal water output per metre run is 0.75–1.5 l/h for porous wall tube, 2–9 l/h for twin tube, and 10 l/h for stitched tube.

6.4.2.2 Low-level sprays

These distribute water over a greater area than seep or drip systems.

(a) The simplest method uses plastic tube with small holes punched into the walls. It is run at medium pressure, which exudes the water in a series of small jets. Output and jet throw can be varied with water pressure, normal outputs being 60–120 l/h per metre and corresponding jet throws 120–400 mm, for a tube having four 0.8 mm holes at 130 mm spacing. Because the output rate per unit length of this system is many times greater than the trickle systems discussed in section 6.4.2.1, it is often found that the water-carrying capacity of the tubing severely limits the length of run.

(b) Spray lines, similar to those used overhead, can be placed at soil level. These are suitable only for crops that do not have dense lower foliage, so as to avoid blocking the spray distribution.

6.4.2.3 Capillary distribution

Pot plants or modules can be watered from below if they are placed on a layer of wet sand or water-conductive fabric (capillary matting). This is normally used on benches, although some large pot plant operations use capillary matting laid over polyethylene sheet on the house floor.

Nowadays the capillary system is normally used to supplement the lateral movement of water applied by one of the other low-level systems. It was, however, originally designed to distribute water directly from a reservoir, using one of the following methods.

(a) The sand acts as a support for the plant over a layer of water on the bench. Water can freely percolate sideways through its lower layers, and is drawn upwards by capillary attraction of the compost in the pot. The layer of water in the base of the sand is maintained by either a float valve and header tank, or by application from a drip nozzle system.

(b) Capillary matting has the capability to draw water upwards by 10–20 mm. This means that the bench or floor need not be absolutely level, and the water can be supplied from a trough under one edge of the bench, into which the matting edge hangs.

(c) The flooded bench is a variation of the capillary bench. This consists of a shallow, water-tight tray, placed at a slope of 1 in 200. Water is applied to the upper end and drains from the lower end. Its application rate is such that a water level of 25 mm is maintained on the bench by the flow restriction caused by the closely spaced pots. Water draining from the bench is held in a tank and returned to the head of the bench by a pump. Pump flow rate should be 5 m^3/h per metre of bench width.

The bench is periodically flooded to suit the evapotranspiration of the pot, and is allowed to drain when the pot compost is fully resaturated.

6.4.3 Nutrient film technique (NFT)

The plants are suspended in a channel along which there is a flow of water and nutrients. The channel is evenly sloped at 1 in 75 and discharges into a sub-floor holding tank from which the solution is continually circulated by a pump. The channel should have an enclosed top to prevent light reaching the roots. The nutrient status and pH of the solution is continually monitored by electronic analysers, and these control the injection of nutrients and acid. In some systems the solution is also heated.

An alternative system uses the nutrient film equipment to supply water by drip irrigation to a crop growing in an inert fibrous material (such as Rockwool).

6.4.4 Adding nutrients to irrigation systems

It is normal for the plant nutrients to be added to the water as it flows to the irrigation system. Two systems are used: displacement and positive injection.

6.4.4.1 Displacement injection

The nutrient is held in a barrel (figure 6.4) with a discharge tube rising from the base. Water from the irrigation line is bled into the top of the barrel and displaces the nutrient downwards, driving it up the discharge tube. There need not be a physical barrier between the water and nutrient, as the densities of the two are sufficiently different to prevent mixing. Some barrels contain a rubberised bag to hold the nutrients and this is squeezed by the incoming water. The bag types are suited for adding miscible liquids, like acids, to the system.

The barrels range in size between 10 and 160 litres; the actual size used depends on the irrigation layout, but there should be sufficient capacity for the maximum throughput at one watering.

Dilution rate is controlled by adjusting the water input rate. Some adjusters meter the amount of water going into the barrel while others alter the pressure drop across the diluter, effectively diverting more or less water through the barrel. In most units the full water flow passes through the head, but at least one system incorporates the head in a bypass, so that only a portion of the water flow is affected by the head pressure drop.

Most units are calibrated in dilution ratio — 1:50, 1:100, 1:200 and 1:400 being common. Further adjustments to dilution rate are effected by the strength of the stock solution. Diluters are made for water flows ranging from 0.03–7 l/s.

6.4.4.2 Positive injection

These systems use a pump to inject doses of nutrient at a rate commensurate with water flow. Some use a positive displacement pump, others a centrifugal pump and metering valve.

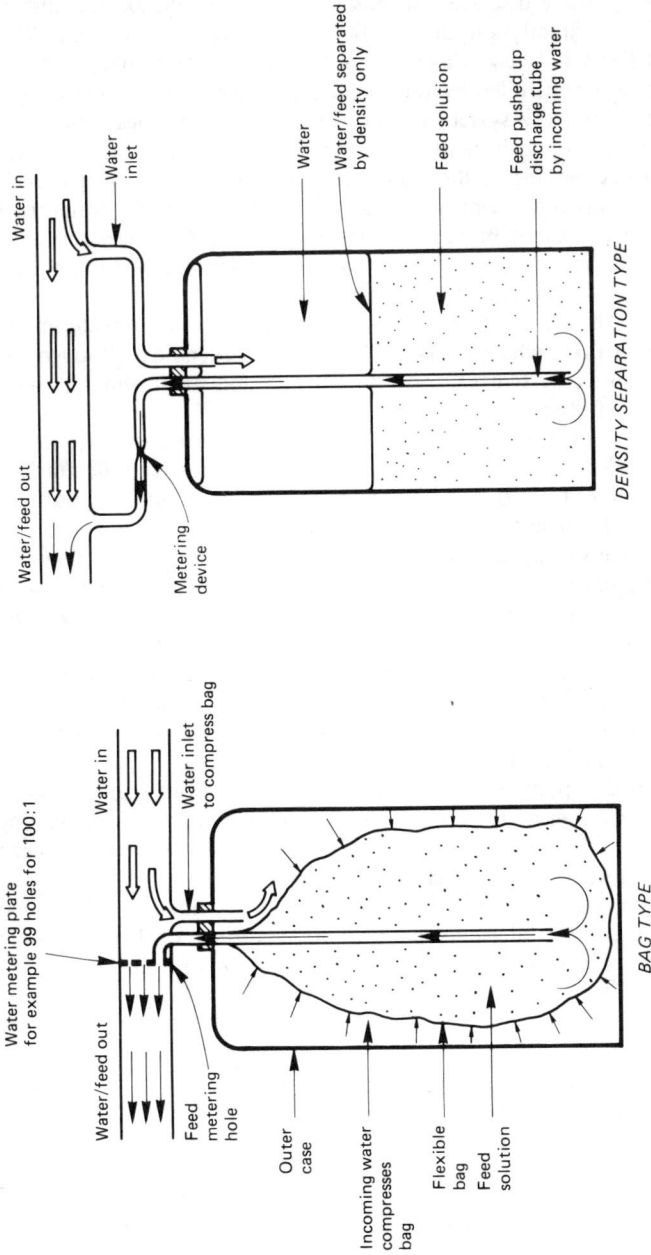

Figure 6.4 Displacement nutrient feed injectors.

(a) The positive displacement pump is usually a reciprocating piston acting either directly on the solution or through a diaphragm. The piston delivers a fixed amount of solution at each stroke, and the dosage rate is controlled by the frequency of the strokes. One system uses water from the system to operate the piston by means of a diaphragm at the opposite end of its rod. A pair of solenoid valves let water into either side of the diaphragm alternately, to cause it to reciprocate. This requires a mains pressure of 270 kPa, and the water used by the motor cannot be returned to the system. An alternative is to drive the piston by a pair of electromagnetic solenoids which are used alternately to reciprocate the piston rod.

The stroke rate is normally governed by a pulse output water-meter in the main flow, which operates the valves or solenoids, although the electromagnetic system can operate with an adjustable timer to set a stroke rate, if the flow is known and remains constant.

(b) The centrifugal pump system uses a metering valve to determine the injection rate. This system incorporates an electronic nutrient sensor system to regulate the metering valve, so that the nutrient strength in the main flow is maintained at a prescribed value.

(c) In one system the pump is used both to draw in nutrient and to supply the system water. This is achieved by the pump drawing both its fresh water and nutrient through a series of tubes of equal length. As the flow is the same through each tube, it is simple for the dilution rate to be set by the ratio of water to nutrient tubes; for example, for 1:100, 99 of the tubes would draw water and 1 would draw nutrient. The system is fitted with a series of control valves which open various combinations of tubes to give a range of dilution rates.

All types of pump system draw stock solution from a tank, and can be arranged to draw from any one of a number of tanks containing different solution strength or compositions, so that different crops can be irrigated without manual change of diluter.

Dilution rate on positive stroke types is usually fixed at 1:200 when using a water-meter of 1 pulse per revolution, although 1:100 is possible by fitting the water-meter with a cam of 2 pulses per revolution.

6.4.5 Water supply

The method for calculating water requirements, methods of holding a water supply and pump and pipework design are similar to those discussed in chapter 5 of the companion volume (*Horticultural Engineering Technology — Field Machinery*).

Water quality is also very important. Crops that are consumed directly without being cooked, such as those used in salads, must use water that is free from harmful organisms (often termed 'potable' water). Water drawn from public mains and stored correctly will be of the required quality, but if drawn from private source or ditches it will probably need to be purified. Even where potable quality is not essential the water will need to be finely filtered to remove particles which might block the fine orifices in dilutors and nozzles. Some supplies might need to be treated with algicide to prevent blockage from algal growth; the use of these compounds might, however, render the water unsuitable for potable applications.

6.5 LIGHTING

Artificial illumination is used for one of three main purposes: to supplement daylight, to replace it altogether, or to alter the ratio between 'day' and 'night' periods (photoperiodicity).

6.5.1 Light requirement

Both the quality and the quantity of the illumination must be suited to correct plant growth. The quantity of light emitted by a lamp is measured in 'lumens'. The more important factor is the 'illuminance'; this is the quantity falling on a given area beneath the lamp, and is measured in 'lux' (lx), the common notation of lumens/m^2. The relationship between lamp output and illuminance is governed by the 'inverse square law'. Because light spreads in two dimensions, the illuminance varies and is reduced in proportion to the square of the distance; for example, doubling the height of a lamp from a surface reduces its illuminance at the surface to one-quarter of the original value.

6.5.1.1 Quantity

The illuminance requirement of a crop will depend on many factors, the chief among these being as follows.

(a) Purpose: supplementary, replacement or photoperiodic.
(b) If replacement: length of the lighting period. Most crops will perform well with either 15 000 lx for 12 h/day, or 8000 lx for 24 h/day. A few crops will tolerate a 'daylength' of 7 hours, enabling the lamps to be run on cheap tariff electricity.
(c) Crop requirement for photosynthetic active radiation (PAR).

The requirements in (b) and (c) are well documented for many crops, the majority having been established by detailed experimentation on optimum response.

It should be noted that the levels for replacement illuminance are 5–10 times those required to light buildings for human occupancy.

6.5.1.2 Quality

Each of the colours of the spectrum occurs at a certain wavelength of light; light wavelength is extremely small and is measured in nanometres (nm). Figure 6.5 shows the wavelengths for daylight; the wavelength band for PAR ranges between 400 and 700 nm, so the whole visible spectrum of daylight is important except for the shortest wavelength around violet. However, few lamp types include either full daylight spectrum or the PAR spectral colours in equal quantities. Considerable research into plant response to artificial light has shown that a certain

The visible near-visible radiations of
the electromagnetic spectrum:

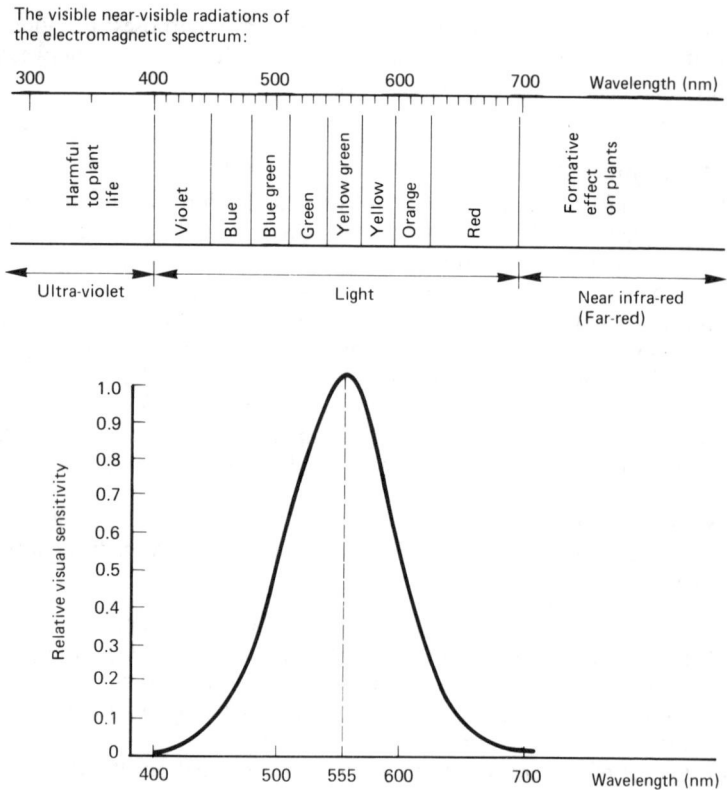

The standard luminosity function, that is, the relative sensitivity of the human eye to the wavelengths of the visible spectrum

Figure 6.5 Visible spectrum wavelengths (*courtesy of The Electricity Council, London*).

imbalance in PAR towards the longer wavelength (red) end is tolerable for photosynthesis. In addition to photosynthesis, some light is required to induce morphogenetic (plant development) effects, and this tends to lie within the shorter (blue) end of the PAR band. The spectral characteristics of a lamp must supply the minimum plant requirements in each wavelength. Sometimes two types can be combined to produce the required effect — for example, combining a tungsten bulb with a fluorescent tube.

In some cases spectral imbalance can be used to advantage. As far red light induces elongation (drawing), it is reduced for those plants like lettuce that have to be sturdy and short. Where some stem elongation is desirable, for example in tomatoes, it should be increased. Other colour patterns can induce flowering, which could be an advantage to flower crops but a disadvantage to vegetables.

It is possible to overcome some of the spectral shortcomings of a lamp type by increasing the total illuminance to a level where the minimum colour requirements are satisfied. This is wasteful of both installed equipment and running costs, and should be considered only as a short-term solution.

6.5.2 Lamp type

Lamp choice is affected by many factors, the main ones being cost of installation, luminous efficiency of power consumed, spectral quality, size and intensity. The latter two govern the distance above the crop at which the lamps must be placed for even illuminance and, where used for supplementary lighting, shading effect on daylight. The present types of lamp suitable for horticulture are discussed below.

6.5.2.1 Incandescent (type GLS)

These are the normal 'light bulbs' used in domestic buildings. The colour spectrum is heavily biased towards the red spectrum. They are cheap to install, compact and, because of the number needed for adequate illuminance, can be placed close to the crop. The power conversion efficiency is low, only about 5 per cent of input energy is converted to radiation energy, most of the remainder being converted to heat, and thus their running cost per unit of useful light is high. The GLS lamp is normally used only in conjunction with other, more efficient, lamp types to increase the red spectrum.

6.5.2.2 Fluorescent tube (type MCF)

These consist of a glass tube internally coated with phosphor, containing a mercury vapour. An electrical discharge along the vapour in the tube reacts with the phosphor coating to produce visible light. The phosphor coating includes various substances in order to produce different spectral colourings. The three commonest types are

(a) 'Daylight' with a high portion of light energy split between the blue and red wavelengths.
(b) 'White' and 'Warm white' with most of the light energy in the yellow and red wavelengths.
(c) 'Natural' or 'Kolor-rite' where spectral colours are the most evenly balanced.

The MCF lamp converts 15–17 per cent of the input energy to visible radiation energy. Most of the remainder is converted to heat by the choke coil which is used to maintain the discharge. The choke can be sited remotely from the tube where illumination is required, but excessive heat is undesirable.

6.5.2.3 High-pressure mercury (type MB)
MB lamps are discharge tube types containing high pressure mercury vapour within a glass tube. Visible light is produced by one of two means.

(a) MBF: the discharge tube is enclosed within a glass envelope, coated inside with phosphor. It converts 12–14 per cent of input energy to light energy, and the choke is externally mounted and consumes an extra 10 per cent of the nominal lamp power. These lamps are globe shaped and reasonably compact. Some have an in-built reflector (MBFR/U) to concentrate the light downwards through an angle of 120°.
(b) MBI: additives within the discharge tube convert the power energy to light energy. Efficiency is higher, with about 18–20 per cent conversion. The colour emission is nearer daylight, and can be further improved by adding a phosphor coating to the outer envelope (MBIF). These lamps are considerably more expensive than the MBF type.

6.5.2.4 Sodium (type SO)
(a) SOX: these lamps use low-pressure sodium vapour, and are the most efficient type of discharge lamp, converting 30–32 per cent of input energy to light energy. However, spectral output is not ideal for replacement lighting as most of the colour is in the yellow/orange wavelength, but is suitable for supplementing winter daylight, as the daylight corrects the spectral imbalance. These lamps are horizontal tubular types, with no internal reflector and thus require large external reflectors, which can themselves shade some of the poor daylight in winter.
(b) SON/T uses high-pressure sodium vapour and is slightly less efficient than SOX, converting only 24–26 per cent of the input energy. The

spectral output spans most of the PAR wavelengths, making it highly suited to horticultural use. The lamp is upright and thus requires a smaller area of reflector, which blocks less daylight.

6.5.3 Installation
The lamps must be mounted so as to provide the required illuminance at the crop, and to distribute the light evenly over the crop area. The installation layout will depend on the purpose of the illumination, and this normally falls into one of five categories.

6.5.3.1 Daylight supplementation
Table 6.1 gives examples of the layout of lamps for the supplementary lighting of some common crops.

6.5.3.2 Photoperiodic (nightbreak) lighting
As it normally requires only low illumination levels for this purpose, it is common to use clear glass tungsten (GLS) lamps arranged for an illuminance of 60–100 lux. Table 6.2 shows the arrangement of various GLS lamp sizes to give a satisfactory illuminance.

6.5.3.3 Daylight replacement
Owing to the high illuminance requirement the most common lamp type is the fluorescent tube, because of cost, light quality and the headroom requirement. These tubes are mounted in close banks above the crop. A typical layout for tomato plants is shown in figure 6.6. As the lighting totally replaces daylight, a totally insulated building can be used; if carried out in a glasshouse, the daylight shading caused by the rig will not be a problem. The insulated building is normally termed a 'growing room', and in addition to the lighting is fitted with temperature and humidity control. To make full use of the space available it is common to place the growing trays, each with its own lighting unit, in tiered racks. These normally have the lower illuminance level for a 24 hour lighting period. Handling plants in and out of tiered racks can be labour intensive, and better handling is achieved by using a moving bench system. In these, the lighting units and tray support racks are permanent, and the growing trays are propelled through on some form of roller; this might be on an 'all in, all out' system, or progressively so that the time taken for passage of a tray equates to the time taken for the plant to complete its required growth.

Growing rooms made from converted buildings and glasshouse-based systems often use a 15 000 lx rig to enable a 12 hour lighting period to be used, and are used for two batches of plants per day. The rig is constructed half the length of the growing bench, and is mounted

Table 6.1

Lamp layout for supplementary lighting
(by permission of the Electricity Council, London)

Crop	Type of lamp	Illuminance (lux)	Large block scheme			Single or double rows of lamps		
			Mounting height (m)	Area/lamp (m²)	Dimension of area (m)	Mounting height (m)	Area/lamp (m²)	Dimensions of area (m)
Tomato plants	400 W HLRG	5000	1.1	1.7	1.3 × 1.3	1.1	1.3	1.2 × 1.1
	400 W SON/T	10 000	1.5	1.9	1.7 × 1.1	1.2	1.0	1.1 × 0.9*
	180 W SOX	10 000	1.2	1.2	1.2 × 1.0	1.0	0.6	0.5 × 1.2**
Cucumber plants	400 W MBFR/U	5000	1.1	1.9	1.4 × 1.4	1.1	1.4	1.3 × 1.1
Lettuce	180 W SOX	7500	1.2	1.8	1.6 × 1.1	1.0	1.1	0.8 × 1.4**
Pot chrysanthemums	400 W MBFR/U	7500	0.9	1.4	1.2	0.9	0.7	0.9 × 0.8

*Lamps parallel to bench or bed.
**Lamps across bench or bed.

Table 6.2

Tungsten (GLS) lamp layout for nightbreak lighting
(by permission of the Electricity Council, London)

Lamp power (W)	Height above plants (m)	Spacing (m X m)
60	0.6-0.9	1.2 X 1.2
100	1.2-1.4	1.8 X 1.8
150	1.5-1.8	3.1 X 3.1

above it, or suspended from an overhead track by wheels, so that it can
be rolled to the alternate site every 12 hours. This can be done automatically by a timeswitch-controlled winch.

6.5.3.4 Growing room ventilation and irrigation
In most growing rooms the waste heat from the lamps is in excess of
temperature maintenance requirements. Some heat input can be prevented by placing chokes and starters in a separate ventilated compart-
ment, but this requires a separate multi-core cable to each lamp, rather
than the two-core ring main used if entire lamps are installed. Excess
heat is removed by blowing air across the gap between the plants and
the lamps, but in some circumstances the velocity will be so great as
to damage plants. If this problem is serious the lamps can be mounted
within a separate glazed area, which can be ventilated independently,
although the lamp numbers might have to be increased to take account
of light transmission loss.

Watering will be important, and the ventilation airflow will further
increase irrigation need. The low headroom of tiered bench systems
precludes most spray systems, and even in single layer 'linear' growing
rooms, sprays should be used with care to avoid damage to the lighting
gear. The best method is either a drip system with capillary matting
or a flooded bench.

6.5.3 5 Low-level illuminance replacement
Some crops require only low levels of illuminance — for example seed
potato sprouting (chitting), where only enough light to contain excessive sprout elongation is required. This can be provided by single
fluorescent tubes hung vertically between the rows of stacked chitting
trays. One tube unit is sufficient for 3-4 columns of trays for early
potatoes or 5-6 columns of main crop varieties, provided it is moved
next to a different column each day.

(a) Spacing to give an average illuminance of 15 000 (11 000) lx

| 76 | 152 | 152 | 152 | 152 | | 6 | 6 | 6 | 6 | 6 | 6 | 3 |
| mm | mm | mm | mm | mm | | in | in | in | in | in | in | in |

2.4 m (8 ft) 125 W tubes

Mounting
height
450–600 mm
(1.5–2 ft)

Floor or Bench

(b) Spacing to give an average illuminance of 8000 (5500) lx

| 76 | 230 | 305 | | 12 | 12 | 9 | 3 |
| mm | mm | mm | | in. | in. | in. | in. |

2.4 m (8 ft) 125 W tubes

Mounting
height
450–600 mm
(1.5–2 ft)

Floor or bench

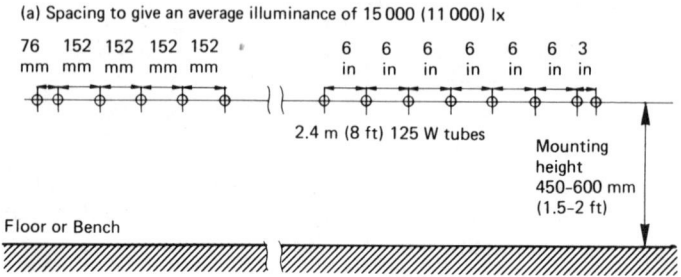

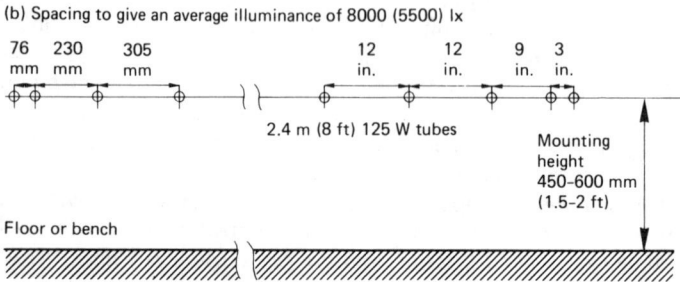

**Fluorescent tube spacing for linear rigs, showing
the ends only**

(a) Spacing to give an average illuminance of 15 000 (11 000) lx

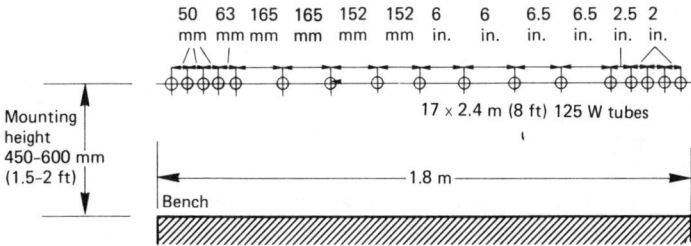

(b) Spacing to give an average illuminance of 8000 (5500) lx

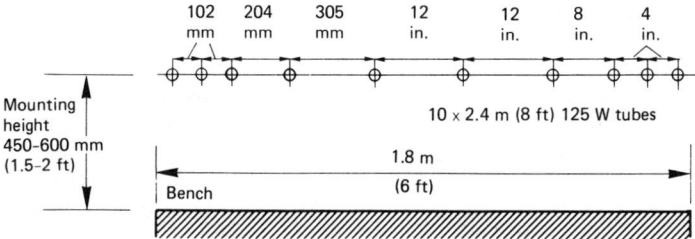

Fluorescent tube spacing for over-bench lighting on a 1.8 m (6 ft) wide bench

Figure 6.6 Light layout for a growing bench (*courtesy of The Electricity Council, London*).

7 EQUIPMENT AND SYSTEMS FOR CROP STORAGE

7.1 CROP DRYING

Some crops such as bulbs, onions and most seeds require to be dried prior to storage and marketing.

7.1.1 Root crop drying

This involves both removing the moisture from adhering soil and drying off old foliage and roots. While this can be carried out naturally by laying the harvested crop on the soil surface, many growers utilise artificial drying systems to ensure that the crop is thoroughly dried without the risk of bad weather.

7.1.1.1 Onions and narcissus bulbs

The artificial drying of onions and some bulb crops involves two stages of moisture removal.

(a) Stage I removes the 'free' water that is held as moisture in adhering soil, and on the surface of the product. The rate at which this moisture can be removed depends on the energy applied, both in terms of airflow and, within limits, heat.

The high air temperatures in stage I are often beneficial in controlling crop disease. For example, it restricts development of the fusarium moulds that cause neck rot in onions or basal rot in bulbs. An additional benefit of heat in, for example, onions, is to improve the skin finish and general appearance by enhancing their skin colour.

(b) In stage II the water that is held within the cells of the roots and foliage is removed. The removal rate of this water is governed by the rate at which it diffuses through the cell wall. It is not improved by airflows above a certain level and only influenced by heat if this significantly reduces relative humidity.

The humidity can also be important to crop appearance. While it must be sufficiently low for the air to have the capacity to absorb moisture, if too low it can overdry the skins of onions and cause them to crack and fall off, or cause the dehydration and shrivelling of bulbs. The recommended temperatures and airflows for drying onions and narcissus bulbs are shown in table 7.1.

Stage I should take 3 days when the crop is in a bulk heap, and 1 day when it is in boxes. Stage II can take several weeks and during its later stages the cell sap moisture release will be so slow as to require only intermittent ventilation.

It is usual to size the fan for these crops to dry either one-third of the store at stage I airflow, or to stage I dry the product of 3 days harvesting, whichever is the larger.

The method for calculating fan output is

$$\text{either} \quad m^3/s = \frac{\text{Store tonnage} \times 450}{3 \times 3600}$$

$$\text{or} \quad m^3/s = \frac{\text{Hectares lifted in 3 days} \times \text{yield} \times 450}{3600} \qquad (7.1)$$

Where stage I stores are designed for high rate harvesting, the fan output will be unnecessarily high for stage II if provided by one fan. It is, therefore, usual to install two or more fans so that all are used for stage I and only one for stage II.

The heat input needed to ensure that the recommended temperatures are met can be calculated from the ambient design temperatures given in table 5.5.

The method for calculating maximum heater capacity is

$$kW = m^3/s \text{ (from equation (7.1))} \times \text{temperature lift } (^\circ C) \times 1.3* \qquad (7.2)$$

As heaters are installed for maximum temperature lift, there must, therefore, be a means of reducing heat output during warmer weather. One simple method is to supply the heat load with a number of small heaters and switch some off when lesser outputs are required.

Increasing use is being made of modulating oil or gas burners (see section 4.3) firing directly into the airstream. These are under thermostatic control, and so can maintain the required duct temperature irrespective of ambient conditions. This type of heater is usually manufactured in the form of one large burner unit; however, when using a multiple fan installation, there should be a separate heater or burner

---

*Mean value of specific heat of air on a volume basis, at the drying air temperature.

Table 7.1

Recommended drying conditions for onions and narcissus bulbs

Crop	Stage I		Stage II		Relative humidity of air (per cent)
	Airflow (m³/h per tonne)	Crop temperature (°C)	Airflow (m³/h per tonne)	Crop temperature (°C)	
Onions	450	30	175	Slowly reduce to below 5	60–80
Narcissus bulbs	450	35	175	Rapidly reduce to below 18	60–70

unit for each fan. This is because it is extremely difficult to distribute the efflux from one heater evenly among the fans, which can lead to some of the crop becoming severely overheated.

The heater might also be used during stage II to add a small amount of heat to reduce the relative humidity (see section 7.8.3). The temperature rise required for this will be much less than for stage I, and usually a rise of 5°C will be adequate.

7.1.1.2 Tulips and other bulbs

Bulbs with only one skin, like tulips and anemones, cannot be bulk dried as described above. This is because, before all the top bulbs are dry, the low relative humidity of the incoming air will cause those at the base of the heap or bin to overdry and shed their skins, and so be devalued or dehydrated. Tulips are normally shallow layer dried at ambient temperatures at 65–70 per cent relative humidity.

7.1.2 Seed drying

Peas and seed crops contain water only within the cell spaces, and thus their drying method will resemble that of stage II in onions.

The amount of moisture in the seed (moisture content) is closely related to the relative humidity of the air that surrounds it, and is termed the 'equilibrium moisture content'. These values are shown for peas and grass seed in table 7.2.

Table 7.2

Equilibrium moisture content of seeds

Relative humidity (per cent)	Crop equilibrium moisture content (per cent), wet basis			
	Peas	Ryegrass	Onion	Rapeseed
90	24	26	23.5	17.4
85	19	21	19.3	14.3
80	17	18	16.2	11.9
75	15.5	15.5	14.1	10.2
70	14	14.5	12.6	8.8
65	13	13.25	11.5	8.0
60	12.75	12	10.8	7.4
55	12.0	11.25	9.5	6.9
50	11.25	10.5	9.6	6.6
45	10.5	10.0	8.8	6.1

The seed-drying process depends on this relationship to both execute the process and control it. Drying of the crop is achieved by passing air through it with a relative humidity less than that of the existing seed equilibrium. Control of the final moisture content is achieved by controlling the relative humidity of the drying air to that of the desired equilibrium moisture content.

For example, air at 70 per cent relative humidity will dry grass seed to 14.5 per cent moisture content or peas to 14 per cent moisture content. The process works in both directions, as seed will absorb moisture from air at higher relative humidity; for example, a batch of peas at 15 per cent moisture content will be rewetted to 17 per cent moisture content if blown with air at 80 per cent relative humidity.

7.1.2.1 Bulk drying

This is a similar method to that for bulbs and onions, except that air of controlled relative humidity is blown into the mass. If the relative humidity of the incoming air is too high, it is reduced before it enters the crop by the addition of a small amount of heat, under the control of a humidistat.

The airflows are similar to those used in stage II for onions — 0.05 m³/s per tonne — but owing to the closer packing of the seeds, it requires a higher pressure to force it through the mass. The fan will need to develop a pressure of 200 Pa for every metre depth of peas, and 800 Pa per metre depth of brassica seed. The depth that can be dried is related to the moisture content and speed of the drying front. Normally this limits peas to 2.5 m, freshly harvested seeds to 1.2 m, and small seeds, like brassicae, to 1 m.

Attempts to increase the drying rate by adding too much heat will only lower the relative humidity of the air below that which is desired. This will in turn dry the bottom layers of the bulk to a very low moisture content, but not increase the drying rate of the upper layers. In fact, if the heat addition is very high, the saturated air can cool and condense into water on the upper layers, thus increasing their moisture content.

7.1.2.2 Continuous flow

Seeds can be dried using high volumes of hot (50–90°C) air. The heat added lowers the relative humidity drastically below the equilibrium moisture content, so the drying is carried out in a thin layer of seeds, and the process stopped when the correct moisture content is reached.

In most systems the seeds are carried through the hot airflow on a perforated conveyor or between two vertical perforated sheets as a thin column. The speed at which the seeds pass through the hot section is adjusted to suit the required moisture content removal. It is possible to dry small amounts of seeds in a batch process. using a perforated tray to hold the seeds in the hot air blast. The tray is emptied and refilled for each batch. The temperature of the drying air must be related to the requirements of the seeds. If the air is too hot, germination will be impaired. Also large seeds like peas and beans can be split by the expansion of the water vapour tapped within the seed coat. When a large amount of moisture has to be removed, it is better to pass it through the drier two or three times, removing a small amount at each pass.

7.1.3 Drying flowers and ornamentals

The main requirement when drying these products is to maintain the structure and appearance. Because flowers and ornamentals are fragile, they need to be carefully arranged in the drier, so the foregoing drying methods will be unsuitable. Some subjects will dry satisfactorily if they are hung in bunches in a dry atmosphere, the air conditions being controlled to ensure that the product dries before it moulds, but not being so severe as to discolour or otherwise spoil it. Subjects with fleshy leaves or petals must be supported during drying, to prevent moisture content differentials causing them to curl. The usual method is to bury them carefully in an absorbent material, such as silica gel sand.

7.2 CROP STORAGE METHODS

7.2.1 Crop requirements

Long-term cool storage is possible for many types of root vegetable: fruit, such as apples and pears, some nursery stock species, and some flower bulbs. Most 'leafy' crops, soft fruit and flowers can be stored only for a few days.

Deterioration of the product starts as soon as it is harvested. the time for this to become significant in ambient conditions depends on the product; a strawberry or cauliflower might be unmarketable in 2–3 days, while for an onion or potato it might take several months for noticeable deterioration to occur.

Because the product is alive when harvested, it continues to respire, so the first signs of deterioration will be moisture loss. Most fruits also continue to develop or ripen, typified by changes in taste, colour or texture. Tubers and biennial roots will eventually show signs of regrowth. Cut or damaged surfaces will oxidise, with a distinct colour change, and sap or moisture exuding from these areas can promote development of moulds or other rots. In some fruits the ripening process produces ethylene, which can be trapped within the mass and in turn lead to even more rapid ripening.

These events can often be prevented or suppressed by controlling the temperature, humidity or atmospheric composition.

7.2.1.1 Temperature

Under 'cool storage' the crop is held at a temperature that allows it to live, but at a slow rate, and does not materially affect its cell structure. 'Cold storage' is normally carried out at temperatures lower than $-10°C$, which will kill most crops by freezing the cell moisture; this also causes irretrievable damage to the cell structure, so that the character of the produce is changed after thawing. The cell sap freezing point depends on the amount of salts contained in the sap; in most crops it is slightly below the freezing point of pure water ($0°C$). Onions, for example, do not freeze solid until $-2°C$. In some crops damage will occur above water freezing point. Tomatoes, for example, can be severely damaged at $+2°C$.

The recommended storage temperature for a selection of vegetables is shown in table 7.3, and those for fruit and white cabbage under controlled atmosphere in table 7.4.

Table 7.3

Storage conditions of vegetables

Crop	Temperature (°C)	Relative humidity (per cent)	Storage period
Red beet	1–3	over 95	4–7 months
Winter white cabbage	0	90–95	7 months
Carrots (topped)	0–1	over 95	6–7 months
Leeks	0–1	over 95	6–8 weeks
Onions (bulb)	−1–0	60–80	10 months
Potatoes (ware)	3.5–4.5	90–95	7 months
Potatoes (processing)	7–10*		

*Processing potatoes require relatively high storage temperatures because of 'sweetening'. This is a reaction to cold, by which some of the tuber's starch is converted to sugar to provide extra energy. The sugar formed can caramelise during cooking to produce black crisps or chips. The high storage temperature is, however, above that needed to suppress growth, and artificial sprout suppressants have to be introduced to the mass.

7.2.1.2 Humidity

The relative humidity of the air in the store is also important to storage life. Many crops require high humidity to counteract moisture loss. Carrots require such a high humidity that even humidification of the store air is insufficient, and they are best stored in polyethylene-lined bins.

Table 7.4
Recommended temperature and gas conditions for controlled atmosphere stores
(based on data from ADAS, East Malling Research Station, and Food Research Institute)

	Temperature (°C)	No scrubber		Using a scrubber			Note
		%CO$_2$	Terminate	%CO$_2$	%O$_2$	Terminate	
Apples							
Bramley's Seedling	3.5–4.5	8–10	May	5	–	–	
Cox's Orange Pippin and its sports	3.5–4.0	5	Early Jan.	5 / <1	3 / 2	February / Late March	1
Crispin	3.5–4.0	8	April	–	–	–	
Egremont Russet	3.0–3.5	6–8	January	5	3	Early March	
Laxton's Superb	3.5–4.5	6–8	March	7–8	3	Late March	
Worcester Pearmain	0.5–1.0	7–8	February	5	3	Mid March	
Pears							
Beurré Hardy		–	–				
Conference		–	–				
Doyenne du Comice	–1 to –0.5	–	–	<1	2	Late April	2, 3
Williams bon Chrétien		–	–				
White cabbage	0			5	3	July	

Notes
1. Core flush risk after cool seasons or after prolonged storage in 5 per cent CO$_2$ regimes. Use 2 per cent O$_2$ level for storage beyond February. For this regime ensure O$_2$ level does not fall below 1.6 per cent; carry out regular independent checks of O$_2$ levels using portable analyser and drawing atmosphere sample direct from store.
2. Ensure that CO$_2$ level remains below 1 per cent and O$_2$ does not fall below 1.8 per cent. Cool to –1°C before establishing low O$_2$ regime.
3. Unscrubbed CA storage is no longer recommended for pears.

Lily bulbs are also highly susceptible to moisture loss, and are often stored in wet peat at $-2°C$, where the peat freezes and prevents moisture loss from the bulb.

Potatoes and white cabbage are best stored at 90–95 per cent relative humidity, the former to discourage sprouting, the latter to dry the outer leaves into a 'skin' which prevents further dehydration or mould spoilage.

Onions and dry bulbs require a lower relative humidity of between 65 and 75 per cent to prevent storage moulds developing.

7.2.1.3 Controlled atmosphere (CA)

The ripening process of apples, pears and some vegetable crops can be further inhibited by modifying the oxygen and carbon dioxide levels in the storage atmosphere. The recommended atmospheres for some commonly stored products are shown in table 7.4.

It is desirable to control the levels of ethylene in CA stores or those stores in which the air leakage is minimal because of their construction. Ethylene has the effect of encouraging ripening. This is obviously undesirable in long-term storage. Alternatively some crops like tomatoes, bananas or flower bulbs might require an enhanced ethylene level just before removal from the store, to encourage ripening or flower initiation.

7.2.2 Ambient air cooling

The simplest method for holding crops through winter and early spring is to ventilate the store with cold ambient air. This involves a fan system which is controlled automatically by a differential thermostat system. This compares the temperatures of the crop and the outside air. If the outside air is significantly cooler (typically 2–3°C) than the crop, and the crop is above its desired temperature, then the fan blows air into the store until the crop and the outside air approach the same temperature. The differential temperature setting must take into account the heat rise over the fan (see section 7.5), and ensure that the outside air will have a significant cooling effect. Most systems also incorporate a 'frost protection' over-ride, so that the crop cannot be ventilated with air at a temperature that might damage it.

As this system operates only when the outside conditions are cool, the crop must be insulated against heat gain during times of high ambient temperature. The safe storage period using ambient cooling will depend on the crop temperature requirements; for example, it can hold potatoes from October until early April, but onions from only November to late February.

7.2.3 Refrigerated cooling

Refrigerated cooling can guarantee a crop storage temperature for the whole of the required storage period, independent of ambient temperature.

7.2.3.1 Direct cooling

The store air is passed through a cooling coil. This can be either 'direct expansion' in which the refrigerant gas flows through the coil or indirect expansion in which the refrigerant chills a mixture of water and salt (brine) or water and glycol antifreeze, and the cooled liquid is circulated through the coil.

In most systems the store air is forced over heat exchanger coils using in-built fans, or as part of the main store air movement. It is possible in some situations to site banks of refrigerant pipes in the store ceiling, so that the cold air they produce drops through the stored produce by convection.

One unfortunate side effect of cooling the air in high humidity stores by refrigeration is dehumidification. This is caused by the air being cooled below its dewpoint during its passage through the coil, and shedding some of its moisture in the form of condensation or ice, depending on the coil temperature.

It is impossible to eliminate this effect, as the coil must operate below air temperature to have any cooling effect, but it can be minimised by designing for the least possible air temperature drop (TD) across the coil. The recommended TD for high humidity storage is 1–2°C. The coil airflow rate is, however, limited by the maximum speed at which the air can travel through it. This maximum is not only dependent on increased air resistance, because at very high speeds the condensing water can be removed as droplets which will saturate anything directly downstream or cause ice build-up in the discharge ducting. The limiting airspeed is normally 2–4 m/s.

It should be noted, however, that the 'temperature drop' quoted for a direct expansion coil usually refers to the difference between the air temperature and the refrigerant gas temperature, instead of the 'air on/air off' difference. The two values are not directly comparable, as the air TD depends on the coil design and airflow through it. A rough estimate of air TD can be obtained using equation (7.2) if the coil rating in kW and the airflow in m^3/s is known; alternatively the airflow needed to produce a required TD in a coil of given rating can be estimated.

It will be seen that the combined effects of low air TD and air velocity limits will result in a coil with a large face area.

7.2.3.2 Wet air indirect systems
While this system has been developed predominantly for rapid cooling
(see section 7.3), it has also proved to be well suited to maintaining the
temperatures of high humidity stores holding, for example, carrots or
nursery stock. The 'ice bank' type will also enable the refrigeration unit
to operate only during 'off peak' power periods, but will still maintain
the cooling effect during the rest of the day.

7.2.3.3 Jacketed store
In this sytem the crop is held within a sealed, non-insulated chamber,
sited inside the insulated structure (figure 7.1). There are spaces between
all surfaces of the chamber (walls, ceiling and floor) and the corresponding parts of the store that form the 'jacket' through which cold air
can circulate. As the air within the jacket is sealed from the crop
chamber, it does not need to be of high humidity and, therefore, can
be cooled with a refrigeration unit chosen for maximum cooling efficiency rather than for minimum dehumidification effect. The crop in the
chamber is cooled by internal air circulation over the cold jacket
surfaces. In most stores the circulation is solely due to convection, no
fans being used because they would represent an additional heat load.

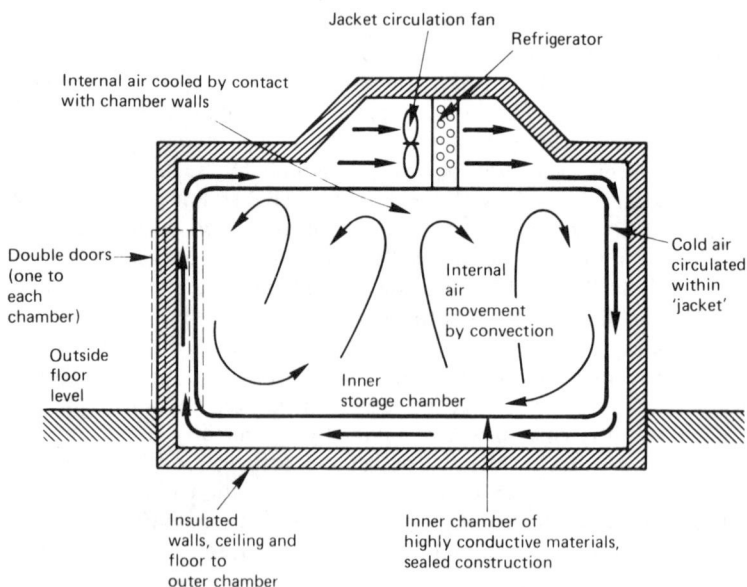

Figure 7.1 Jacketed store.

The vapour given off by the produce is held within the chamber atmosphere, with any surplus condensing on the chamber walls. It is normally allowed to collect on the floor so that it can re-evaporate if the relative humidity of the chamber falls for any reason. The jacket space needs careful design so that the cold air is circulated evenly around all the chamber surfaces. In poorly designed systems it is possible to freeze areas of the chamber surface if the full blast of cold air is concentrated on them.

7.2.4 Calculation of cool store refrigeration capacity
The cooling load is made up of four items:

(a) Structural heat gain.
(b) The heat generated by fan motors, lights, workers, machines operating inside, etc.
(c) The heat given off by the crop respiration (metabolic heat).
(d) The heat to be removed, if cooling.

(a) Structural heat gain
This consists of heat in-leakage through the walls, roof and floor, and also that brought in as warm air draughts.
The heat gains in W/°C temperature difference are

Side wall 1:	length × height × U value	= W/°C
Side wall 2:	length × height × U value	= W/°C
Ends:	length × average height × 2 × U value	= W/°C
Roof:	length × width of one side × 2 × U value	= W/°C
Floor:	length × width × U value	= W/°C
Air in-leakage:	length × width × average height × air changes/h × 0.36	= W/°C
	Total heat gain per °C	= W/°C

$$(7.3)$$

Where the crop is to be cooled during the autumn and held until the summer, it is usual to calculate the heat gain at both these times, because part of the summer cool-holding capacity can be used for cooling in autumn when the outside temperatures are lower.

Heat gain at cooling time (kW) =

$$\frac{\text{heat gain per °C (from equation (7.3)) × design temp. diff. (°C) (autumn)}}{1000}$$

$$(7.4a)$$

Heat gain during hottest time of storage (kW) =

$$\frac{\text{heat gain per }^\circ C \text{ (from equation (7.3)) } \times \text{ design temp. diff. (}^\circ C\text{) (summer)}}{1000}$$

(7.4b)

(b) Heat generated by ancillaries
The heat load from fan motors on the cooler unit might have to be guessed initially, and then recalculated when a more accurate size of cooler unit has been established.

Heat from ancillaries = motor kW + light kW + etc   (7.5)

(c) Respiration (metabolic) heat
The heat given off by a range of common crops is given in table 7.5.

Table 7.5

Respiration rates and specific heats of selected crops
(based on ADAS data)

Crop	Respiration heat (W/tonne) at a temperature (°C) of				Specific heat (kJ/kg)
	5	10	15	20	
Beet red	20.0	31.5	48.7	54.4	3.76
Brussels sprouts	85.9	143.2	214.8	257.7	3.67
Cabbage spring	74.5	85.9	105.9	114.6	3.92
Calabrese	166.1	300.7	572.8	687.4	3.85
Cauliflower	97.3	128.9	191.9	360.8	3.88
Lettuce	63.0	74.5	143.2	243.4	4.01
Peas (in pod)	174.7	372.3	515.5	730.0	3.30
Spinach	200.5	229.1	343.7	429.0	3.93
Sprouting broccoli	343.7	486.8	787.6	1217.2	3.85
Sweet corn	157.5	257.7	406.6	601.4	3.30
Watercress	103.1	229.1	389.5	592.8	3.97
Carrots	48.7	54.4	68.7	94.5	3.80

$$\text{Respiration heat (kW)} = \frac{\text{tonnes of crop} \times \text{respiration heat rate (table 7.5)}}{1000}$$

(7.6)

(d) Cooling load
This is determined from the crop weight, container weight, their specific heats (from table 7.5), the required temperature reduction and the time during which this can be achieved. The 'pulldown' time is somewhat subjective, but in the absence of other information a drop of 1–2°C per day for vegetables and 3–5°C per day for fruit will produce a reasonable performance (for 'rapid cooling', see section 7.3).

Cooling load (kW) =

$$\frac{\text{tonnes} \times 1000 \times \text{temp. reduction (}^\circ\text{C)} \times \text{specific ht (kJ/kg }^\circ\text{C)}}{3600 \times \text{pulldown time (h)}}$$

$$(7.7)$$

Note: calculation (7.7) has to be done for both the product and the container.

(e) Total heat load

Total load (kW) at pulldown =
kW loads from equations (7.4a) + (7.5) + (7.6) + (7.7)   (7.8a)

Total load (kW) at hottest time of storage =
kW loads from equations (7.4b) + (7.5) + (7.6)   (7.8b)

(f) Plant capacity

The refrigeration unit must be capable of extracting the calculated heat load in a daily running time net of periods for defrosting. Defrost allowance depends on store and evaporator temperatures, as shown in table 7.6.

Table 7.6

Defrost allowance times

Defrost method	Store temp. (°C)	Evap. temp. (°C)	Plant running time in 24 h
None	Above 2	Above −1	22
Off cycle	Above 2	Below −1	16
Powered	Below 2	Below −1	20

Thus for a power defrosted store the plant capacity should be 24/20 times the heat load calculated from equation (7.8a) or (7.8b).

Sometimes an extra margin is allowed to cover plant deterioration or uncertainties in calculation data. This margin should not exceed 10 per cent and is often assumed to be covered within the defrost allowance.

Refrigeration plant duty (kW) =

$$\text{load from equation (7.8a) or (7.8b)} \times \frac{24}{\text{plant running time (h)}}$$

$$(7.9)$$

7.3 RAPID COOLING SYSTEMS

There is an increasing interest in cooling fruit and vegetables immediately after harvest so that they can be delivered to the retailer in a chilled form with minimum loss of quality. This technique is popularly termed 'cold chain distribution'. The first stage in the cold chain is to lower the produce temperature from the ambient at which it has been harvested to 7°C or less within 6–18 hours.

7.3.1 Conventional, direct expansion stores
The normal direct or indirect expansion cold store is not well suited for this because its refrigeration capacity will have been designed for cool holding and possibly slow cooling. There are occasions where a large store will cool a small amount of product — for example, using a 30 tonne apple store for cooling two or three pallet loads of strawberries. This is achieved by placing thin layers of produce on to trays that have proud cornerposts which create a series of horizontal gaps when stacked (potato chitting trays, for example). The pallet loads of trays are stood in line, and the top and sides covered by a sheet to form a tunnel. One end of the sheeted stack is placed against the cooler inlet so that the recirculating cold air is drawn through the 'tunnel'. In stores with high-level coolers the same effect can be achieved using a separate fan to *draw* through the stack, or the crop can be put into boxes and force ventilated by the means described in section 7.4.2.

An additional problem stems from the dehydrating effect of the cooler, which can cause loss of quality in most types of produce.

7.3.2 Wet air cooling (figure 7.2(a), (b))
The air is cooled by direct contact with water chilled to 0.5°C in a 'cooling tower'. This is a vertical column filled with a matrix of plastic extrusions; these divide the water flow into a number of thin streams to give it maximum exposure to the air flowing through the tower. This method gives a better transfer of heat between the air and the water than if the water was atomised in the airstream. The airflow is either across the tower (crossflow) or up the tower (counterflow). The latter method is more effective as the air is progressively cooled and, immediately prior to leaving the top of the tower, is in contact with the coldest water.

The air leaves the tower at a temperature close to the water temperature and fully saturated. The cooling capacity of a tower is dependent on the chilled water supply rate, fan capacity and tower cross-section. There are two methods for producing chilled water.

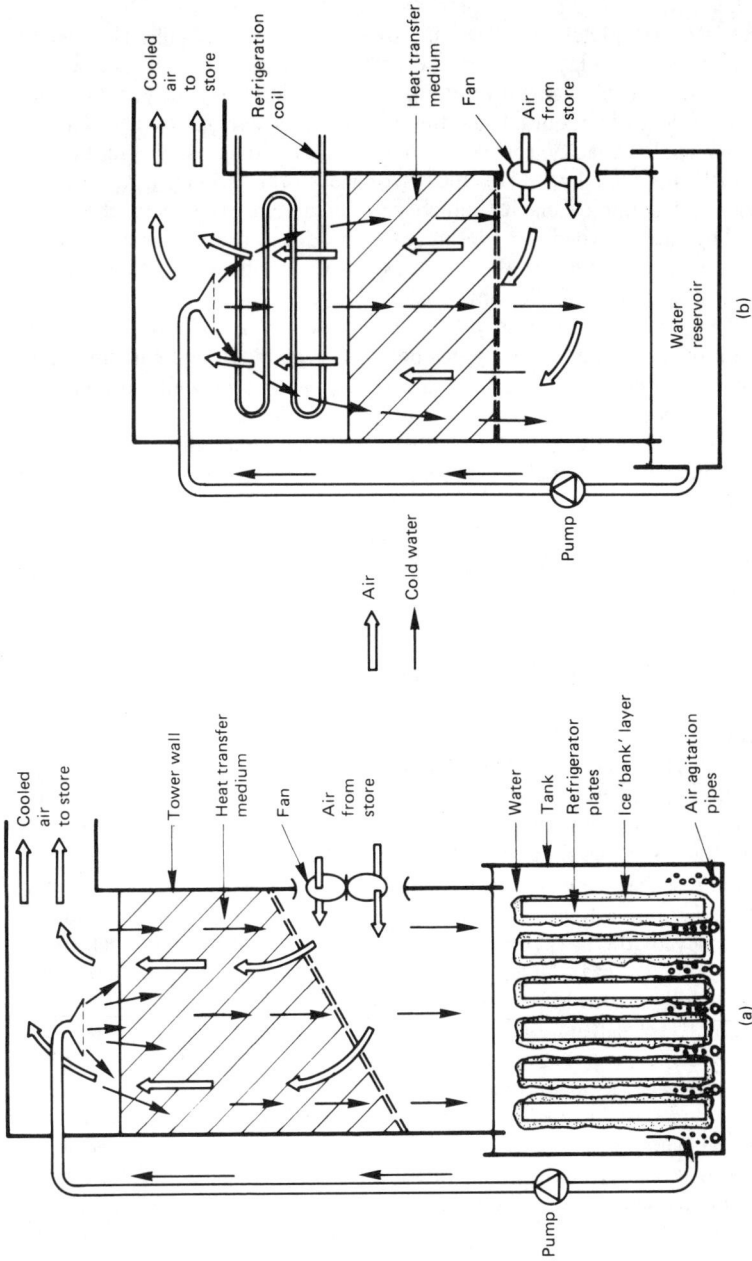

Figure 7.2 (a) Ice bank cooler. (b) Spray chiller cooler.

7.3.2.1 Ice bank (figure 7.2(a))

Refrigeration plates are fitted in rows across a water tank. The water freezes on the plates to form a series of ice blocks with free water between. The ice can be built up and used independently, when the cooling load is required by the tower. It is normal to use a relatively small capacity refrigeration unit to build ice slowly but continually on the plates. The blocks of ice so formed give a reserve, or 'bank' of cooling capacity which can be melted off to give the high cooling rates needed for the incoming produce. The refrigeration unit is controlled by sensing the ice thickness on the plates, so that it runs until it has built a 50–60 mm layer of ice.

The ice is melted evenly from the plates by a combination of air agitation (from perforated pipes between each plate) and ensuring that the returning water is distributed evenly across the tank surface. In most cases the cooling tower is placed above the tank so that the water runs back directly, but if the tower is smaller than the tank a water distribution system will be needed.

The alternative to using a small compressor running continuously is a larger unit which runs only during periods of cheaper power availability; the cost benefit of this latter will however be reduced somewhat by the more expensive plant.

7.3.2.2 Spray chiller (figure 7.2(b))

The water is chilled by spraying it over refrigeration pipes. These are either placed in the top of the tower, above the medium, or across the top of the chilled water tank, to cool the returning water. The refrigeration plant operates at an evaporation temperature of $-5°C$, so the chilling pipes run with only a thin glaze of ice. This system does not have the reserve cooling capacity of the icebank.

Because heat transfer from the plates to the water through a layer of ice is poorer than the direct plate/water transfer, the refrigeration efficiency of the ice plate compressor will be relatively low. Therefore it is normal to find a larger compressor on an ice bank plant than on the direct chiller of the same cooling capacity.

The tower can be used to cool air to temperatures other than $0.5°C$. Higher temperatures are achieved by mixing the chilled water going to the tower head with warmed water returning from the tower.

Produce coming to the cooler from harvesting or packing will normally be handled in boxes or palletised trays. If these are stacked in a store with a 'free blowing' air distribution system, the cold air will not be able to penetrate to the centre of the mass to produce the necessary cooling effect. If rapid heat removal uses any cold air system, the air must be forced through the produce mass, the most common system for this being based on the box ventilation systems described in section 7.4.2.

7.3.3 Hydrocooling

This can be used on crops that are washed as part of their preparation for market, such as carrots and leeks, or are handled wet, such as watercress. This method is less well suited to leafy produce, because the water it retains makes handling difficult and might lead to anaerobic deterioration in the pack. Heat transfer between produce and water is much faster than between produce and air. Using hydrocooling the field heat can be removed in 20–30 minutes instead of the several hours that would be needed using even forced cold air.

The crop can be either immersed in a tank of chilled water or deluged with chilled water as it passes along a perforated conveyor.

In either case pieces of crop, soil and other contaminants are washed off, which leads to general fouling of the water and high counts of bacteria. Because of the high refrigeration load and cost of mains water, the bulk of the chilled water is recirculated or stays within the immersion tank over long periods of cooling. Only a small amount of water is renewed by replacement of the water carried out with the product.

The problem is worst in immersion systems because the water stays within the tank and the debris either accumulates as sediment or floats on the surface. The conveyor system uses a separate water-holding tank, thus there is opportunity to screen the water returning from the conveyor to remove a large percentage of solid debris. Some systems also include water treatment facilities, which are able to remove harmful bacteria but do not lower the pollution level caused by the plant debris.

In either system it is usual to chill the water using refrigeration pipes in the holding tank; these can be operated as ice bank plates to provide a reserve capacity for fluctuating loadings.

7.3.4 Vacuum cooling

This relies on the cooling effect of water vapour evaporating from the produce. Evaporation is possible only by reducing the air pressure around the product to below its water saturation vapour pressure. At the temperatures associated with produce cooling, the pressure has to be reduced to about 500 Pa (absolute), about (1/200th) atmospheric pressure, to create the necessary evaporation down to $0°C$. This requires a sophisticated vacuum pump capable of handling both air and the water vapour removed.

To avoid overloading the pump with water vapour it is recondensed on refrigeration coils placed within the chamber.

The produce to be cooled is placed within a sealed chamber built to withstand the forces created by the vacuum. In the U.K. cylindrical chambers are used, while rectangular shaped chambers are used in the U.S.A. The cylinder is a stronger structure but involves wasted space when it contains a rectangular load. The U.S. shape more closely fits the produce load, thus reducing the surplus air to be exhausted.

Vacuum cooling is more effective on produce that has a large surface area to mass, such as a lettuce, rather than a compact shape, such as a courgette. Cooling times of 20–40 minutes are typical on suitable produce. At 500 Pa (abs.) the water evaporation rate can cool the product to below freezing, so control probes are placed in the crop, which stop the process when the required temperature is reached. The vacuum cooler is able to abstract heat from produce in packages, provided that there is provision for some air escape, and is thus able to cool produce at the point of despatch in its final package.

The produce loses between 1 and 3 per cent of its weight because of the water removed, but this is undetectable in terms of produce quality. Some crops can be sprayed with water before cooling, so that part of the evaporation takes place from the added water rather than totally from within the crop.

U.K. produced cylinder chambers are made to hold between two and five pallets of produce. The chamber might have one door, with the product going in and out at the same end, or two doors for a through flow pattern. The pallets are carried into the chamber on powered roller conveyors.

7.3.5 Cryogenic cooling

This uses the latent heat of evaporation of a gas, usually liquid nitrogen or solid CO_2 (dry ice). These gases are also extremely cold in these forms, the 'boiling' temperature of liquid nitrogen being $-196°C$ and that of $CO_2 - 78.5°C$. Despite this, the majority of heat is extracted by the latent heat needed to return the liquid or solid back to a gas, rather than the effects of warming to ambient temperature.

The produce is cooled by conveying it through a tunnel into which the gas evaporates. At the above temperatures the produce will freeze and thus be ruined as a 'fresh market' product. This problem is prevented by careful control of the evaporation rate and conveyor speed.

The system is relatively cheap to install but expensive to run. Its main advantage is in cooling crops like soft fruit, which have a short seasonal requirement, and where the grower has no other uses for a high capital cost system during the rest of the year.

7.3.6 Calculation of rapid cooling plant capacity

The heat removal calculation (7.7) assumes that the crop will give up its heat faster than the refrigeration will take it. In rapid cooling systems the cooling rate will be governed by the produce heat release characteristics, especially the temperature difference between the product and the cooling air. When the crop comes into the store there is a wide temperature difference with the cold air and cooling will be rapid, but as it approaches the cold air temperature, the rate decreases greatly. This is represented graphically in figure 7.3.

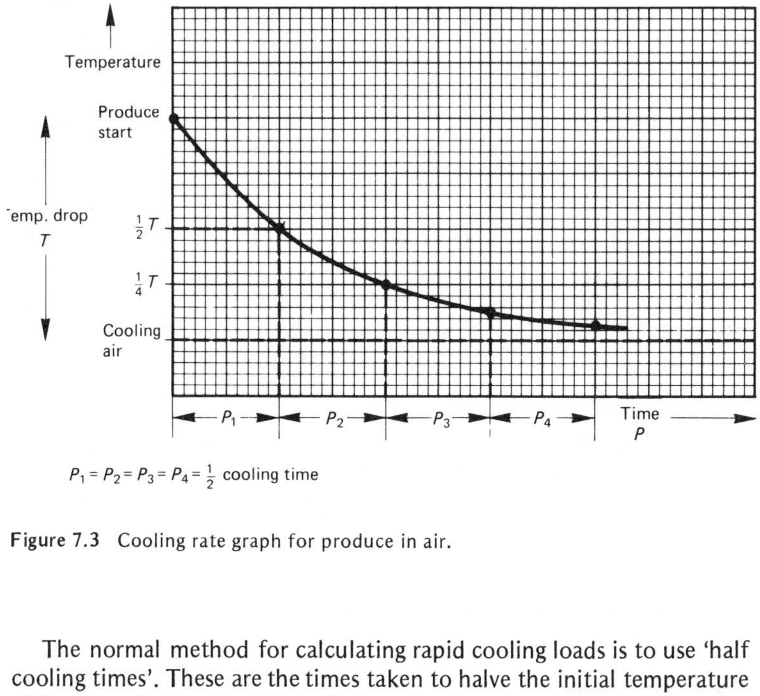

$P_1 = P_2 = P_3 = P_4 = \frac{1}{2}$ cooling time

Figure 7.3 Cooling rate graph for produce in air.

The normal method for calculating rapid cooling loads is to use 'half cooling times'. These are the times taken to halve the initial temperature difference. It has been found that, for any crop, each half cooling period is the same length (figure 7.3), so that if it takes 2 hours to reduce a crop temperature to 50 per cent of its original value, it will take a further 2 hours to reduce it to 25 per cent, a further 2 hours to reduce it to 12.5 per cent and so on. The plant capacity calculations are always based on the temperature drop in the first half cooling period, and the length of this period.

The half cooling time is based on Newton's Law of Cooling, and is, within limits, independent of the produce characteristics, and obtained from the graph curve shown in figure 7.3. The curve can be translated to

$$\text{Half cooling time (h)} = \frac{-0.693 \times \text{target cooling time (h)}}{\text{natural log (ln)} \, \dfrac{(T_2 - T_0)}{(T_1 - T_0)}} \qquad (7.10)$$

where T_0 = cooling air temperature (°C)

$\quad\quad\;\; T_1$ = produce starting temperature (°C)

and $\quad T_2$ = produce target temperature (°C)

The natural logarithm can be found from a scientific calculator or tables; it will appear as a negative value, thus cancelling the initial minus sign.

For example, when T_0 = +0.5°C, T_1 = 24°C, T_2 = 4°C and the target time is 10 hours, the half cooling time is 3.4 hours.

If directly refrigerating the cooling air or water, the plant capacity is calculated by equation (7.7), to give half the temperature drop in 3.4 hours. If a storage (ice bank) system is used, the above capacity will relate to the heat exchanger size, and the refrigeration plant can still be based on the number of hours between each batch being loaded into the cooler.

As most air-based systems cool deep layers of crop in boxes, there will be a delay while the 'cooling front' rises through the mass. The air-flow rate into each box must therefore be based on cooling the topmost layer within the half cooling time. The airflow rate will also depend on the cooling characteristics of the crop, these being determined by practical cooling experiments. This part of the cooling calculation is extremely complex, and ADAS have designed computer programs that calculate the optimum sizes of the various components of rapid coolers.

7.4 AIR DISTRIBUTION AND CIRCULATION

7.4.1 Bulk stores

7.4.1.1 Methods
Air for ventilating or drying the crop is introduced at the base of the heap through a system of floor level ducts or 'laterals'. There are three methods for constructing the duct system.

(a) 'Above ground' laterals are placed in lines on top of the concrete floor as the store is filled. They can be made as tunnels of perforated steel sheet or steel mesh covered, if the mesh is too large for the crop, with hessian, slatted timber in a triangular shape, or tubes of corrugated steel with perforations.

(b) Subsurface or 'level floor' laterals are formed by covering trenches with a perforated material. As these are permanently installed, the cover has to withstand the loads imposed by any wheeled vehicles likely to use the building. A suggested minimum design load is 5 tonnes per wheel. The covers can be spaced slats of concrete, timber or steel for root crops. Seed crops with small grain size use heavy grids covered with finely perforated materials or closely spaced steel slats.

(c) False floors are an extension of the above, where the lateral trench is widened to the point where the whole floor is a series of 'lateral tops' supported on transverse beams. These floors can be made of lengths of timber or concrete sections, with open gaps for root crops, or with perforated mesh across the gaps for seed crops. The false floor can be laid over an existing concrete floor to form a 'drive over' air distribution system. On new installations the flat 'concrete' sub-floor is simpler and easier to construct than a series of sub-floor lateral trenches.

7.4.1.2 Bulk store air distribution system design

Both the main air duct and the lateral system must be designed to supply sufficient air for the purpose, and distribute it evenly without imposing undue restriction on the fan. In most cases a main duct design air speed of 10 m/s is the optimum for avoiding high frictional resistance without creating uneconomically large ductwork, and in many cases laterals are designed to this velocity also, although in some cases 5 or 7.5 m/s is used.

The main air tunnel has to convey the full airflow requirements of the crop if the fans are sited at one end. Each lateral duct has then to carry the portion of this airflow for the crop it is ventilating.

The steps used to design the cross-section of all the ductwork are as follows.

(a)

$$\text{Fan airflow } (m^3/s) = \frac{\text{crop airflow requirement } (m^3/h \text{ per tonne}) \text{ (from table 7.7)} \times \text{crop tonnage}}{3600} \quad (7.11)$$

(b)

$$\text{Main tunnel cross-section } (m^2) = \frac{\text{fan output } (m^3/s) \text{ (from equation (7.11))}}{\text{design airspeed } (m/s)} \quad (7.12)$$

Table 7.7

Crop airflow requirements

Crop	Airflow (m³/h per tonne)
Onions, narcissus bulbs (drying stage I)	450
Onions, narcissus bulbs (drying stage II)	175
Red beet	265
Seeds	175
Potatoes (Dutch practice)	150
(U.K. practice)	70
(U.S. practice)	20

For long runs of main airduct the cross-section can be recalculated at intervals to take account of the portion of the initial airflow already discharged. By this method the tunnel is made in a series of decreasing steps.

(c) The first step in determining lateral cross-section is to calculate the tonnage of crop it serves.

$$\text{Tonnage/lateral} = \frac{\text{depth of crop} \times \text{lateral length} \times \text{lateral spacing}}{\text{bulk density of crop (table 3.1)}}$$

$$(7.13)$$

The airflow per lateral is calculated in equation (7.11), using the tonnage from equation (7.13) and its cross-section calculated by equation (7.12).

(d) The air tends to travel along a duct until it is caused to escape by increasing resistance created by the closed end. In a parallel duct, sufficient resistance to cause escape might exist only in the latter part of its length, thus little air will escape at the inlet end. This problem can be reduced by progressively reducing its cross-sectional area, by tapering or stepping; this creates a better resistance profile and hence a more even air output per metre run. The step sizes are worked out as in (c) above, at a number of distances along the lateral. Tapering can be calculated by the same method, but a 'rule of thumb' tapering is to decrease the cross-sectional area to one-third of its original area at the stopped end. Some of the effect of tapering can be obtained by progressively decreasing the size of the outlets towards the stopped end.

(e) Lateral covers should have a minimum free area of perforation, to allow the air to escape without hindrance. The commonly accepted minimum is to have 5 per cent of the total floor area represented by lateral air escape free area. The method for calculating the actual free area requirement of the lateral covering is as follows.

Firstly calculate the percentage of the overall floor area that the lateral surface area represents.

$$\text{Lateral surface area factor (per cent)} = \frac{\text{aggregate surface area of all laterals}}{\text{overall floor area (m}^2)} \times 100$$

$$(7.14)$$

$$\text{Perforation area of lateral (per cent)} = \frac{\text{required free area (per cent)}}{\text{lateral surface area factor (per cent)}} \times 100$$

$$(7.15)$$

Example — a floor measures 18 m long x 9 m wide, with laterals 0.3 m wide and 8.5 m long at 2 m centres, needing an air escape area of 5 per cent.

Using equation (7.14)

$$\text{Lateral surface area factor} = \frac{8.5 \text{ m long} \times 0.3 \text{ m wide} \times 9 \text{ laterals}}{18 \text{ m} \times 9 \text{ m}} \times 100 = 14.2 \text{ per cent}$$

Using equation (7.15)

$$\text{Perforation free area} = \frac{5}{14.2} \times 100 = 35.2 \text{ per cent}$$

Where proprietary perforated mesh is to be used, the free area calculated above and the maximum hole size to retain the crop will be sufficient to specify the mesh. If gapped slats are to be used, the gap width for a given slat width can be calculated as follows

$$\text{Slat gap (mm)} = \frac{\text{slat width (mm)} \times \text{required free area (per cent)}}{100}$$

$$(7.16)$$

Thus if the laterals in the above example were to be fitted with 75 mm wide slats, using equation (7.16)

$$\text{Slat gap (mm)} = \frac{75 \times 35.2}{100} = 26.4 \text{ mm}$$

(f) The perforation or gap must be small enough to retain the crop without its becoming wedged or sitting partially submerged in the hole. This latter is important where loading shovels are used on flat floor systems, because any object so positioned will be sliced by the bucket. Conversely, gaps for root crops should not be so narrow as to allow loose soil to pack in.

The shape of the perforation is also important. A correctly sized round hole can still allow a spherical object, like a pea, to nestle partially in it and effectively block its airflow. The best shape for most seeds is either a diamond or a long slot.

(g) The spacing of the ducts depends on the airflow requirements for the crop. For drying airflows or high rate ventilation (over 100 m³/h per tonne) spacings should not exceed 1 m or half crop depth, whichever is less. For low rate ventilation (less than 100 m³/h per tonne) the spacing can be 2 m or three-quarters crop depth.

The duct run should not discharge air for the first 500–600 mm of its length, and so should stop the same distance short of the opposite wall. This reduces the tendency for the air to escape by the slightly easier path formed where the crop meets the wall surface.

(h) Air inlets and outlets to the store
It is recommended that the air inlet to the fanhouse, exhaust vents in the building and any recirculation vents between the main building and the fanhouse be sized for an airflow of 5 m/s. The sizes of these openings can be calculated from equations (7.11) and (7.12).

The size calculated refers to the *clear* area of the vent. Any louvre blades or other impediments to flow must be taken into account, and the overall opening size calculated by aggregating the free areas existing between the louvres, plus the sum of the louvre blade thickness.

7.4.2 Box, pallet and tray store ventilation systems

There are five main methods for stacking these stores to ensure that the crop is adequately ventilated.

7.4.2.1 Free circulation

The containers are stacked in blocks and the air is circulated generally around them in the building. This method is simple and allows the building to contain separate stacks of several types of produce without destroying the ventilation pattern. With 'free circulation' air movement the air travels generally around the store, rather than being forced through the produce. The object is to maintain an even environment throughout the store so that the crop responds to its surrounding (see also section 7.4.3.2). As a result, this method is to be recommended only for storage of produce and is not suitable for crop drying or where large amounts of heat are to be extracted.

The ventilation pattern can produce either a vertical or a horizontal airflow. In this type of store the main airflow requirement is to prevent vertical temperature gradients. These are caused by warm air rising towards the roof; it is possible for the roof temperature to be 10–15°C above that at floor level in an unventilated store. Vertical systems, sometimes called 'heat syphons', simply remix these gradients. Horizontal systems can allow the gradients to remain unless they are specially designed to draw in at floor level and discharge at higher levels. In some sophisticated horizontal pattern stores, the discharge ducting is along the wall, built with outlets to suit the gangways between rows of boxes.

7.4.2.2 Underfloor ducting

Boxes are placed over sub-floor laterals similar to those used in bulk stores. The boxes are usually stacked only one high for drying and two or more layers high for storage ventilation. The boxes generally have two-way entry pallet bases, and are loaded with the bases running in the same direction as the duct. The last pallet fork space and any unused portion of the duct are sealed by jamming in foam rubber blocks. Loading by this method does not use the full width of a floor store as the forklift requires room at the wall end to manoeuvre. An alternative is to stack the boxes in a solid block over a number of ducts, and to wrap polyethylene sheet around the sides, which effectively forms a bottom-ventilated drying bin.

7.4.2.3 Forced blowing of closely stacked boxes

A number of boxes are placed together and connected to a fan. The fan can be connected in one of three ways:

(1) Two-way entry pallet boxes placed in line, with pallet spaces connected. The fan is fitted to one end of the run via a fishtail, and the other end is blocked.

(2) As above, except that both outer ends of the pallet base are blocked and the fan is placed in a lid over the central box in the run. Air travels down through this box and under those to either side.

(3) Four-way entry pallet boxes are arranged in a square, with all the outer fork entry slots sealed. The fan blows down a central box, and the air moves in all four directions beneath the box square.

The design of most boxes allows only one layer to be ventilated by these means, but where boxes are made for 'up/down' blowing (see section 7.4.2.4), two layers are possible.

7.4.2.4 Letterbox wall

The letterbox wall uses specially built boxes which can be blown with positive ventilation by connecting the pallet spaces to an air supply duct.

The boxes are placed against an air supply duct, (figure 7.4) which has an outlet slot corresponding to each pallet space in the stack; this gives it the name 'letterbox wall'. The boxes have to be made specially for this purpose, the main point being their ability to fit tightly together

LETTERBOX WALL

Bottom deck sheet needed

Air stop

Main air duct

Bin

Air flap

Air slot 'letter box'

Air blown in along pallet

Air exhausts from space between bin and next base

DRYING WALL BOX

Air exhaust, if upwards blowing, by proud cornerposts or recess in side panels

Clad with T & G board or WBP grade ply

Slatted floor

Side panels extend to base of box

Bearers finish flush with faces

Bottom deck sheet (if required)

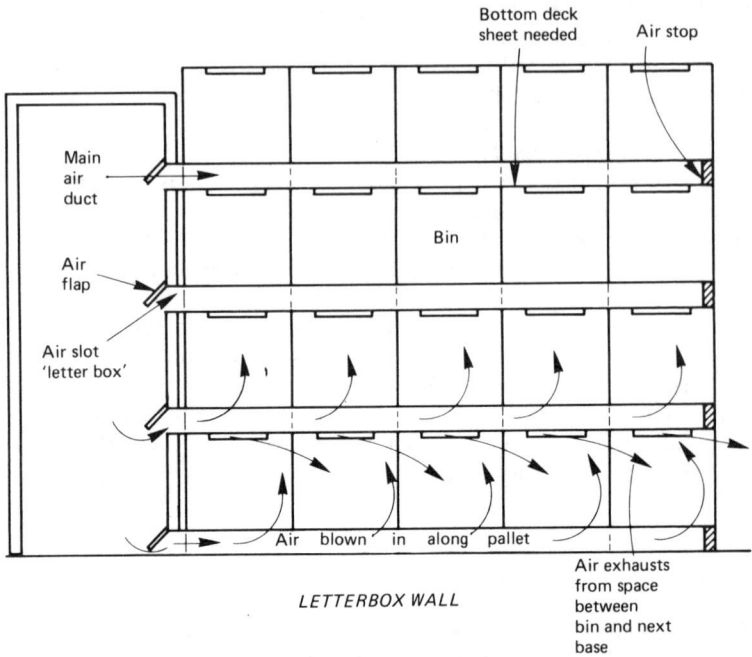

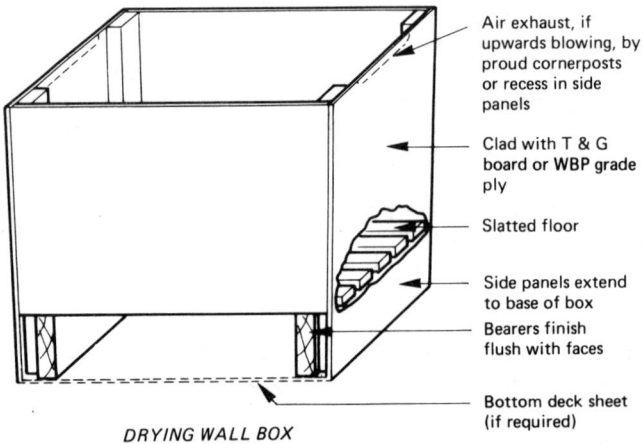

Figure 7.4 'Letterbox' ventilating wall and associated box.

at all points to minimise air loss (figure 7.4). The sides are extended down to cover the pallet base as well, and the pallet runners finish flush and square with the box face.

The box sides must be air-tight, the only effective material for this being ply or other sheet materials. Closely placed boarding, even if tongue and grooved, is unsuitable because gaps will be formed as a result of the timber expanding and contracting with moisture.

The remaining box design depends on the method of air distribution within the stack.

'Up only' blowing (figure 7.4) uses each pallet base as an inlet duct and the air is exhausted by leaving a gap between the top of the sides and the box above. This gap can be formed either by a recess in the top of the side or by the corner posts protruding 20 mm above the sides. The base of the pallet must be air-tight also; this can be built as part of the box only if it is not to be used on a forward rolling forklift tipper, where the forks hinge to tip. For this tipper, an open base pallet is used, and a sheet of 12 mm ply is placed between it and the box beneath to effect the air seal. Some systems use a separate pallet as the duct; this is placed between each box in the stack and feeds into an open-bottomed pallet-based box above.

'Up/down' blowing (figure 7.5) uses alternate pallet spaces as air inlets and exhausts. This requires a box with an open pallet base and sides which fit flush against those of the boxes above and below.

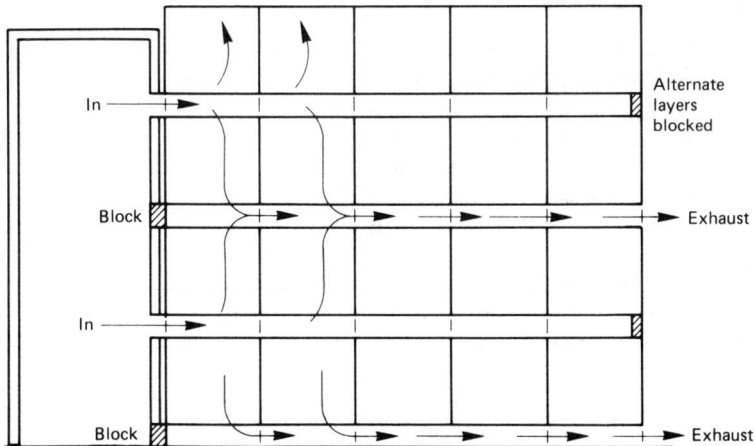

Figure 7.5 Up/down (two-directional) blowing.

The letterbox wall does not have to withstand crop thrust, but does have to resist the buffering forces as the boxes are pushed tightly together by the forklift. It is essential that it does not move as a result of this buffering, otherwise it will break the airseal to those rows on either side. The best method of construction is heavy vertical supports corresponding to the positions of the box corners, with the front, back and top clad with light sheet material. The normal cladding is plywood, but the front face of some walls have been clad with butyl rubber sheet. This effects a good air seal, as it is blown against the box stacks by air pressure in the wall.

The opposite ends of those pallet spaces acting as inlet ducts are sealed with foam rubber blocks. Each letterbox is fitted with an air control flap, to enable the operator to choose the box runs to be ventilated.

It is acknowledged that even the best constructed systems will not be air-tight, up to 50 per cent air leakage is allowed for by *doubling* the design airflow rates shown in table 7.7.

Fans can be placed at one end of the wall, feeding all the letterbox slots, or the wall can be compartmented vertically and small axial fans placed along the top of the wall to serve each section.

Air distribution in a letterbox wall can be uneven. It is normal for those boxes furthest from the fans to receive more air than those nearest it. This problem is caused by a combination of streamlined airflow and low back-pressures in the system, and is worsened by high air velocities and the air spinning or forming a concentrated jet as it leaves the fan. There are several methods available to reduce these problems, the main ones being

(a) Maintaining a low air velocity when blowing only a few boxes, by reducing the fan output accordingly (see section 7.5.4).
(b) Placing the fan at a distance from the first letterbox that allows its discharge efflux to decay to an acceptable speed or to stop rotating. The distance for this to occur is at least 2 fan diameters for an axial fan or 2 m for a centrifugal type.
(c) Creating severe air turbulence by siting the fan so that it discharges into the wall via a 90° bend. This, however, increases fan back-pressure and requires a more powerful fan for the desired output.
(d) Controlling the air inlet or outlet to each bin by adjusting either the gaps in the box base or the outlet slots at the top of the sides.
(e) Making the air in 'up/down' systems exhaust at the same end as the letterbox wall, as shown in figure 7.6. This theoretically gives the air flowing to the furthest box in the row added resistance by making it take the longest return path.

The normal 150 mm pallet base height limits the airflow to that which is sufficient for a row length of 6–7 boxes when drying. The

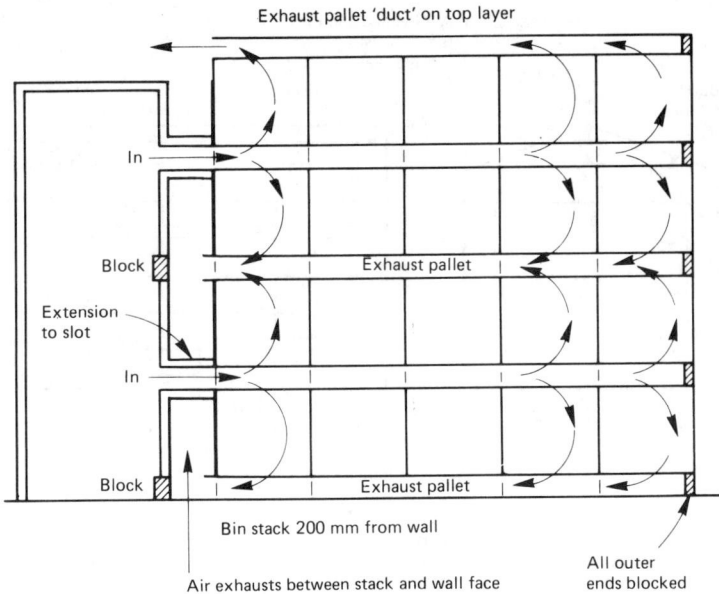

Figure 7.6 Equalised air distribution on a 'letterbox' wall.

practical stacking height limit is 4 boxes; above this, small discrepancies in floor level or box squareness will be magnified to the point where the upper boxes cannot be sealed together adequately.

7.4.2.5 Induced flow

Induced flow uses the pallet spaces for air carrying, like the letterbox, but without using the ducted wall. The boxes are placed in a solid block, with all pallet spaces pointing along the length of the store (figure 7.7(a)). The gaps between the sides of the box stack and the building walls, and the stack top and the roof, are blanked with sheeting. This creates a sealed chamber across the end of the building, and air can only move into this through the pallet spaces. A fan draws the air from this sealed chamber and blows it through ducting to the opposite end; this creates a horizontal air movement, involving flow along the pallet spaces. Only alternate spaces are left open at the fan end, so that the air is drawn along these; it, however, enters all the spaces at the opposite end and that in the blanked runs must thus pass through the boxes to reach the suction chamber. This flow is enhanced by the

A = Recirculation
B = Exhaust
C = Fresh air in

END SECTION
OF EMPTY BUILDING

SIDE SECTION

End of boxes
forms 'letterbox' wall
Alternate layers blocked

(a)

Airflow is redistributed at each break

(b)

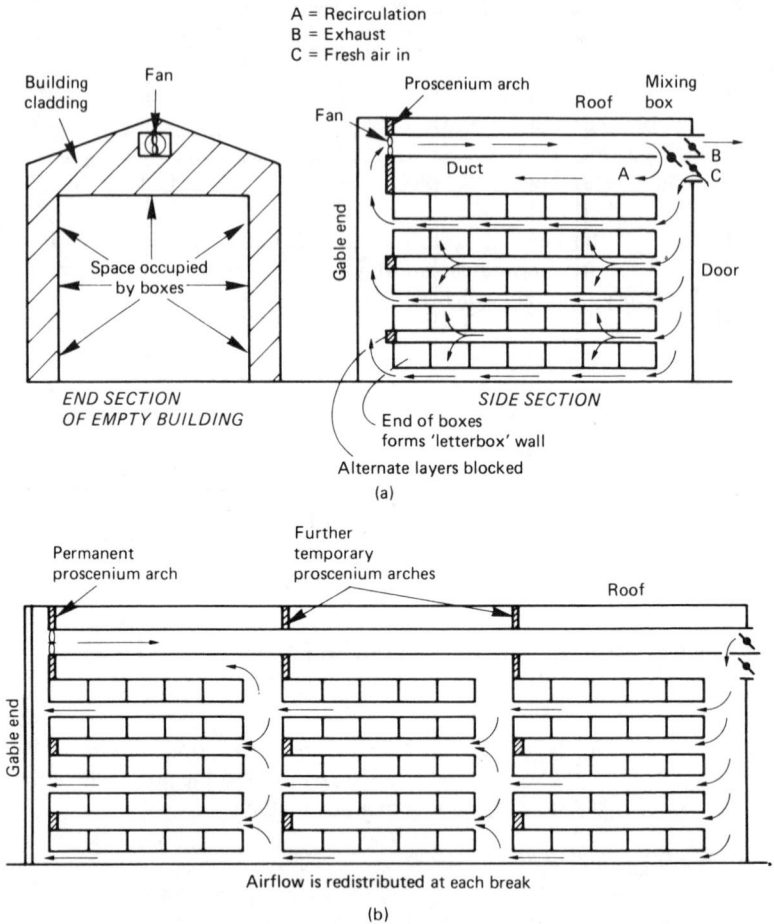

Figure 7.7   (a) Induced box ventilation. (b) Division of long runs in an induced
             ventilation store.

venturi suction created by the high velocity along the open pallet
spaces.

The effect has been found to be most pronounced at the start and
finish of each run. Large stores with long runs of boxes are split into
short blocks, and further blanking is installed after each block, to form
a series of chambers (figure 7.7(b)).

This system is suitable for storage but not drying.

7.4.3 Introducing cooling into stores

7.4.3.1 Bulk stores

Refrigeration can be applied in the form of an evaporator coil in the discharge between the fan and the main duct. For reasons described in section 7.2.3, the coil face area will normally be very large, to produce the cooling effect without severe dehumidification, and requires a specially enlarged main duct. There is also a potential for freezing the crop, because the cold air from the coil is discharged directly into it. If the coil ices severely and restricts airflow, it will produce a small volume of very cold air, which might miss any frost protection cutouts fitted.

The problem of coil face area can be mitigated by totally sealing the fanhouse and placing the coil in the return air vent between the store and the fanhouse. By this method, however, the fan heat will be added to the air after cooling, and the resulting slight rise in temperature will lower the humidity by a few per cent.

A further option is to use a dual discharge, free-blowing, cooler in the roofspace to cool the air above the crop, and to circulate this periodically through the crop. By this method, any heat coming in through the roof as a result of solar gain is captured before it affects the crop. It has been found that the crop is partially cooled by natural convection occurring within the crop bulk, where warm air rising from the mass is replaced by cooled roofspace air. Periodic fan ventilation completes the cooling effect and evens any temperature differences within the stack caused by the natural ventilation. Some potato stores using this system have needed the fan to run for only 15 minutes every 6–8 hours to maintain stack temperature.

7.4.3.2 Box, pallet and tray stores

Where cooling is by ambient air, the cold air can be simply introduced by a fan directly into the building, but a more satisfactory system is to use ducting (figure 7.8). This both ensures uniform cold air distribution and improves removal of warm air from all parts.

Where a refrigeration system is used, the coolers are fitted with their own fans and are often sited in the upper parts of the store, towards one side or one end. The cold air is discharged across the store at ceiling level and as it is denser than the warmer air around the produce, drops through the crop by convection. A version of this type of cooler, called the 'dual discharge' evaporator, discharges air in two horizontal directions, and so can be sited towards the centre of the store.

Air distribution from these types of cooler is non-uniform, often leaving areas of the store without adequate ventilation, owing to air short-circuiting (figure 7.9). This effect can be minimised by designing

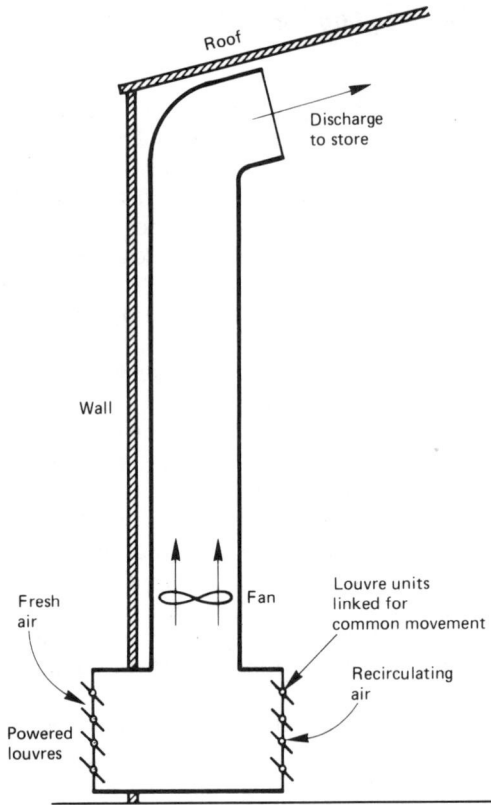

Figure 7.8 Vertical box store ventilation system.

the cooler unit to pick up its return air from ground level and discharge through a series of ducts at roof level. It is possible also to use an independent fan and ductwork system similar to that shown in figure 7.8, to circulate the store air, with the cooler unit discharging its cold air into the circulation created by the main system (see also section 7.4.2.1).

The output of the air circulation fans is normally calculated in terms of building air movement, as the number of empty store volumes circulated per hour, rather than per tonne of produce therein. It has been found that 12–20 volumes/hour is suitable for long-term storage of most crops, and 20–50 volumes/hour is needed where more rapid temperature changes are to be effected.

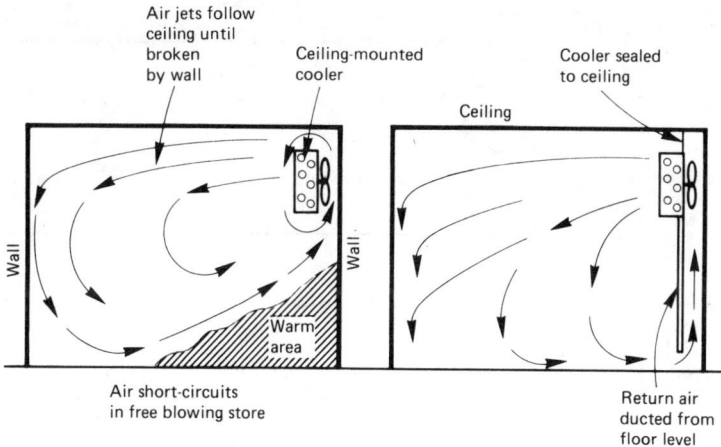

Figure 7.9 Air distribution from ceiling coolers.

The fan output is calculated thus

$$\text{Fan output } (m^3/s) = \frac{\text{empty store volume } (m^3) \times \text{volumes/h}}{3600} \qquad (7.17)$$

7.4.4 Air-handling units

Many stores that use ambient air for cooling or drying will be equipped so that outside air is used only when needed, and the store air recirculated at other times. Some systems are capable of mixing varying portions of outside air with recirculating air to give better temperature control.

The vent openings for air intake and exhaust can be controlled by power-driven doors or louvre blades. Some systems fit 'pressure operated' louvres, which are opened by the action of the fan and fall closed when it stops; these can prove restrictive to the fan when open, and can allow considerable air leakage in strong winds when 'closed'. Powered louvres open and close positively, but there are many more surfaces to seal when closed than there are for the four edges of a single door.

It is possible to link the vent drive motors with the fan controller, so that it will not run until the vents are fully open; this should prevent pressure damage to the building structure.

The simplest method to change from fresh air to a recirculation system, or vice versa, is to use three vents (figure 7.10). Two are in the

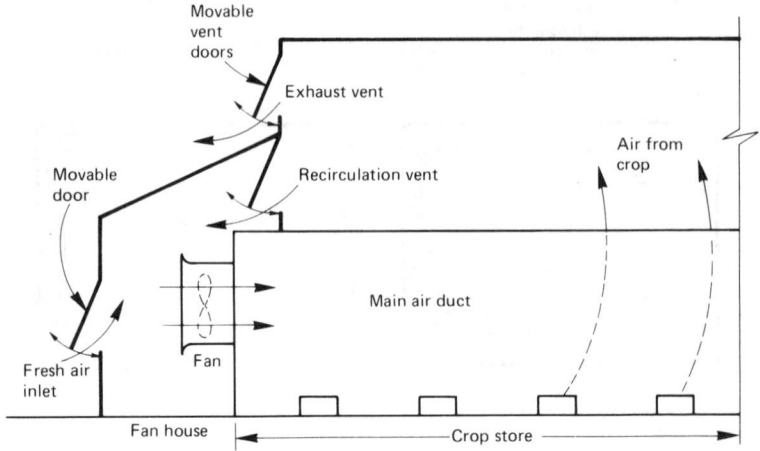

Figure 7.10   Bulk store air mixing and control.

fanhouse — one from outside, the other from the store — and the third is to exhaust air from the store. These are not normally sited so that they can be driven from a common motor, so there is always a risk of the vents not operating in the desired sequence.

A better system uses an air-mixing box, an example of which can be seen in figure 7.8. This has a flap or louvres to determine which air intake vent is to be used. If these are driven by a modulating motor, both vents can be partway for air mixing. The system in figure 7.8 depends on air exhaust through a separate vent. It is possible to combine the exhaust vent into the air-mixing box also (figure 7.11) and use one motorised door or set of louvres. This method also ensures that the airflows within the building are always in the same direction, irrespective of whether the system is on fresh air, recirculation or mixing.

7.5 FANS

7.5.1 Types of fan
The fans used in crop stores will be one of two basic types: centrifugal or axial flow.

7.5.1.1 Centrifugal
The airflow is created by the centrifugal action of a spinning impeller, the air being introduced into the centre of the impeller and expelled

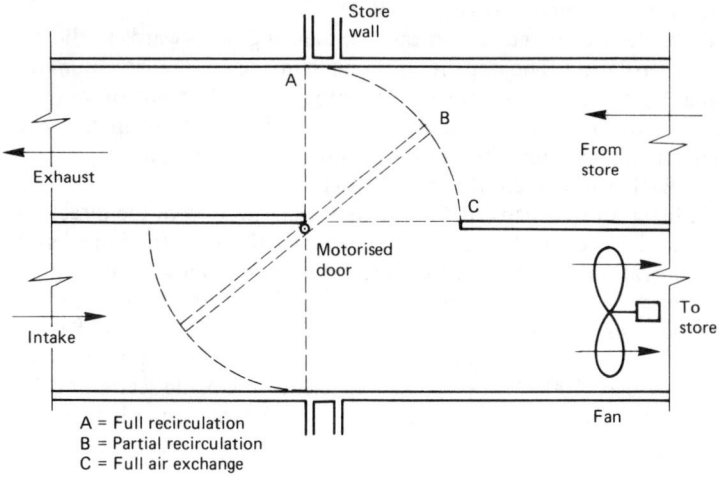

Figure 7.11 Parallel duct mixing box.

through a tangential outlet in the case surrounding it (figure 7.12).
The rotor blades can have one of three basic shapes.

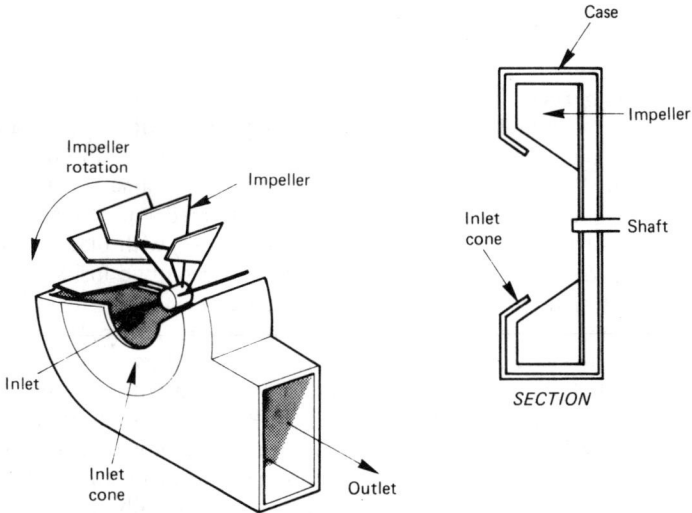

Figure 7.12 Centrifugal fan.

(a) 'Forward curved' (figure 7.13(a))
The blades are curved so that their tips are angled forwards to the direction of rotation. The impeller is normally made up of a large number of small blades, and this has led to its other common name of 'multivane fan'. These fans are normally slow running, quiet in operation and generate high volumes but at low pressures (up to 500 Pa).
(b) 'Backward curved' (figure 7.13(b))
The blade tips are curved so that they trail away from the direction of rotation. Fewer blades (5–12) are normally fitted to the impeller. The fan operates at a higher rotor speed than the forward curved type; this creates a similar airflow but at a much higher pressure. Most backward curved fans in horticultural use can operate at 1500–2000 Pa; those used in industry for applications like forge blowing can generate pressures of over 5000 Pa. For greater efficiency the blade section might be of aerofoil section (like an aeroplane wing) rather than being formed from a flat sheet of metal.
(c) 'Paddle blade' or radial (figure 7.13(c))
The fan blades are flat and arranged along the radial lines of the impeller; like the backward curved, few blades are used. These fans are normally used for handling dirty air, because the blade shape does not interfere with the flow of solid material, and there is a reduced chance of blockage. The speed needs to be high to produce an airflow comparable to the other fan types, but the pressures generated can also be as high as a backward curved type. The efficiency of power use is very low compared to the curved bladed fans.

7.5.1.2 Axial flow

These use a windmill type of action in which the airflow is generated by an impeller fitted with angled blades; the air moves through the impeller in the direction of its shaft axis, hence the name 'axial flow'.

(a) The simplest type of axial fan is often termed a 'propeller'. This has a simple blade resembling an aircraft propeller, with blades either of flat section or of aerofoil section. It may be mounted inside a hole in a flat steel plate (diaphragm mounting, figure 7.14(a)) or inside a ring encompassing the blade tips (bellmouth, figure 7.14(b)). The diaphragm plate allows some air to leave the blade tips by centrifugal action, and thus lowers its performance. The bellmouth prevents this air loss, and converts it into axial motion. Propeller fans are normally made in sizes between 150 mm and 1 m diameter, and operate at speeds from 2900 rpm to 720 rpm. They are normally incapable of generating air pressures much above 250 Pa, thus they are normally used for the simple ventilation of buildings, and not for blowing air through crop bulk mass or complex ductwork.

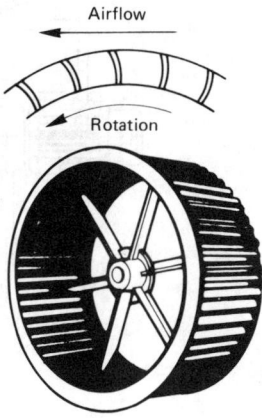

15A Forward
curved
(multivane)

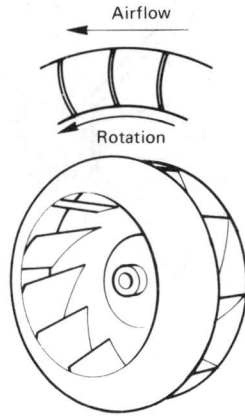

15B Backward
curved

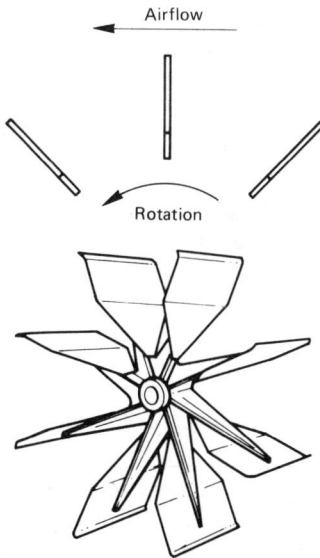

15C Paddle
bladed

Figure 7.13 Centrifugal fan impeller shapes.

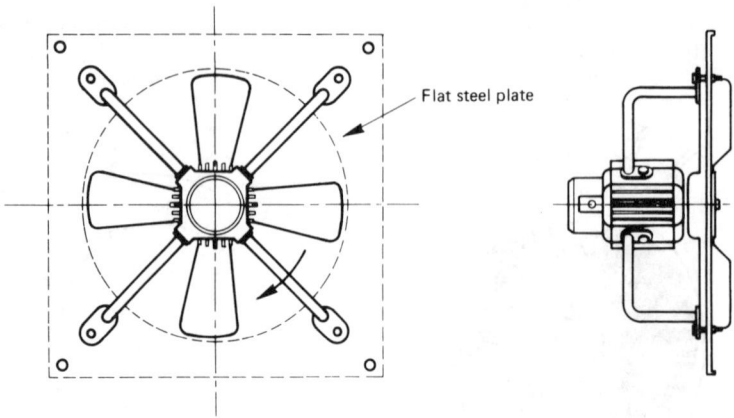

16A Ring or Diaphragm

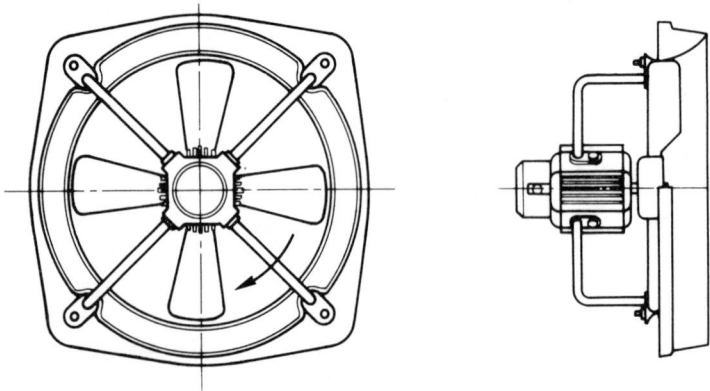

16B Fan with bellmouth

Figure 7.14   Propellor fan mountings (*courtesy Woods of Colchester Ltd*).

(b) The true 'axial flow' fan consists of an impeller with aerofoil section blades mounted within a close fitting cylindrical casing. The casing is at least as long as the blade width (short case type) and often extends to contain the motor as well (long case type). The case prevents losses by centrifugal action, and also prevents air from flowing around the blade tips back to the suction side. These contribute to higher operating pressures, up to 500 Pa being possible from a single impeller.

In most axial flow fans the volume and pressure flow rates can be varied by adjusting the blade angle. A narrow angle to direction of rotation produces low airflow but high pressure, a wide angle the converse. Most fans are purchased with blade angle set to produce the specified duty but, where the original application of the fan has changed, it is possible to reset the angles, provided that the motor has sufficient power for the new duty. When resetting blades, all must be at the same angle, as any blade at a different angle will be understressed or overstressed compared with the others, and this will unbalance the rotor. Fans are produced that have an instantly variable blade pitch system, so that the fan duty can be adjusted to suit the system requirements. In some cases the blade angle can be varied while the fan is running.

(c) The pressure characteristic of an axial fan impeller can be increased by using 'guide vanes'. These are a set of angled blades set in a static ring either in front of or after the impeller, so that the rotating airstream created by the impeller is turned to flow parallel with the case. Guide vanes can increase pressure by 20–30 per cent without increasing the volume flow, and they require a correspondingly greater motor power input to the impeller.

(d) Pressure can also be increased by 'multi-staging' (figure 7.15), in

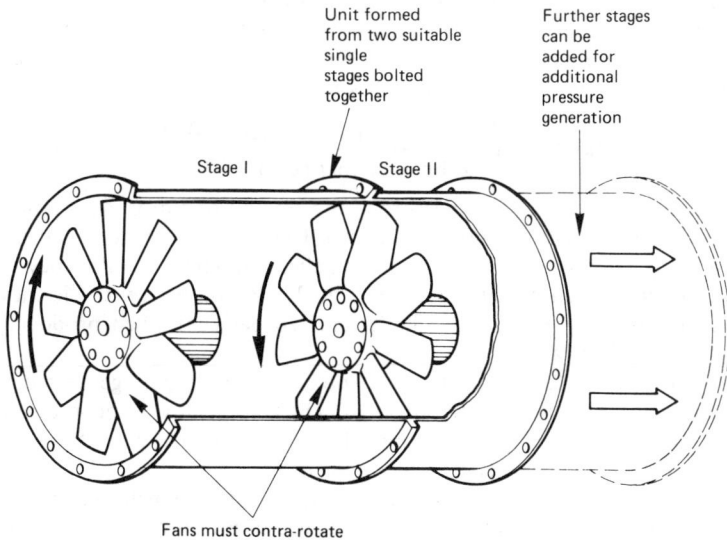

Figure 7.15   Two-stage axial flow fan (*courtesy Woods of Colchester Ltd*).

which two or more impellers are mounted one after another in the same case. Each impeller rotates in the opposite direction to the one before it, so that the rotating airstream from one is intercepted by the blades of the next. The pressure increase by multi-staging is 1.7 times the single impeller pressure with two impellers, and 2.5 times with three impellers; the volume flow remains the same as that of one impeller, but the total power increases accordingly.

7.5.2 Fan laws and theory

The relationships of impeller speed with volume flow, pressure and power input are as follows.

Change in volume flow is proportional to the change of rotor speed. Change in pressure is proportional to the square of the change of rotor speed.

Change in power consumed is proportional to the cube of the change of rotor speed.

For example, if a fan producing 10 m³/s at 200 Pa and consuming 5 kW when running at 500 rpm was to be doubled in speed to 1000 rpm, the output would rise to 20 m³/s (10 × 2), pressure to 800 kPa (200 × 2²) and the power absorbed to 40 kW (5 × 2³).

The power absorbed by a fan is the product of volume flow rate, pressure and impeller efficiency. At ambient air temperatures and pressures, the power input is calculated as follows

$$\text{Power (kW)} = \frac{\text{volume flow } (\text{m}^3/\text{s}) \times \text{pressure (Pa)}}{\text{efficiency (per cent)} \times 10} \qquad (7.18)$$

Impeller efficiency is a measure of the amount of motor input power converted to airstream power; this can depend on the duty it is being asked to perform. For example, an impeller could have an efficiency of 82 per cent when producing 10 m³/s at 220 Pa; 60 per cent efficiency when producing 6 m³/s at 330 Pa; and 70 per cent when producing 12 m³/s at 100 Pa.

The direct relationship between pressure and volume generated is peculiar to the fan type (figure 7.16). The volume flow is theoretically proportional to the pressure, but the impeller design and efficiency creates the curvilinear relationships shown.

The axial and forward curved or paddle bladed centrifugals show a larger change in volume for a small change in pressure than the backward curved type. As a result the power consumption of the former types will increase with reducing back-pressure, because the volume flow has increased to a greater extent than the pressure fall. In the

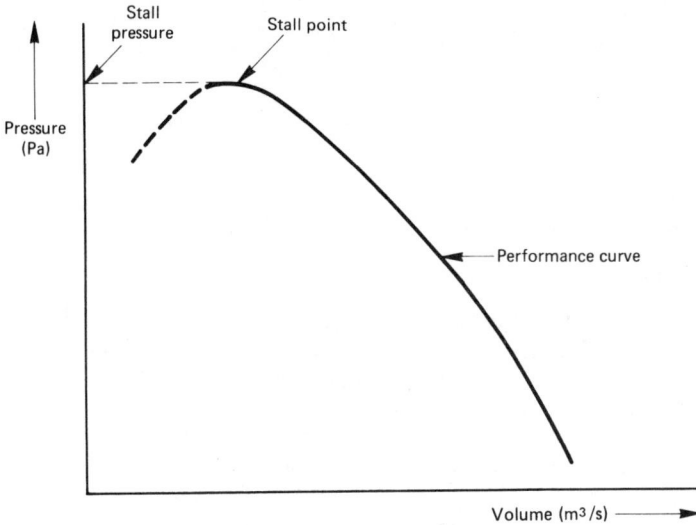

Figure 7.16 Theoretical fan curve.

backward curved type the volume rises proportionately to, or even at a lesser rate than, pressure fall, so that the input power requirement remains the same or might even fall.

The backward curved types are thus referred to as being 'non-overloading', while the other types have either a motor large enough for maximum conditions, or are carefully selected for a set system resistance, and steps are taken to ensure that this does not fall during operation.

7.5.3 Fan selection

The fan is chosen to provide the required volume flow rate (m³/s), against a certain pressure (Pa). Fan performance is shown in tabular or graphical form, with volume on one axis and pressure on the other. The performance figures might also include the variations due to impeller speed, and blade angle if axial, on a single page so that direct comparisons can be seen. A sample is shown in figure 7.17.

The power absorbed and efficiency at this duty is often quoted also, so where there is a choice between several sizes of fan to do a particular duty, it is possible to select the best one for motor size and efficiency. It will often be found that low power and high efficiency are obtained

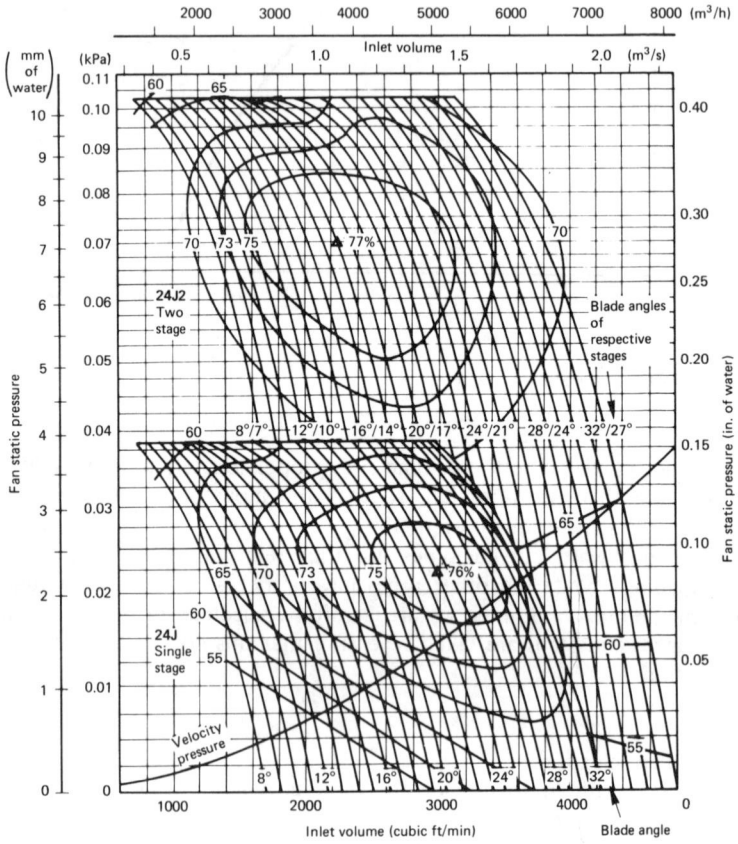

Figure 7.17   Actual fan performance curves (*courtesy Woods of Colchester Ltd*).

from large fans running at low speeds, but these tend to be more expensive than smaller high-speed types.

7.5.4 Fan installation

(a) Noise

Normally this is related to the tip velocity of the impeller, thus a small high-speed impeller can be noisier than a slightly larger one running slowly, but which is producing the same duty. Some fan catalogues quote sound levels in deciBels (dB), so that the 'quietest' impeller can be chosen. It must be appreciated, however, that the deciBel sound scale is logarithmic, so that every increase of 10 dB represents a doubling of sound level. Because there are several methods of sound measurement the unit often carries a suffix, such as dBA, to denote the scale used.

Noise problems can be reduced by fitting silencers. As most noise emanates from the inlet or outlet, the silencers are usually in the form of lengths of ducting lined with acoustic deadening material. These, however, will add to the fan resistance and require higher motor powers to maintain the output duty. Noise control is, however, a complex subject and problematical situations are best left to specialist consultants.

(b) Volume variation

This is usually done by impeller speed control, blade angle adjustment (axial flow only) or throttling the flow. Impeller speed control is difficult on direct driven fans, with induction a.c. motors. Only small axial flow or propeller fans can be fitted with motors that are capable of speed control. Large fans have to be indirectly driven with a variable ratio drive.

The most common method is flow throttling by either in-built dampers or restrictions placed across the fan inlet. Increasing the resistance of a fan is likely also to reduce power requirement, thus contrary to popular belief, throttling will not cause motors to overload or burn out. The only exception to this is in directly driven axial flow fans which rely on the moving airstream to cool the motor; in this case a total airflow stoppage can cause the motor to overheat.

A common practice is to throttle by placing a board across part of the inlet. While this is acceptable in terms of performance, prolonged use can cause the impeller to break owing to fatigue caused by the flexing of each blade as it runs through the shadow behind the board.

It is possible to fit inlet guide vanes to both axial and centrifugal fans. These pre-spin the air in the direction of impeller rotation, which reduces its performance. Inlet guide vanes are usually made adjustable from in-line with flow, for maximum flow, to completely blocking the flow. This system also reduces motor input power to a greater extent than does throttling.

(c) Inlet impediments
The smooth flow of air into the inlet of a fan is far more important than air turbulence at the outlet. These include heaters and tightly curved inlet ducts. These problems can be avoided if the fan is installed so as to be at least 1.5 times the impeller diameter from any blank wall or bend in the ductwork. Louvred inlet vents also disrupt flow, and these should also be at least this distance away from the fan inlet. Inlet airflow is improved by fitting a 'bellmouth', which is an outwardly flared cone to smooth airflow at the edges of the inlet duct.

(d) Fan reversal
Centrifugal fans will continue to move air in the same direction whichever way the impeller is rotating. However, the airflow rate in the wrong direction will be 30–40 per cent of that in the correct direction, the rest of the input energy being wasted in the form of heat. The correct impeller rotation is rotation towards the case outlet (figure 7.12).

The axial fan will reverse airflow if its impeller rotation is reversed. However, the blade aerofoils will be operating in the wrong direction, and thus the airflow will be reduced to around 75 per cent of that in the intended direction.

(e) 'Stalling'
This refers to the air flowing through the fan, not to its impeller ceasing to rotate. The fan is said to be stalled when the resistance rises to such a level that it baffles flow. The pressure at which this occurs is represented by the point where the performance curve significantly changes slope. As stalling produces little or no airflow, the power consumed by the fan also decreases markedly. The fan can often be heard to run slightly faster than normal owing to lack of airflow. However, during stalling, the air within the fan is recirculated around the impeller and is heated by friction, and this can ultimately affect airstream-cooled motors of axial fans.

(f) Frictional heating
The air flowing through the fan is warmed by friction as it travels through the impeller blades, and also through the motor in an axial fan. The frictional heating effect varies inversely with impeller efficiency, so that the highest efficiency produces the least heating. The heat rise can vary between 0.5°C at high efficiency and 2.5°C when the fan is performing beyond its intended duty. Heat rise is important when a fan is being used to cool a crop, and because it also has the effect of reducing the relative humidity of air passing through it.

7.6 REFRIGERATION

Most modern refrigeration plant works on the 'heat pump' principle, in which a gas is in turn compressed to liquid and then expanded back to gas within a closed system.

7.6.1 Components that form the basic refrigeration cycle

The four basic parts of the refrigeration system are discussed below (also see figure 7.18).

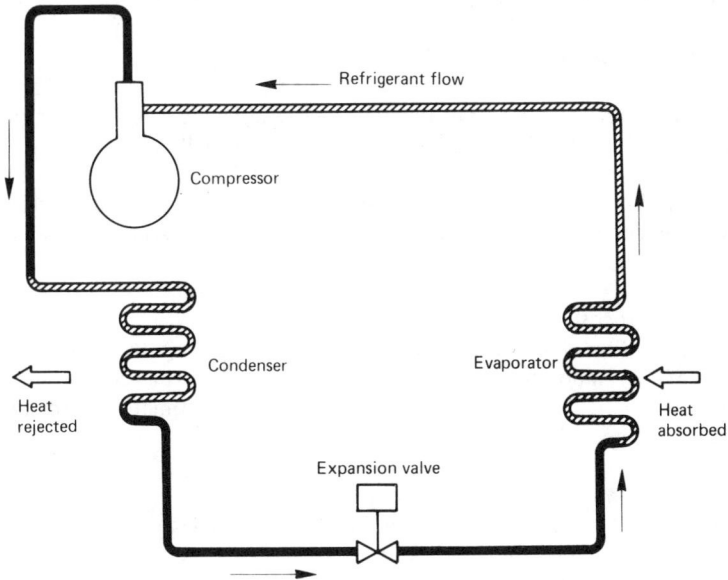

Figure 7.18 Vapour compression refrigeration cycle.

7.6.1.1 Compressor

The gas is compressed to a pressure at which it will liquefy on being cooled in the condenser. During compression the gas is heated. Most compressors used in horticulture are piston type (similar to an internal combustion engine). They might be subdivided into 'open' or 'hermetic' types, which refers to the relationship between the motor and the gas within the compressor. In an 'open' compressor the motor (electric or internal combustion engine) which drives the compressor is outside the refrigeration system; in the 'hermetic' type, the motor (always electric) is directly coupled to the compressor shaft and both are placed within a hermetically sealed chamber containing the refrigerant. The open compressor requires a refrigerant-tight rotary seal on its drive input shaft, whereas the hermetic requires to have only its wires sealed into the chamber wall. A third type, the 'semi-hermetic', uses a separate motor within its own sealed casing, which is directly bolted to the compressor by a gas-tight seal, and refrigerant gas is allowed to flow into the motor also. The hermetic type is the cheapest to produce but can prove difficult to service if the motor fails. If motor failure includes burning of the wiring insulation, the resulting carbon residues pass into the refrigerant system and can cause blockage in other components.

7.6.1.2 Condenser
The condenser removes the heat produced by the compressor, and also the latent heat of condensation from the gas, allowing it to form liquid. Condensers of the size used in horticulture are usually air cooled, with variable speed fans which control the amount of heat to be removed. Industrial condensers are water cooled; this is a more compact system, but the cooling water must in turn be cooled in a separate cooling tower.

7.6.1.3 Expansion device
The expansion device meters the liquid refrigerant to the lower pressure of the evaporator so that it can evaporate. The expansion device is usually a variable orifice valve which is adjusted automatically to suit the conditions in the evaporator.

7.6.1.4 Evaporator
The evaporator is where the liquid metered through the expansion device boils under the reduced pressure created by the compressor suction. On boiling, the refrigerant absorbs latent heat of vaporisation, which produces the cooling effect. The 'direct expansion' air cooling evaporator is in the form of a finned tube 'radiator' with the gas inside the tubes and air being blown over the finned surfaces. The evaporator can also be used to chill water directly; the water chiller is more compact and cheaper than the direct expansion air evaporator but requires a secondary (indirect) air-cooling system to be of use in cool storage.

7.6.2 Other components of the refrigeration system
In addition to the basic circuit, other devices or techniques are fitted to improve performance.

(a) Unloading allows a multi-cylinder compressor to run at partial capacity by using only some of its cylinders. The remaining cylinders are 'unloaded' either by holding down the inlet valves or by recirculating their output directly back to the inlet. Unloading is often used where there is more than one evaporator, or circuit, within an evaporator, so that the refrigerant flow can be reduced to suit the number of circuits operating.

(b) The liquid receiver holds the liquefied refrigerant, and acts as a reservoir to even the flow fluctuations caused by the expansion valve adjusting.

(c) 'Pumping down' is a technique used on all but very small systems. This uses a solenoid valve on the receiver outlet, so that when the system requires to be stopped this valve is closed and the compressor 'pumps down' all the refrigerant from the system into the reservoir. The compressor is then switched off by the pressure in the receiver. Pumping down prevents refrigerant remaining in the circuit, where it might condense and be drawn into the compressor as liquid.

(d) A dryer or superheater is used because liquids are, for all intents and purposes, incompressible and liquid refrigerant drawn into the compressor will cause a hydraulic lock and burst the cylinder. The dryer is a small heat exchanger in which the hot gas from the compressor is used to warm gas returning from the evaporator to ensure that any drops of liquid remaining are evaporated.

(e) Defrosting is essential for evaporators running at $1-2°C$ or below, because ice will gradually accumulate in the form of hoar frost from the condensing atmospheric water vapour. If this is not regularly cleared, the evaporator coil will eventually become solidly blocked with ice. The weight of this ice or its expansion as it cools can also cause damage to the evaporator coil.

The common method for defrosting is by electric heating elements embedded in the coil; other techniques include a bypass, whereby the hot gas from the compressor is diverted through the evaporator instead of the condenser, or given a hot wash using water heated in a water-cooled condenser. The two latter methods are more efficient in power use but complex to install.

Defrosting is normally done at fixed intervals, actuated by a time-clock which is set manually to provide the optimum running time before excessive icing is experienced. It is terminated by a sensor which senses the absence of ice by a sharp rise in coil temperature.

(f) Refrigerant is normally carried in copper piping. This is of a higher purity and wall thickness than is used for normal water pipe. Non-permanent pipe joints are made by mechanical (screwed) assemblies where the pipe end is flared outwards to fit a spigot on the other part of the joint and clamped down on to the spigot of a screwed collar nut. Permanent joints are made by brazing into fittings, the solder joints used on water pipes being unsuitable.

(g) A 'sight glass' is fitted into the liquid flow line of some systems. This enables the liquid flow to be observed, as bubbles or larger blocks of vapour can indicate that the refrigerant charge requires to be topped up.

(h) The oil separator returns, to the crank case, any oil droplets which have been carried out of the compressor by the refrigerant. This occurs in most compressors because it is easier to allow the refrigerant to mix freely with the crank case oil than to try to stop it leaking past the piston.

7.6.3 Refrigerants

Most modern refrigerants are based on various compounds of fluorine, hydrogen and carbon (fluorinated hydrocarbons). Each compound is designated by a 'refrigerant number', such as R12, R22 or R502, the number referring to the chemical groupings within the compound. Each has its own pressure/temperature relationship and heat-carrying capacity. For example, R12 operates at a lower pressure than R22, allowing the use of simpler compressor components, but moves only about half the heat per volume flow of R22, requiring the fitting of larger pipework. The pressure/temperature relationships are shown in table 7.8.

Table 7.8

*Pressure/temperature relationships for Freon
(du Pont de Nemours) refrigerants*

Pressure (kPa (gauge))	Temperature (°C)		
	R12	*R22*	*R502*
0	−30	−40	−
50	−22	−33	−38
100	−14	−27	−30
150	− 7	−21	−23
300	+ 6	− 7	−11
450	+17	+ 2	− 2
600	+26	+ 9	+ 6
750	34	16	13
900	41	22	19
1050	−	28	24
1200	−	33	29

It is usual for gauges fitted on the compressor to measure its suction and delivery pressures, so that it can be calibrated in both pressure and the corresponding temperatures of the three common refrigerants. Thus the 'suction' gauge reading can be related to the evaporating temperature, and the delivery gauge reading can be related to the condensing temperature.

As refrigerant pressure and temperatures are related, any leakage in the system will cause a pressure drop in the refrigerant which in turn will cause the system to operate at a lower than design temperature.

Refrigeration systems must be kept free of contaminants, especially water vapour which can form ice blockages in the expansion valve and evaporator. Strict precautions are taken to ensure that contaminants are excluded from the system before and during installation. Water is excluded by drying and sealing all components, including piping, during manufacture, and then purging the whole system after assembly with refrigerant gas. Any swarf or deposits of welding flux that have entered the system during assembly are caught by filter cartridges placed in the system.

7.6.4 Coefficient of performance (COP)

The refrigeration unit will 'pump' a much greater amount of heat energy than the mechanical energy absorbed by the compressor motor. The COP is the ratio of energy moved to energy absorbed. Theoretically the system can have a COP of 13 — that is, it will move 13 kW of heat for each 1 kW absorbed by the compressor motor. However, owing to slight leaks in the compressor and other inefficiencies in the system, the practical COP will be between 2.5 and 4. Normally the COP will be greater when the temperature differences between the evaporating and the condensing processes are smallest, so that a unit with a COP of 2.5 evaporating at $-20°C$ and condensing at $+40°C$ could have a COP of 3.5 if it was evaporating at $0°C$ and condensing at $+30°C$.

7.6.5 Component selection

This is a complex matter, as each component has to be matched with the others in the system in terms of both refrigerant flow and energy transfer. These steps are fully explained in textbooks on refrigeration system design and component manufacturers' handbooks.

7.7 HEATERS

Airstream heating can be done with direct or indirectly fired gas or oil heaters, electric element heaters or heat exchangers running from steam or hot water. These are described in chapter 4.

7.8 HUMIDITY

There are several methods for expressing the moisture vapour content of air; these include relative humidity, vapour pressure deficit and dewpoint temperature. Of these, relative humidity (rh) is the most widely used, although dewpoint is the most easily and accurately measured.

7.8.1 Psychrometry
The relationships between the atmosphere and the water that it contains fall within the science of psychrometry.

7.8.1.1 Psychrometric definitions
Relative humidity refers to the ratio between the amount of water that the air is holding and the amount that it could hold at the same temperature. At the upper limit, when the air can absorb no further water, the rh is given a value of 100 per cent, thus the rh of any air sample lies somewhere between 0 per cent (absolutely dry) and 100 per cent.

Relative humidity is also dependent on air temperature; as air is warmed, the amount of water vapour needed to saturate it to 100 per cent rh also increases. For example, when cool air at 75 per cent rh is warmed, the amount of water vapour it contains remains unchanged, but a greater amount will be needed to saturate it. Thus the amount of existing vapour might now represent only 50 per cent of the amount needed to saturate it — that is, the rh will now be 50 per cent. Conversely, when air is cooled its ability to hold water decreases, so cooling air will effectively increase its rh, even though no water is added in the process.

Dewpoint refers to the temperature below which the air is unable to hold all the water it contains in the form of vapour. The excess water which cannot be held as vapour, forms droplets of *dew*.

7.8.1.2 The psychrometric chart

This chart represents, by graphical means, the complex relationships between atmospheric water and the air, and also enables the engineer to determine other factors, such as the specific volume and specific enthalpy (total heat content) of air at a given condition. An example of the chart is shown in figure 7.19.

The purposes of the various lines and scales are as follows.

Dry bulb temperature ($^{\circ}$C): scale along bottom axis, grid lines running vertically.

Moisture content (kg of water per kg of dry air): scale along right-hand axis, grid lines running horizontally.

Saturation curve (rh = 100 per cent): left-hand, curved axis.

Wet bulb temperature ($^{\circ}$C): scale on saturation curve, grid lines running diagonally down to right. The wet bulb scale is taken from the points of intersection of the corresponding dry bulb scale with the saturation curve.

Relative humidity lines (percentage saturation): follow a similar shape to the saturation curve, scale on top axis.

Specific volume (m^3 of air per kg): running upwards at a slight angle to the vertical.

Specific enthalpy (kJ/kg): scale around edges of sheet, no drawn grid lines, enthalpy at any condition found by ruling across between same values on each side.

The conditions of a sample of air can be established by measuring only two parameters (usually wet and dry temperatures) and plotting the intersection point on the chart; the other conditions can then be read off.

Table 7.9 shows the consequences on the parameters of changing the conditions of a sample of air, initially at point A on figure 7.19. Plotting the effects of such alterations of a parameter can help the engineer to see either the consequences of an action, for example, the fall in rh caused by the air being warmed through a fan, or the action needed to effect a change, such as the amount of water needed to increase the rh by x per cent.

7.8.2 Humidification equipment

This is the process of adding water to the air. Several methods are used.

(a) Water is added in the form of a fine mist of droplets which evaporate readily. The droplets can be generated by hydraulic nozzles, a compressed air/water (sonic) nozzle or a spinning disc. In each method heat is required from the air to turn the mist into a vapour. In some cases

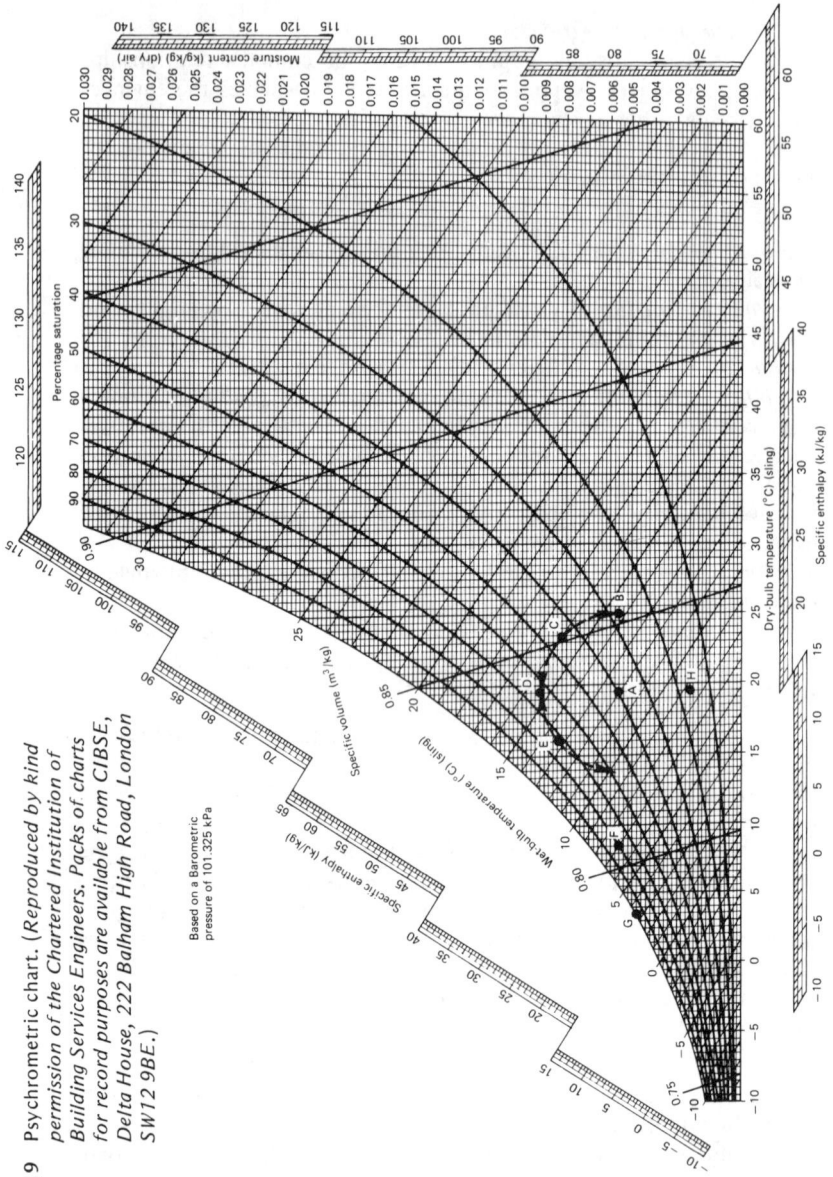

Figure 7.19 Psychrometric chart. (*Reproduced by kind permission of the Chartered Institution of Building Services Engineers. Packs of charts for record purposes are available from CIBSE, Delta House, 222 Balham High Road, London SW12 9BE.*)

Table 7.9

Changes of air condition as represented on a psychrometric chart (to be read in conjunction with figure 7.19)

Typical action to effect a change of condition	From A to	Effects of action on					
		Dry bulb	Wet bulb	rh	moisture content	specific volume	specific enthalpy
Heating by indirect fired heater	B	Up	Up	Down	Same	Up	Up
Heating by live steam or direct firing	C*	Up	Up	**	Up	Up	Up
Humidification by water injection	D	Same	Up	Up	Up	Up	Up
Wet pad cooling	E*	Down	+	Up	Up	+	+
Cooling above dewpoint	F	Down	Down	Up	Same	Down	Down
Cooling to below dewpoint, dehumidification by refrigeration	G	Down	Down	Up to 100 per cent	Down	Down	Down
Dehumidification by silica gel	H	Same	Down	Down	Down	Down	Down

Notes * This point can be anywhere in this quarter.
   ** Depends on the direction of C relative to A.
    + Depends on the direction of E relative to A.

like, for example, discharge from a cooler unit, there is very little heat energy available in the air to do this. Mist droplets that do not evaporate can be carried into the crop and cause damage by forming water pockets.

(b) Water vapour can be directly added by injecting steam into the airstream, although this can also raise the air temperature slightly.

(c) By drawing the air through a moistened fabric, this process both filters and cools the air in addition to humidifying it.

Control of humidifiers is normally imprecise and most machines are run continuously, with provision for recovering excess water droplets from the discharge airstream.

7.8.3 Dehumidification equipment
There are three ways to reduce the rh of the air.

(a) Heating the air so that the rh falls but the water vapour content remains unchanged.

(b) Using a refrigeration unit to cool the air below its dewpoint, in order to reject a portion of its water content, and then a heater to restore it to its desired temperature. The cooler operating temperature will determine the dewpoint (100 per cent rh) of the air leaving the coils, so that the subsequent reheating will reduce the rh to the desired level.

Self-contained dehumidifiers working on this principle use the condenser to reheat the air to the desired rh. These units do not need separate siting for the components or long runs of fixed pipework, but are incapable of performing cooling.

(c) Moisture can be absorbed by a hygroscopic chemical such as silica gel, which can then be regenerated (redried) by heating. In small rooms it is sufficient to place trays of the gel to absorb water, and regenerate the gel as necessary in an oven. Large stores use a continuous process whereby the gel is moulded into pockets in a large wheel. This is mounted so that part is in the store air circulation duct, and the rest is within a hot air duct for regeneration; the wheel slowly rotates so that each pocket of gel absorbs moisture and is then redried.

The warming method does not remove moisture, and thus the rh can return to a high level, with the air conditions also becoming warmer. The cooling/reheating method is usually suitable only for reducing rh levels to 30-40 per cent. Where very low rh levels are required, for example in long-term seed stores, the absorption system is the more effective.

7.9 ATMOSPHERE CONTROL

7.9.1 Oxygen and CO_2

Most crops in controlled atmosphere stores use oxygen from the store atmosphere and produce CO_2. As this gradually depletes the oxygen level, and increases the CO_2 correspondingly, in most stores it will be necessary to remove the surplus CO_2. The rate of oxygen consumption can also be too slow for some produce, requiring a reduction in the level of store oxygen by artificial means.

(a) Controlled ventilation or 'flushing' can be used only where the sum of the CO_2 and oxygen contents still add up to the 21 per cent oxygen level of atmospheric air — that is, where the atmospheric oxygen has been directly replaced by CO_2. These stores operate by allowing the CO_2 to reach the desired level, and then maintain it by flushing through with fresh air at a controlled rate. The store is fitted with two valved pipes, a 'fresh air' inlet and a 'foul air' outlet. The fresh air inlet is normally connected to the suction side of the store air circulation fan, to ensure that the air exchange takes place. The valves can be controlled by hand or by an automatic gas sensor. In the latter case it is normal for them to be modulated so that the desired flushing rate is maintained constantly. This is better than an 'off/on' valve control, where the CO_2 and O_2 levels will fluctuate.

(b) Carbon dioxide is removed by a 'scrubbing' process in which the atmosphere is passed through absorbents. Two types of absorbent are used — lime (calcium hydroxide) and charcoal. In the former case the CO_2 forms a chemical bond with the lime, whereas it forms only a physical bond with charcoal, which can be regenerated by exposure to fresh air.

Lime scrubbing is done in a chamber that contains palletised bags of lime adjacent to the store, the store air being blown through this chamber as necessary. The chamber air ducts can be isolated from the store, so that the lime in it can be changed. Some large installations use a single chamber to serve several stores through a system of interconnecting air ducts.

The charcoal scrubber normally consists of a pair of vessels arranged so that one is in use while the other is being regenerated with fresh air.

(c) Oxygen control is needed where respiration alone is insufficient to maintain low oxygen levels, and also where there is only slight fresh air in-leakage. There are three methods for doing this.

(i) The use of nitrogen (an inert gas in terms of crop storage) to flush out the oxygen-laden atmosphere.

(ii) Open flame flushing using outside air to flush the store, which has first passed thorugh a gas burner. This uses the atmospheric oxygen in the gas combustion process to produce water vapour and CO_2. A suitable burner will reduce the oxygen level from the normal 21 per cent to 1–2 per cent.

(iii) The catalytic burner, which also consumes excess oxygen by combustion of gas, although this burner is used inside the store to deplete the oxygen level directly. As a normal burner flame will not run satisfactorily at low oxygen levels, these burners contain a catalyst to maintain combustion.

Both of the combustion type oxygen controllers produce extra CO_2, which has to be removed by the scrubber, and heat, which has to be removed by the cooler plant. Nitrogen-flushing systems require high exchange rates to remove sufficient oxygen for those crops that require only a very low oxygen level.

7.9.2 Ethylene control

There are two methods for reducing the levels of this gas.

(a) Chemical absorption using similar equipment to that for CO_2 scrubbing. The chemicals are very expensive when compared with the cost of lime.

(b) Use of catalytic burners similar to those used for oxygen control. The catalyst, however, has to be maintained at a high temperature (200–250°C) to be effective. This can prove difficult both with regard to maintaining temperature during intermittent running, and discharging the waste heat to the cooler system.

APPENDIX A: METRIC CONVERSION FACTORS

Length	1 mm	=	0.0394 inches
		=	0.1 centimetres
	1 m	=	3.28 feet
		=	1.09 yards
	1 km	=	1093.6 yards
		=	0.62 miles
Area	1 m²	=	10.76 square feet
		=	1.196 square yards
	1 ha	=	10 000.0 m²
		=	2.47 acres
		=	11 956 square yards
Volume	1 litre (l)	=	1.76 Imperial pints
		=	2.11 U.S. pints
			(1 U.S. liquid pint = 0.859 U.S. dry pints)
		=	0.22 Imperial gallons
		=	0.26 U.S. gallons
	1 ml	=	1.0 cubic centimetres
		=	0.0352 fluid ounces
	1 m³	=	35.31 cubic feet
		=	1.31 cubic yards
Mass	1 g	=	0.035 ounces
	1 kg	=	2.204 lb
		=	35.26 ounces
	1 tonne (t)	=	2204.6 lb
		=	0.984 Imperial (long) tons
		=	1.102 U.S. (short) tons
			(1 short ton = 2000 lb)
		=	19.6 Imperial hundredweights
		=	22.05 U.S. cwt

Force	1 Newton (N)	=	0.101 kilogrammes force
		=	0.225 lb force
	1 kN	=	0.10 tons force
Pressure	1 N/m^2 (Pa)	=	0.10 mm water gauge
	1 kPa	=	4.02 inches water gauge
		=	0.144 lbf/square inch (psi)
		=	0.01 bar
		=	0.0102 kgf/cm^2
		=	0.102 m water gauge
	1 MPa	=	144 lbf/square inch
Energy	1 kJ	=	0.948 British thermal units (Btu)
		=	0.238 kilocalories
	1 MJ	=	0.278 kWh
Volume flow rate	1 litre/s	=	13.2 Imperial gallons/min (gpm)
		=	791.9 Imperial gallons/h (gph)
		=	15.8 U.S. gallons/min
		=	949.9 U.S. gallons/h
	1 m^3/s	=	35.31 ft^3/s (cusec)
		=	2118.6 ft^3/min (cfm)
Mass flow rate	1 kg/s	=	7936.5 lb/h
		=	3.54 ton/h
Moisture content	1 g/kg	=	7.0 grain/lb
	1 kg/kg	=	7000.0 grain/lb
Pressure drop per unit length	1 Pa/m	=	0.01 ft water/100 ft
Thermal resistance	1 °C m^2/W	=	5.68 °F ft^{2}h/Btu
		=	1.16 °C m^{2}h/kcal
Specific heat capacity	1 kJ/kg °C	=	0.24 Btu/lb °F
		=	0.24 kcal/kg °C
Specific volume	1 m^3/t	=	35.9 ft^3/ton
Velocity	1 m/s	=	196.9 ft/min
		=	2.24 mph

Heat capacity	1 kJ/°C	=	0.53 Btu/°F
		=	0.24 kcal/°C
Power, heat	1 W	=	3.41 Btu/h
flow rate		=	0.86 kcal/h
	1 kW	=	1.34 horsepower
		=	1.36 metric horsepower
		=	0.28 ton of refrigeration
		=	1.0 kJ/s
Illumination	1 lux (lx)	=	0.093 ft candle
Calorific value	1 kJ/kg	=	0.43 Btu/lb
		=	0.24 kcal/kg
Thermal con-	1 W/m² °C	=	0.18 Btu/ft² °F
ductance		=	0.86 kcal/h m² °C
(U value)			
Thermal con-	1 W/m °C	=	6.93 Btu inch/h ft² °F
ductance		=	0.86 kcal/h m² °C
(k value)			
Density	1 kg/m³	=	0.06 lb/ft³
	1 t/m³	=	0.028 ton/ft³

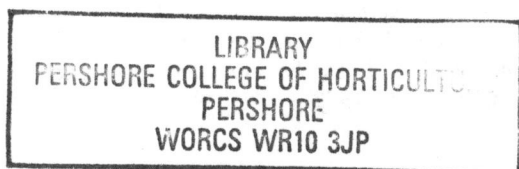

APPENDIX B: FURTHER READING

R. C. Balls, *Horticultural Engineering Technology – Field Machinery*, Macmillan, London, 1985 (companion volume).

C. Bishop and W. Maunder, *Potato Mechanisation and Storage*, Farming Press, Ipswich, 1980.

J. Robertson, *Mechanising Vegetable Production*, Farming Press, Ipswich, 2nd revised edn, 1978.

P. Atkinson, *Feedback Control Theory For Engineers*, Heineman Educational Books, Exeter, 1982.

W. H. Wolsey, *Basic Principles of Automatic Control (with special reference to heating and air conditioning)*, Hutchinson Educational, London, 1975.

I. McFarlane, *Automatic Control of Food Manufacturing Processing*, Applied Science Publications, Barking, Essex, 1983.

R. V. Buckley, *Control Engineering Theory, Worked Examples and Problems*, Macmillan, London, 1982.

A. L. Ryall and W. J. Lipton (eds), *Handling Transportation, and Storage of Fruits and Vegetables, Vol. 1: Vegetables and Melons*, AVI Publishing Co., Westport, Connecticut, 1979.

W. J. Lipton and J. Werner (eds), *Handling, Transportation, and Storage of Fruits and Vegetables, Vol. 2: Fruits and Tree Nuts*, AVI Publishing Co., Westport, Connecticut, 1982.

M. A. Hellickson and J. N. Walker (eds), *Ventilation of Agricultural Structures*, American Society of Agricultural Engineers, St. Joseph, Michigan, 1983.

J. E. Haines, *Automatic Control of Heating and Air Conditioning*, McGraw-Hill, New York, 2nd edn, 1961.

P. M. Goodall (ed.), *The Efficient Use Of Steam*, IPC Science and Technology Press, Guildford, 1980.

B. B. Daly, *Woods Practical Guide to Fan Engineering*, International Publishing Service, New York, 3rd edn, 1978.

S. W. R. Cox and D. E. Filby, *Instrumentation in Agriculture*, Crosby-Lockwood, St Albans, 1972.

C.I.B.S.E. Guides, a series of reference works providing authoritative and topical data for engineers, published by The Chartered Institution of Building Services Engineers, London. The following will be of particular interest:

A2, Weather and Solar Data, 1982.
A3, Thermal Properties of Building Structures, 1980.
A4, Air Infiltration, 1971.
A5, Thermal Response of Buildings, 1979.
A10, Moisture Problems (under revision).
B1, Heating, 1972.
B3, Ventilation and Air Conditioning (Systems and Requirements), 1972.
B7, Corrosion Protection and Water Treatment (under revision).
B13, Combustion Systems, 1972.
B14, Refrigeration and Heat Rejection, 1972.
B16, Miscellaneous Equipment, 1972.
C1/2, Properties of Humid Air, 1975.
C3, Heat Transfer, 1976.
C4, Flow of Fluids in Pipes and Ducts, 1977.
C5, Fuels and Combustion, 1976.

Grow Electric Handbooks, published by The Electricity Council, Farm Electric Centre, Coventry.

Electricity in Horticulture, 1982.
Growing Rooms, 1981.
Lighting in Greenhouses, 1981.
Potato Storage, 1983.
Ventilation for Greenhouses, 1979.

Advisory Leaflets for Horticulturists, published by the Ministry of Agriculture, Fisheries and Food, Alnwick, Northumberland.

B2099 Management of Ware Potato Stores, 1982.
B2105 Greenhouse Ventilation, 1979.
B2114 Boilers for Nursery Use, 1980.
B2127 Greenhouse Heating Systems, 1976.
B2133 Fuels and Firing Equipment for Nurseries, 1981.
B2140 Watering Equipment for Greenhouse Crops, 1980.
B2284 Windbreaks for Glasshouses and Plastic Structures, 1980.

Refrigerated Storage of Fruit and Vegetables (RB324), Her Majesty's Stationery Office, London, 1979.

INDEX

244